The Young Nietzsche's Education

The Young Nietzsche's Education

An Interpretation of Nietzsche's
Untimely Considerations

JOZEF MAJERNÍK

SUNY
PRESS

Published by State University of New York Press, Albany

© 2025 State University of New York

All rights reserved

Printed in the United States of America

No part of this book may be used or reproduced in any manner whatsoever without written permission. No part of this book may be stored in a retrieval system or transmitted in any form or by any means including electronic, electrostatic, magnetic tape, mechanical, photocopying, recording, or otherwise without the prior permission in writing of the publisher.

Links to third-party websites are provided as a convenience and for informational purposes only. They do not constitute an endorsement or an approval of any of the products, services, or opinions of the organization, companies, or individuals. SUNY Press bears no responsibility for the accuracy, legality, or content of a URL, the external website, or for that of subsequent websites.

EU GPSR Authorised Representative:
Logos Europe, 9 rue Nicolas Poussin, 17000, La Rochelle, France
contact@logoseurope.eu

For information, contact State University of New York Press, Albany, NY
www.sunypress.edu

Library of Congress Cataloging-in-Publication Data

Name: Majerník, Jozef, 1991– author.
Title: The young Nietzsche's education : an interpretation of Nietzsche's
    Untimely Considerations / Jozef Majerník.
Description: Albany : State University of New York Press, [2025] | Includes
    bibliographical references and index.
Identifiers: LCCN 2024044577 | ISBN 9798855802467 (hardcover : alk. paper) |
    ISBN 9798855802481 (ebook)
Subjects: LCSH: Nietzsche, Friedrich Wilhelm, 1844–1900. Unzeitgemässe
    Betrachtungen.
Classification: LCC B3313.U53 M35 2025 | DDC 193—dc23/eng/20250103
LC record available at https://lccn.loc.gov/2024044577

For Matthew, an *Erzieher* and a friend

. . . and to live at all means to be in danger.

—Nietzsche, *Untimely Considerations*

Contents

Acknowledgments	ix
Abbreviations	xi
Introduction	1
Summary of the Argument	4
Note on the Title	10

I. *David Strauss the Confessor and the Writer*:
    Nietzsche's *Kulturkritik* — 13
      I.1. Richard Wagner and the Origins of the *UC* — 14
      I.2. *DS* 1–3: Nietzsche's Critique of German Culture — 19
      I.3. *DS* 4–12: The Portrait of the Cultivated Philistine — 26

II. *On the Utility and Liability of History for Life*:
    The Human Soul and Its Modern Deformation — 43
      II.1. *HL* 1: The Erotic-Historic Soul — 44
      II.2. *HL* 2–3: *Historia Magistra Vitae* — 52
      II.3. *HL* 4–9: The Problem of Scientific History — 63
      II.4. Curing the Historical Sickness — 75

III. *Schopenhauer as Educator*: The Good Life According
    to the Young Nietzsche — 87
      III.1. *SE* 1: Erotic-Historic Self-Knowledge — 87
      III.2. *SE* 2–4: The Educator — 96
      III.3. *SE* 5: The "Schopenhauerian" Affirmation — 105
      III.4. *SE* 6–8: The Life of Culture — 115

viii | Contents

IV. *Richard Wagner in Bayreuth*: Wagner, Tragedy, and
Free Human Beings of the Future   129
    IV.1. Becoming Richard Wagner   135
    IV.2. Wagner's Tragic Art   140
    IV.3. Wagnerian Musical Education   153
    IV.4. Finale: The Free Human Beings of the Future   161

V. The Failures—and the Successes—of the
Untimely Considerations   167
    V.1. The Failure of the Project of the *UC*   170
    V.2. The Sickness of the Thought of the *UC*   176
    V.3. The Successes of the Thought of the *UC*   190
    V.4. The Thought of the *UC* as a Means to Overcome Itself   203
    V.5. Conclusion   213

Bibliography   217

Index   225

Acknowledgments

Above all, I would like to thank my mother, Zuzana Majerníková, who has lovingly and selflessly supported my studies and ambitions for decades by now. I would never be in the position to write these acknowledgments were it not for her.

I owe a great deal of gratitude to the members of my dissertation committee: Heinrich Meier, Nathan Tarcov, and Robert Pippin. Their many insightful comments and suggestions on the earlier versions of this study have improved it immensely. A special thank you is due also to James Conant and David Wellbery, who have helped me better to understand Nietzsche, Goethe, as well as the overall cultural and intellectual landscape of 19th century Germany.

I would also like to thank to Garrett Allen, Mat Messerschmidt, Matthew Post, and Daniel Watling, my dear friends who have taken interest in my work. Conversations with them have enriched not just this study, but my thinking in general. The same is true of the John U. Nef Committee on Social Thought and its people as a whole: a wonderful space of intellectual openness and curiosity that not only facilitated many great conversations, but also allowed me to pursue my intellectual interests with all the freedom I could ever wish for.

Last but not least, I would like to thank Martine Prange, in whose class at Leiden University in Fall 2012 I first read *Schopenhauer as Educator* and immediately fell in love with it. I have loved the *Untimely Considerations* ever since, and the entire present study was, in principle, started at that moment.

However, any errors contained herein are my sole responsibility.

This work was produced at the Institute of Philosophy, Slovak Academy of Sciences, in connection with the project "Philosophical Anthropology in the Context of Current Crises of Symbolic Structures," supported by the Slovak Research and Development Agency under the contract APVV-20-0137.

Abbreviations

Throughout this study I refer to Nietzsche's works according to their established English abbreviations. Quotations from the *Untimely Considerations* are taken from R.T. Gray's translation (Nietzsche, 1995), modified if appropriate. The *Considerations* (which, unlike most of Nietzsche's other works, cannot be accurately cited by their internal divisions alone) are cited first by reference to the *Kritische Studienausgabe* (KSA), to which I refer simply in the format x.y, where *x* is volume number and *y* is page number (i.e., omitting the abbreviation KSA), and then by reference to the page number in Gray's translation. Quotations from Nietzsche's other published works are taken from existing translations (modified if appropriate), but cited by the abbreviation of the given work and its internal division; in most cases this means the number of the aphorism. Works not published in the KSA are quoted according to the *Kritische Gesamtausgabe Werke* (KGW), and letters are quoted according to the *Kritische Gesamtausgabe Briefwechsel* (KGB). Translations of these are my own.

Quotations from other works in German are taken from existing translations if possible (modified if appropriate); if no translation of the given work is listed in the bibliography, the quotations are translated by me.

Emphases in all quotations are original unless indicated otherwise.

Nietzsche's Published Works and Authorized Manuscripts

AC   *The Antichrist: A Curse on Christianity*

AOM   *HA II, Part One: Assorted Opinions and Maxims*

BGE   *Beyond Good and Evil: Prelude to a Philosophy of the Future*

xii | Abbreviations

BT   *The Birth of Tragedy Out of the Spirit of Music*

CW   *The Case of Wagner: A Musician's Problem*

D   *Daybreak: Thoughts on the Prejudices of Morality*

DS   *UC, First Piece: David Strauss the Confessor and the Writer*

EH   *Ecce Homo: How One Becomes What One Is*

FEI   *On the Future of Our Educational Institutions: Six Public Lectures*

GM   *On the Genealogy of Morality: A Polemic*

GS   *The Gay Science*

HA   *Human, All Too Human: A Book for Free Spirits*

HL   *UC, Second Piece: On the Utility and Liability of History for Life*

SE   *UC, Third Piece: Schopenhauer as Educator*

TI   *Twilight of the Idols, or How One Philosophizes with a Hammer*

UC   *Untimely Considerations*

WB   *UC, Fourth Piece: Richard Wagner in Bayreuth*

WS   *HA II, Part Two: The Wanderer and His Shadow*

Za   *Thus Spoke Zarathustra: A Book for All and None*

Editions of Nietzsche's Writings

KGB   *Nietzsche Briefwechsel. Kritische Gesamtausgabe.*

KGW   *Nietzsche Werke. Kritische Gesamtausgabe.*

KSA   *Friedrich Nietzsche, Sämtliche Werke. Kritische Studienausgabe in 15 Bänden.*

Other Works

PP   Arthur Schopenhauer, *Parerga and Paralipomena*

WWR   Arthur Schopenhauer, *The World as Will and Representation* (2 vols.)

Introduction

Friedrich Wilhelm Nietzsche (1844–1900) is undoubtedly one of the most influential thinkers of the modern age. We often tend to focus on the sharp critical strands he developed in his late works, such as his diagnosis of the European nihilism, his critique of Christianity as the ultimate source of this nihilism, or his genealogical dismantling of apparently exalted moral values to the *pudenda origo*, the "shameful origin," from which they stem (cf. *D* 102). But, as influential as Nietzsche's critique of earlier moral systems has been, his ethical thinking nevertheless contains also a more constructive dimension that tends to be overshadowed by the critical moment. This constructive dimension is signaled by slogans such as *be yourself!* or "become what you are," *amor fati*, or "eternal return of the same," and its general purpose is to educate his readers to love life—both their own life, and life (or being) as a whole—in a way that is not possible under other, more conventional ways of ethical self-understanding. This study is focused on the origins and foundations of this constructive dimension of Nietzsche's ethics as they appear in his second book—the collection of four long essays, written between 1872 and 1876, collectively known as the *Untimely Considerations*. In doing so, I aim to articulate in a detailed manner how Nietzsche, at this stage of his productive life, imagines the new, life-affirming ethic—an ethic that is, unlike its popular Kantian and utilitarian rivals, not just a set of lifeless ratiocinations, but a concrete and individualized *way of life* (which, as Pierre Hadot has emphasized, is essential to Greek philosophy in general, and which was applied specifically to Nietzsche by Hutter, 2006). What Nietzsche promises us here is the path to a life that would be suited to our particular nature and satisfy its particular needs, as well as a life freely chosen by ourselves: in a word, a life that would be genuinely *our own* and hence genuinely happy.

2 | The Young Nietzsche's Education

At first sight, however, the *Untimely Considerations* do not appear to have much of a coherent vision at all. The first one, *DS*, is for the most part a scathing review of D. F. Strauss's latest book, and scholars like Colli (1999, p. 905) or Brobjer (2008, p. 58) have called it Nietzsche's least interesting work. And while *HL* and *SE* have found their fair share of critical attention, *WB* is commonly considered to be a rather uninteresting, fawning hagiography of Wagner, a testament of Nietzsche's naive youthful devotion to the maestro. Moreover, the *UC* are, as a whole, undoubtedly Nietzsche's most neglected work. This has been noted by those who have devoted some attention to them (Breazeale, 1997, vii; Large, 2012, p. 86). And deeds—or rather lack thereof—provide even stronger evidence of this neglect: When I first conceived this study, in the spring of 2016, not a single book had ever been published about the *UC*. That made it 140 years since their completion without a dedicated interpretation or commentary. Catherine Zuckert's 1976 article, based on her 1970 dissertation (to which I had access through the University of Chicago library), was the only interpretation of the *UC* as a whole known to me. The other articles on the *UC* were either accounts of a particular aspect of these essays (Siemens, 2001; Ansell-Pearson, 2013),[1] or simply introductions provided for the *UC* or for the individual essays when they appeared in English translations (Nietzsche, 1990, ed. Arrowsmith; Gray, 1995; Breazeale, 1997).

A major reason for this scholarly neglect is the assumption that insofar as the *UC* can be considered a single project at all, it is a fragmentary and abortive one. Evidence from the *Nachlass* is cited to show that Nietzsche planned a much larger number of the *UC* (13 in the most developed extant plans),[2] most of which were never even started, and insofar as their unity is discussed, it is only in terms of certain themes that appear across these four

---

1. Siemens's focus is the theme of agonism in the *UC*, while Ansell-Pearson claims that for the early Nietzsche, the sublime defines "the very practice of philosophy" (2013, p. 227). He then however goes on to define the sublime as simply "the truly important and significant [as opposed to] the fleeting and fashionable" (ibid., p. 231). Obviously, Nietzsche's philosophy—as any other philosophy—is concerned with what the author considers truly important. Ansell-Pearson thus says frustratingly little of substance about the argument of the *UC*.

2. The note 7 [189], 7.212 is a plan of eleven essays without a common title, and the note 16 [2], 7.393 is a plan of nine such essays. The notes 19 [300]–19 [303], 7.512; 19 [317], 7.516; and 26 [23], 7.585 all contain various possible titles for the essay series. Finally, the notes 19 [330], 7.520; 29 [163], 7.699; and 32 [4], 7.755 each are topically quite similar plans of thirteen essays, which are to be titled *UC*.

Introduction | 3

essays. We can add to these some of Nietzsche's own later statements, such as "I count those untimely considerations as *juvenilia*" (letter to Elise Fincke from 20 March 1882, KGB III.1, p. 181), or "when I once wrote the word 'untimely' on my books, how much youth, inexperience, underhandedness was expressed in this word! Today I understand that [. . .] precisely thereby I belonged to the most modern of the moderns" (note 2 [201], 12.165). But even more stringent dismissals of their value have appeared in the literature—for example, Fink (2003, p. 33) characterizes them as merely "metaphysics of art on the basis of Schopenhauer's philosophy," and Picht (1988, pp. 98–99) wonders whether Nietzsche's actual philosophy begins with *HA* or with *Za*. Thus, when I started working on this study, the reader of the *UC* was faced with the scholarly consensus that these essays are rather uninteresting juvenilia and artifacts of Wagner's influence on the young Nietzsche (given that *DS* was written at Wagner's behest and *WB* appears to be entirely uncritical of Wagner). What more is there to be said about these four youthful errors?

That argument, however, doesn't tell us the entire story. For one, Nietzsche himself tells us that the first three of the *UC* are where his thinking actually begins (*HA* II Preface 1), in the sense that their concerns came to occupy his thinking even before those of *BT*. This already is reason enough for a careful study of the *UC*: to begin at the beginning is a sound principle. The *UC*, the texts in which Nietzsche first articulates the central concerns that animate his thinking throughout his productive life, promise to give us a view of the entire field of Nietzsche's intellectual concerns and of how he conceived of the possibilities of moving within this space. And, fortunately, scholars have begun to appreciate this promise and to pay more serious attention to the *UC* in the recent years. Two book-length interpretations of these essays have been published recently (Brooks, 2018; Church, 2019), as well as a two-volume commentary on the *UC*, which belongs to the *Nietzsche-Kommentar* series (Neymeyr, 2020).[3] Other literature on the early Nietzsche, such as Taylor, 1997; Church, 2015;[4] and Lampert,

---

3. These two volumes offer an overall thematic commentary, as well as detailed *Stellenkommentar*, to each of the four *UC*. I've found that Neymeyr generally tends to overemphasize the dependence of the *UC* on Schopenhauer and Wagner (perhaps because of the plethora of references and allusions to their writings, which she has carefully catalogued), but I've found her commentary to be of great utility nevertheless.

4. Generally speaking, I refer to Church, 2019, rather than to Church, 2015, because Church, 2019, is a later work that is moreover focused solely on the *UC*, and on the *UC* as a single whole.

4 | The Young Nietzsche's Education

2017, is also of some use to those seeking a better understanding of the *UC*. And while I am happy about this newfound critical attention directed at the *UC*, I believe there is much more to say about these four essays of Nietzsche. It is my hope that this study will contribute to a more complete understanding of their arguments, their structure, the project proposed in them, and the thought and intentions behind it.

In more general terms, the topics at the center of Nietzsche's attention in the *UC*—understanding and becoming oneself, the character and purpose of our projects, coming to terms with the culture we live in even though we are sorely aware of its dissatisfactory character, the question of how to relate to great thinkers and artists of (not just) our own times, and more generally the problem of genuine humanity or human greatness under the conditions of modernity—are central also to how we, as modern people, think of and relate to ourselves. Moreover, *SE* is the *locus classicus* of the exhortation to "be yourself!," and thus it is a key source of existentialism and other forms of ethics of authenticity. It has to be said, though, that the difference between Nietzsche's and the existentialists' vision of human goodness or greatness shows that Nietzsche was no existentialist.

In all these regards, then, a deeper understanding of the *UC* is a contribution to the understanding of the sources of our own conceptions of subjectivity, and thereby to our self-knowledge. The thematic concerns just mentioned are my own concerns as well: I still remember how amazed and moved I was when I first read about what it means to *be yourself* in the opening chapter of *SE*. Ever since then, those words of Nietzsche's have become my constant companion, and this book is a product of my thinking through the *UC* and their doctrines. As such, it aims to speak to others like me, to young souls who struggle with the nature of the world they live in and of their own existence—and it aims to help them better to understand and *become* themselves. At the same time, it aims to be an invitation to the reading of the *Considerations*.

Summary of the Argument

As I imply above, it is my opinion that these four essays do form a single, coherent whole, and a principal aim of this study is to interpret them as such. First of all, although Nietzsche did plan 13 essays for the series, the vast majority of the topics the planned essays were to address are present, or at least touched upon, in the four essays that have been completed (Brooks,

2018, p. 14). The three interpreters who have already treated the *UC* as a whole have found significant overarching themes in them, centered on their conception of education and on Nietzsche's hopes for a reform of German culture on this basis (in cooperation with Wagner's Bayreuth project), and consider them neither failed nor incomplete (Brooks, 2018, p. 20; Church, 2019, p. 10). They have also noted that the essays can be divided into two distinct halves, roughly a "no-saying" one (*DS* and *HL*) and a "yes-saying" one (*SE* and *WB*) (Brooks, 2018, pp. 12–13; Church, 2019, pp. 1–2).

I agree with these observations of Zuckert, Brooks, and Church. However, I think that the case for a substantial philosophical unity of the *UC* can be taken much further. My hermeneutical starting point is the observation of Leo Strauss (1988, p. 230) that careful readers are careful writers, and that what a careful writer tells us about how *they* read books is an important guiding thread for the reading of their own works. In this regard I take a new approach to interpreting the *UC* by highlighting the importance of the three questions posed by Nietzsche at the beginning of *DS* 4 (1.177/23), questions that guide his reading of D. F. Strauss's book *The Old Faith and the New*. If we take our bearing from these questions, the *UC* come to light not as a merely theoretical book in which Nietzsche expounds his "philosophy" to whoever might happen to be interested in it, but rather as a practical *project* that strives to effect a transformation first in the souls of its readers and through them hopefully in the German culture at large. In this I depart from Zuckert (1976) and Church (2019, p. 15), the latter of whom treats the *UC* as a piece of "practical philosophy in the distinctly Kantian sense." That is to say, this study aims to be a thorough interpretation of the *UC* that is aware of the differences between their teaching, the project that they present, and the thought behind them. The main models for this approach are Lampert's interpretation of *BGE* (2001), and Meier's interpretations of *Za* (2017) and of *EH* and *AC* (2019). Besides being a hermeneutical innovation, I believe my approach will provide a new way of access to Nietzsche's first formulation of his positive project.

Second, contrary to Brooks's and Church's emphases on culture (Brooks's book is titled *Nietzsche's* Culture *War* [emphasis added]; and Church's reading of the *UC* as neo-Kantian heavily emphasizes culture as the realm of freedom against nature as the realm of necessity), I demonstrate the importance of *nature* in the thinking of the *UC*. On my interpretation, Nietzsche's view of the nature-culture relation is not the Kantian dichotomy, but rather the ancient, complementary view: culture as the cultivation of nature (cf. Cicero, *Tusculan Disputations* II.13), or as a "new and improved *physis*" (1.334/167).

6 | The Young Nietzsche's Education

Thus, I understand nature not in the modern, biologistic or naturalistic sense, but rather in the ancient sense, as that which brings itself forth out of itself (Heidegger, 2008, p. 317). My focus in particular is on the nature of the human soul as it is understood in these essays, which is the core from which all other arguments and plans proposed by Nietzsche unfold. The nature of the soul to be cultivated—soul understood as the structure of human desiring and understanding—is one of the central subjects of the *UC*, and the account of the imperative *be yourself* in *SE* 1 is rightly one of the most celebrated passages in these essays. In this regard I emphasize that *HL* 1 deals not just with human historicity, but also with human ahistoricity, and that the conjunction of these two elements in fact forms a coherent and sophisticated account of the motive forces and inner structures of the human soul. I understand this "ahistoricity" as, essentially, *desiring*: the forces within the soul that demand the satisfaction of some lack we feel within us. Historicity, on the other hand, refers not just to our dealing with the past, but also to our general dealings with all things external to us and with figuring out the best ways of getting around in the world; it is, fundamentally, *historia* in the original Greek sense, "learning by inquiry," and thus the embryonic form of all higher intellectual operations (notably including the operations of *measuring, reasoning*, and *valuing*). It is *magistra vitae, vita* meaning life as essentially desiring of growth beyond whatever it had already become. In this respect I follow in the footsteps of Fink (2003) and Heidegger (2016), both of whom sought to uncover the structures governing human experience of the world that underlie Nietzsche's discussions of (not only) historical phenomena in the *UC*, and especially in *HL*.

On my reading, then, *HL* 1 and *SE* 1 are the central *loci* of Nietzsche's psychological theory in the *UC*, dealing with the nature of the soul not just in terms of its parts, but also in terms of the ways in which it *grows (phuei)* and unfolds itself, and how this growth can be cultivated and directed (cf. Parkes, 1994, p. 2). This psychological theory, which is in its basic principles the same as that of the mature Nietzsche, is the basis of Nietzsche's project in the *UC*: It is an account of the "unalterable nature and form [of things]" that has to be known in order to work on the *"improvement of that aspect of the world recognized as being alterable"* (1.445/272).[5] This psychology

---

5. I don't think this means that philosophy is "only secondarily an enterprise concerned with the pursuit of permanent truth, which, if it even exists, is only desirable because it aids in the more fundamental task of altering truth" (Brooks, 2018, p. 206)—quite the opposite.

Introduction | 7

guides the choice of Nietzsche's principal audience, the rhetorical means he uses to appeal to them and their particular concerns, the shape and extent of the cultural reform the *UC* strive to effect, and the means by which to bring this reform about. In short, psychology is "the queen of the sciences" and "the way to the fundamental problems" (*BGE* 23) already in the *UC*.

The argument of this study unfolds over its five chapters. Each of the first four chapters is an interpretation of a single *UC*, and the fifth chapter is a critical evaluation of the project presented in these four essays and of the thinking behind them. The first chapter begins with the personal background of *DS*, considering the extent to which Nietzsche was—and wasn't—influenced by Wagner in his earliest productive period. Afterward, an interpretation of *DS* 1–3—Nietzsche's *Kulturkritik* in a narrow sense of the word—shows why Nietzsche considered D. F. Strauss's book a subject worthy of a lengthy critique, and I interpret Nietzsche's scathing review of it (*DS* 4–12) as revealing apophatically—by thrashing its failures, which are symptomatic of contemporary German pseudo-culture—the broad contours of his own project.

The second chapter, the interpretation of *HL*, deals first with the structure of the human soul, which I call *erotic-historic*. This structure leads Nietzsche to postulate some basic conditions of psychic health, to which the three useful forms of history are particularly conducive. *HL* 4–9 then explores how modern scientific history undermines said conditions, and so provides a complex diagnosis of the sickness of German culture, of which D. F. Strauss is only the most obvious symptom. The root of this sickness is the absolute and insoluble conflict between life and knowledge, which is shown to be one of the central points of Nietzsche's thinking in the *UC*. Finally, I explore some of his hints toward the curing of this sickness, which are presented chiefly in *HL* 10.

The third chapter, whose subject is *SE*, explicates the meaning of the imperative *be yourself!*, the right and wrong methods of getting to know one's erotic-historic soul (and thus of facilitating one's psychic growth), as well as the role that the figure of the educator has to play in this process. This growth has its peak in the figure of the genius (in three forms: the philosopher, the artist, and the saint), i.e., in a person who has grasped in some way the whole of being and has affirmed its value in a "Schopenhauerian affirmation." This best way of life, or even an inkling of its possibility, is then to result in a practical life devoted to culture understood as *"the production of philosophers, artists, and saints within us and around us"* (1.382/213), and hopefully also in the founding of institutions devoted to this new and genuine culture.

8 | The Young Nietzsche's Education

The main subject of the fourth chapter, on *WB*, is Wagner himself. Three thematic lines emerge here: The first is Wagner as the exemplary artist and a man who has become what he is. The second is his art and the unparalleled effect it can have on its audience, namely its capacity to alienate them from their unreflective, comfortable existence and turn them toward a life of culture. And third, this immense educative potential of Wagner's art in its new home of Bayreuth—conceived as an institution of genuine culture—makes it the best possible vehicle for a large-scale renewal of German, and possibly even European, culture. *WB* culminates in a vision of the free human beings of the future, people educated so as to become what they are, and of the renaissance of European culture they will bring about as the result of Nietzsche's and Wagner's current striving.

The Nietzsche that emerges from this interpretation is a rationalist who thinks culture can be reconstructed on a rational basis with the help of art (cf. 1.445/272), but one who sees a fundamental and insoluble conflict between truth and life. He hoped to manage this conflict by a project that was to work in conjunction with Bayreuth—a project in which he was to suffer from the truth in order to provide salutary illusions to the many and so to establish a new, genuine culture. However, these hopes never materialized, and Nietzsche plunged into a deep intellectual crisis at the inaugural Bayreuth festival. The fifth chapter examines why this happened.[6] First, it explores some grave errors in the project of the *UC*, chief among them a misunderstanding of what Wagner was and what he stood for. Second are the problems of the thinking behind the *UC* itself. The central of these is the idea that the conflict between life and knowledge is absolutely insoluble and its manifold consequences, such as the ultimately life-denying character of the thought built on this foundation. Coming to terms with these problems eventually resulted in a substantial change in Nietzsche's conception of the philosophic life: The later Nietzsche no longer thinks truth and life are *necessarily* in conflict, and takes the life devoted to the truth to be the best and happiest kind of life. However, there are also elements of the thought of the *UC* that remained important for the later Nietzsche, mostly related to

---

6. Brooks (2018, 211) and Church (2015, ch. 9; 2019, ch. 6) emphasize the continuities between the thought of the *UC* and that of the later Nietzsche, but in my view they go so far in this respect as to erase the profound differences between the thought of the young Nietzsche and his mature thought. I intend to pay due attention to both the successes and the shortcomings of the *UC*, and thereby also to shed a clearer light on the break that occurred in Nietzsche's thinking after the *UC*.

Introduction | 9

his psychological theory and his understanding of various human types. And finally, I show how two of Nietzsche's ideas that he was to reject later—the attitude of the voluntary suffering of truthfulness, and his yet-inadequate conception of "becoming what one is"—served the indispensable role of ladders on which he climbed to his mature, genuinely philosophic self.

The twofold meaning of the title of this book, "*The Young Nietzsche's Education*," is related to this experience of failure on Nietzsche's part. On the one hand, the *UC* are written by a young man for young people and their goal is to educate said young people, but on the other hand, Nietzsche realizes in the carrying out of this project how much he himself still needs to learn and (re)think—that his own education was radically flawed or incomplete. Nietzsche was forced to admit the failure of the practical or political project of the *UC* and to come to terms with it; he was forced to deal with his pain and embarrassment and to undergo a stringent self-critique instead of enjoying the triumphal success he was hoping for. In this regard he had responded to his failure as a philosopher should—in a truly *responsible* way, and he is a model of such a responsible attitude to those of us who have had to deal with similar failures ourselves.

In sum, I hope to show the thinking of the young Nietzsche in its full attractiveness and intellectual strength, rather than as just an abortive juvenile misstep. The *UC* offer much food for thought not just regarding their failures from which Nietzsche had to learn, but also regarding their successes which he continued to build upon. It should be noted that, contrary to the established scholarly opinion, Nietzsche himself didn't consider these works to be just failures and juvenilia, and always held them (particularly *SE*) to be of great importance. To give a couple of salient examples, in a draft letter intended for Lou von Salomé from December 1882 (KGB III.1, p. 299), he writes that in *SE* she can find "my deepest and most funda-mental sensibilities." In August 1884 he wrote to Franz Overbeck (KGB III.1, p. 518): "I have *lived* just as I have prescribed it to myself (namely in *Schopenhauer as Educator*)." And in the letter to Georg Brandes from 10 April 1888 (KGB III.5, p. 287), he explains that "this short work [*SE*] serves as my sign of recognition: the person who does not find himself addressed *personally* by this work will probably have nothing more to do with me."[7] The note 35 [48] (11.534–35) from mid-1885 is a draft of an introduction for the four finished *UC*, calling them "fishing rods" for new readers, and speaks of the plan to add three new ones to them (cf. also the

---

7. For a more thorough discussion of this issue cf. the end of Chapter V.4.

10 | The Young Nietzsche's Education

note 41 [2], 11.669–78, titled "*A New Untimely Consideration*"). He reissued the four essays (separately) in 1886, at the time when he reissued also his other pre-*Zarathustra* works (Large 2012, p. 102). And although he did not write a preface to introduce them as he did with his other earlier books, the preface to *HA* II can be considered to serve this purpose (Lampert 2017, p. 43). Finally, in *EH* UC 3, *SE* is described as containing "my innermost history, my *becoming*," and *WB* as "a vision of my future." I aim to do justice to Nietzsche's claims to the effect that the *UC* "deserve the highest attention regarding my development" (letter to Karl Knortz from 21 June 1888; KGB III.5, p. 340).

And, besides their importance for Nietzsche's later development, they are in their own, if somewhat flawed, way a serious reflection on the fundamental philosophical question of *pos bioteon*, of the best way of life—and on the related, eminently practical task of leading the suitable readers toward it, the task of education [*Erziehung*]. The *UC* understand ethics as a complete way of life focused on and tailored for the particular individual as individual. They are, moreover, an educational project that aims to bring about the highest possibilities of human existence by teaching the readers to cultivate their souls toward these possibilities in accordance with their own nature and needs, and by preparing suitable external conditions for them to do so. The real prize of the *UC* is not the goal to which they want to lead us, but rather the path—the activity of questioning and confronting the nature of the world and of ourselves, which is to say the activity of *thinking*, which they both exemplify and invite us to. Understanding the project of the *UC* is invaluable to all those who seek and attempt (*suchen und versuchen*, to put it in a Nietzschean way) new ways of cultivating human souls—their own as well as the souls of others—in the Here and Now.

Note on the Title

The overall title of these four essays, *Unzeitgemässe Betrachtungen*, is notoriously difficult to adequately translate into English. Various translators and scholars over the years have rendered it as *Thoughts out of Season* (A. M. Ludovici), *Untimely Meditations* (R. J. Hollingdale and S. Brooks), *Untimely Considerations* (C. Zuckert), *Unmodern Observations* (W. Arrowsmith), and *Unfashionable Observations* (R. T. Gray and J. Church). In my view, the best rendering of this title is *Untimely Considerations*.

Introduction | 11

The word *unzeitgemäss* means inappropriate or inadequate to the present time or age. Translations of this word as "out of season," "unmodern," and "unfashionable" stress Nietzsche's opposition to the prevailing trends and tendencies of his time, while also underlining his desire to intervene in the said time (e.g., Gray, 1995, pp. 377–79 or Ansell-Pearson, 2013, pp. 227–28). On this view, translating it as "untimely" removes the word from the present temporal context on which it is to act by connotations of a certain inadequacy or misfortune this word carries (as, e.g., in the phrase "an untimely death"). However, Large (1994, p. 33) argues that Nietzsche "is constantly aware of his own writing as occupying an anomalous, often cultivatedly ambivalent position in time," and that the term *unzeitgemäss* carries a futural tendency that alienates it from contemporary times even though Nietzsche's argument clearly is a very "timely" intervention into contemporary German culture (e.g., at 1.247/ 87, or much later in the title *Streifzüge eines Unzeitgemässen* ["Skirmishes of an Untimely One"] from *TI*). Large's reading thus justifies the translation "untimely," and even does justice to the alienating tendency of the word that gives other translators a pause and leads them to be more inclined to other translations.[8] Thus, the word "untimely" best captures the future-oriented dimension of Nietzsche's argument in the *UC*, which is on my reading of particular importance, not least because the human soul as Nietzsche understands it in the *UC* is fundamentally oriented on the future.

As for the second part of the title, the Latin root of the word "consideration" captures both the visual and the intellectual connotations of the word *Betrachtung*. The same could be said of the word "observation"; however, this nowadays tends to mean a disinterested, scientific kind of observing and lacks the sense of a personal, polemical investment that Nietzsche's usage of *Betrachtung* carries (1.466/291).[9] I therefore refer to these essays as *Untimely Considerations* and by the abbreviation *UC*.

---

8. Neymeyr (2020, 2.369) has a similar understanding of Nietzsche's usage of the word *unzeitgemäss*. Interestingly enough, Ansell-Pearson (2013, p. 228) lapses back into the usage of "untimely" right after he argues for the translation "unfashionable."

9. Cf. Siemens (2001, pp. 80–84) on Nietzsche's usage of the word *betrachten* with a focus on the agonistic elements inherent in it.

I

David Strauss the Confessor and the Writer

Nietzsche's *Kulturkritik*

Whatever one generation learns from another, no generation learns the essentially human from a previous one.[1]

David Strauss the Confessor and the Writer, the first of the *UC*, deals with an apparently very "timely" subject: it is a critical review of David Friedrich Strauss's now long-forgotten book *The Old Faith and the New*. This apparent datedness is the main reason for the scholarly neglect of it: Giorgio Colli's claim that *DS* is "the weakest work ever published by Nietzsche, precisely because of its 'timely' character" (Colli, 1999, p. 905) is exemplary of this attitude. However, Nietzsche's critical analyses of cultural philistinism, the intellectual outlook that underlies it, and the conflict of this philistinism with genuine culture or self-cultivation in this essay are integral to the overall argument of the *UC*. To bring out this relevance, it is useful to recount how *DS*—and the entire project of the *UC*—came about. A key part of the story of the *UC*, and of Nietzsche's entire productive life, is his formative friendship with Richard Wagner. Wagner was instrumental in the genesis of the *DS*, the first of the *UC*, and is the central figure of *WB*. Wagner's project of cultural reform, as sketched, for example, in his *Beethoven*, was also an important influence on Nietzsche's own thinking in *BT* and in the *UC*. A brief account of this friendship will elucidate Nietzsche's perspective and motivating concerns in the *UC*, as well as the importance of Wagner as a person to these essays.

---

1. Kierkegaard (1983, p. 121). Cf. Šajda (2011).

14 | The Young Nietzsche's Education

I.1. Richard Wagner and the Origins of the *UC*

The two men first met at a dinner party in Leipzig on 8 November 1868 (Borchmeyer & Salaquarda, 1994, 2.1225), had an enjoyable conversation about Schopenhauer, and apparently took an immediate liking to each other. Wagner invited Nietzsche for a visit (Janz, 1978, 1.291), and Nietzsche wrote a long letter about the meeting to his friend Erwin Rohde right on the following day. He writes that the evening offered him "pleasures of such a peculiarly piquant sort" that he can do nothing but immediately relate them to Rohde, and he signed the letter as "the idyllist from Leipzig" (KGB I.2, pp. 335–342).[2] A closer contact between them seemed at first quite unlikely, especially because of the distance between Leipzig, where Nietzsche was studying, and Tribschen, where Wagner resided. However, Nietzsche was soon thereafter offered a professorial position in Basel. He accepted this position, and he arrived to Basel on 19 April 1869 (KSA 15.10). This meant, among other things, that he now lived only some 100 kilometers away from Wagner. Nietzsche also found himself in an unfamiliar environment and somewhat socially isolated at his new workplace (Prange, 2013, p. 44; cf. KGB II.1, p. 16). Thus he was more than happy to accept Wagner's invitations to spend some time with him and his wife, Cosima, in Tribschen. Their friendship hereby entered its high point: Between May 1869 and April 1872, when the Wagners moved to Bayreuth, Nietzsche visited Tribschen 23 times (Prange, 2013, p. 45).

The time spent in intimate conversation with Richard and Cosima Wagner was of great importance to Nietzsche. As late as in *Ecce Homo* he expresses glowing gratitude toward the Wagner of the Tribschen period (*EH* Clever 5):

> Speaking of the recreations of my life, I must say a word to express my gratitude for what has been by far the most profound and cordial recreation of my life. Beyond a doubt, that was my intimate relationship with Richard Wagner. I'd let go cheap the whole rest of my human relations; I should not want to give away

---

2. Gray (1995, p. 401) points out that Nietzsche's apparently first usage of the word *unzeitgemäss* refers to Wagner. In the letter to Erwin Rohde from 17 August 1869, he speaks of Wagner as of "my Juppiter" [sic], and describes him as "deeply rooted in his own powers, always looking beyond everything ephemeral, and untimely in the most beautiful sense of the word." (KGB II.1, p. 42).

out of my life at any price the days of Tribschen—days of trust, of cheerfulness, of sublime accidents, of *profound* moments . . . I do not know what experiences have others had with Wagner: *our* sky was never darkened by a single cloud.

Wagner exercised a wide-ranging influence on Nietzsche through these conversations. It involved personal issues, such as when Wagner dissuaded Nietzsche from vegetarianism, to which he was moved by the Schopenhauerian arguments of his friend Carl von Gersdorff (KGB II.1, p. 57). Wagner, also arguing on Schopenhauerian grounds, demonstrated to Nietzsche "all the internal contradictions of that theory and practice" (KGB II.1, p. 58): our very existence is the cause of great suffering, for us as well as for other living beings, and thinking that removing a tiny part of that suffering makes any meaningful difference is a piece of silly optimism. The only good reason for vegetarianism would be dietary, namely if one finds that such a diet allows oneself to live better and more productively. But this doesn't seem to be the case either: one of Wagner's friends had apparently died of vegetarianism, and Wagner himself had "felt in the strongest way" (ibid.) the negative physiological consequences of vegetarian diet when he had experimented with it once. Although Nietzsche admits that "a temporary abstinence from meat on dietetical grounds can be most useful" (KGB II.1, pp. 59–60), in general he agrees with Wagner that "spiritually productive natures with an intensive disposition *have to* eat meat," as it provides them with the energy for their "*nobler and more generally useful efforts*" (KGB II.1, pp. 58–59).[3] More generally, Nietzsche describes his conversations with Wagner as "my practical course of Schopenhauerian philosophy" in a slightly earlier letter to Rohde (KGB II.1, p. 17).[4] Wagner was, in effect, teaching him how to live according to Schopenhauerian principles, and thus how to make philosophy the central determining force of one's way of life, overall as well as in the particulars—an idea that will be of great importance to the thought of the *UC* (cf. 1.417/246).

---

3. Wagner also noted the apparent connection between vegetarianism and receptivity to "'all sorts' of socialism" (KGB II.1, p. 60).

4. Nietzsche expressed his gratitude to Wagner as an impulse to his development also in later letters, such as that to Rohde from 25 October 1872 (KGB II.3, p. 73), where Nietzsche says that Wagner "is for me like a good conscience, punishing and rewarding." He voiced similar sentiments to Wagner himself several years later, in a letter from 21 May 1876 (KGB II.5, pp. 59–60). In the same letter he also says that he celebrates the anniversary of his first visit to Tribschen as "my spiritual birthday."

16 | The Young Nietzsche's Education

WAGNER AND NIETZSCHE'S EARLY WORKS

Wagner also provided ample opportunities for his young friend to contribute to his project of reforming German culture. At the highest level, he expressed the shared goal of their endeavors by asking Nietzsche to "help me bring about the great 'renaissance' in which Plato embraces Homer, and Homer, filled with Plato's Ideas, now really becomes the greatest Homer of all," as he wrote to Nietzsche in February 1870 (KGB II.2, p. 146): a union of mythopoetic art and of philosophy that can articulate the art's true importance as the foundation of a great culture oriented on the production of the genius.[5] In more concrete terms, it was Wagner who inspired Nietzsche to write *BT*, his first book, by suggesting him that it would be good to expand and deepen the arguments of his public lecture *Socrates and Greek Tragedy* in the form of "a larger and more comprehensive work" (KGB II.2, pp. 137–138; cf. 15.19).

BT scandalized the contemporary philological community by its bold speculations, its open admiration for Wagner, as well as by its lack of footnotes and other trappings of conventional classical scholarship. *BT* was attacked on these grounds by the young—even younger than Nietzsche—Ulrich von Wilamowitz-Möllendorff in the pamphlet *Philology of the Future!*, published on 1 June 1872, which "in twenty-eight breathless pages attempted a total demolition of Nietzsche's book and its author's classical credentials" (Silk & Stern, 1981, p. 95). Nietzsche's friends came to his defense: Erwin Rohde wrote another pamphlet, titled *Afterphilologie*, in which he defended the unusual form of *BT*, the philological soundness of Nietzsche's speculations, and attacked the ignorance and malice of Wilamowitz's pamphlet (ibid., p. 99). And even before Rohde's defense appeared, Wagner published an open letter on 12 June 1872 to support Nietzsche on broader cultural grounds (KGB II.4, pp. 13–21). This letter is an example both of Wagner's focusing

---

5. A couple of days later, on 15 February 1870, Nietzsche reacted to these words in a letter to Rohde (KGB II.1, pp. 93–96) as follows: "I may yet turn into a walking hope: Richard Wagner, too, has let me know in a most touching way what destiny he sees prescribed for me. All this is making me very anxious." Prange (2013, pp. 47–49) reads this letter as expressing Nietzsche's doubts about Wagner, because of Wagner's apparent misunderstanding of how Nietzsche periodized Ancient Greek culture, and Nietzsche becoming increasingly aware of the huge gap between their respective outlooks. I believe these words express genuine fear and doubt as to whether he, a young man of mere 25 years, will be able to fulfill such an enormous task; and he was also afraid of losing his intellectual autonomy in service to Wagner's cause.

of his general cultural project to a smaller and more concrete partial task, and of his guidance of the young Nietzsche.

Wagner opens the letter by agreeing with Wilamowitz that classical philology should play an important role in German education, and approvingly quotes the concluding sentence of *Philology of the Future!* to this effect. But although Wagner believes that in philology there is "the tendency to a higher, that is, genuinely productive education" (ibid., p. 16), he sees nothing of this kind in philology as it actually exists in Germany, that is, in the philological establishment in whose name Wilamowitz attacks Nietzsche. This establishment contributes nothing to the work of German artists and poets, its thorough study of the classical languages produces no comparable rigor in the proper usage of German language, and even the other sciences do perfectly well without philology. Philology as a discipline is thus shown to be completely impractical and insular, its only goal being the production of more philologists, who "are useful only to each other among themselves" (ibid.).

Wagner believes there is a way to overcome this mismatch between the high ideals professed by philology and its actual practice. But the usual dry popularizing lectures won't do. It would require someone to step forward and "tell us without scholarly language and awful citations *what* have the initiates of philology learned under the cover of their research, which is so incomprehensible to us laypeople" (ibid.). In other words, to present what one has understood of the Antiquity not just as a collection of facts, but as a force that can contribute to the improvement of education here and now, in a way that is comprehensible to non-specialists and that can have a real impact on German culture at large. However, in doing so, this person would have to step beyond the boundaries of what the establishment considers "philology proper," and would thereby incur their wrath and censure; for the establishment they would be "in no way emancipated, but rather just an apostate" (ibid., p. 17). And this, Wagner says, is exactly what Nietzsche attempted to do in publishing *BT* and what happened to him thereafter.

Nietzsche then is currently the best hope for the realization of the ideals of philology—he is an accomplished philologist and also cares deeply about the advancement of German culture. It is on the basis of these credentials that Wagner turns to him in the name of "those whom I call *we*" (ibid., p. 19), of the Wagnerian "we" who work with him on his project of cultural reform, and poses the question in which the entire letter culminates: "*How does it stand with our German educational institutions?*" (ibid., p. 20). Wagner closes the letter by emphasizing that the task opened up by this question is

18 | The Young Nietzsche's Education

for an entire lifetime, and says that its goal is to determine "of what kind would German education have to be if it is to help the resurrected nation to its noblest goals" (ibid., p. 21), or how to shape educational institutions so they would really form the young to human greatness.

By asking Nietzsche to diagnose the actual state of the German educational institutions (their glowing reputation in the eyes of the public opinion notwithstanding) and to propose a reform that would address their current shortcomings, Wagner invited Nietzsche to answer the question in writing and thus to make another concrete contribution to the Wagnerian project of cultural renewal—this time a critique of the German educational system. This critique was to be an expanded version of his lectures *On the Future of Our Educational Institutions*, which Wagner had read and appreciated.[6] Nietzsche indeed perceived this question as such an invitation: He wrote to his friend Malwida von Meysenbug that by this letter, "the Maestro [i.e., Wagner] has ceremonially and publicly laid down this task on my shoulders" (KGB II.3, p. 127, Feb. 1873).

In the same letter Nietzsche also expressed worries whether this task isn't too large for as young a person as he was (he was 28 at the time, while Wagner was 59), and ultimately he never published *FEI* in any form. But in general, Nietzsche appreciated Wagner's gradual guidance in this respect, and on 24 June 1872 he wrote to Wagner thankfully, stating, "you give me time to mature toward my task" (KGB II.3, p. 15). The Wagners had influence also on other projects Nietzsche was working on in this period. The *Five Prefaces to Five Unwritten Books* were written as a Christmas and/ or birthday present for Cosima Wagner (her birthday was 24 Dec.), and given to her in December 1872 (cf. KGB II.3, pp. 108, 110). Conversely, *Philosophy in the Tragic Age of the Greeks* was abandoned after Nietzsche presented the manuscript to Wagner on a visit to Tribschen between 6 and 12 April 1873 and Wagner wasn't interested in it (Golder, 1990, p. 4). After this misunderstanding, Nietzsche began to work on the first *UC* on D. F. Strauss, which subject was suggested to him by the Wagners, both of whom voiced their contempt for Strauss's latest book to Nietzsche (Schaberg, 1995, p. 32). In a note from 1875 (5 [98], 8.66), titled "For an Introduction of the Complete Edition of the 'Untimely Ones,'" which consists of several bullet-point–like sentences about the origin of the *UC*, the last sentence—apparently describing the final impetus—reads "A few words by Wagner in Strasbourg." Cosima Wagner's letter to Nietzsche from

---

6. Cf. Brooks (2018, pp. 6–12) for an account of Nietzsche's intention behind *FEI*.

12 February 1873 also contains some sarcastic remarks about Strauss's book.[7] Nietzsche thus saw a polemic against D. F. Strauss's new book as a way to ingratiate himself to Wagner (Golder, 1990, p. 5). Nietzsche then worked quickly: He reported to Wagner that he was working on *DS* already on 18 April 1873 (KGB II.3, pp. 144–145), and he received the first printed copies of it on 8 August 1873 (Schaberg, 1995, p. 33). Thus Nietzsche, influenced by the Wagnerian conceptions of cultural reform as the proper form of political reform and education as the production of genius—but quickly outgrowing the Wagnerian formulations of these concerns—embarked on the project of the *UC*. In these four essays he articulates a comprehensive critique of contemporary German culture, as Wagner expected him to do with *FEI*—and, as we shall see, much more than just that.

I.2. *DS* 1–3: Nietzsche's Critique of German Culture

DS opens with a reference to the Franco-Prussian war of 1870–71 that ended in a resounding Prussian victory and in the proclamation of the second German Empire in the Hall of Mirrors at Versailles. This victory was, Nietzsche says, a demonstration of the promising capacities that German nature possesses and that "have nothing at all to do with culture," namely "strict military discipline, natural bravery and perseverance, superiority of leadership, unity and obedience among the led" (1.160/6). However, many aren't satisfied with seeing this victory as merely a triumph of German nature. In the opinion of these many—which is actually the *public opinion*, that is, the dominant view of its time—the war demonstrated also a victory of German *culture* over its French counterpart. Nietzsche thinks this is a serious and pernicious error, and not merely because it is an error—"errors can be of the most salutary and blessed nature" (1.159/5)—but, as we'll see, because of its consequences for the kind of life that is being cultivated in Germany. It is by engaging with this popular error—with the contemporary *doxa*—that we enter the territory of the *UC*: the realm of cultural politics in which the project of the *UC* will unfold.

In the first place, there can be no question about a victory of German *culture* over the French. Such a victory would mean imposing "an original

---

7. "In the German Empire I have encountered great enthusiasm for the book of D. Strauss, which liberates us from salvation, prayer, and Beethoven's music by some quotations from Helmholtz" (KGB II.4, p. 209).

20 | The Young Nietzsche's Education

German culture" (1.163–164/9) on the French, and nothing of that kind has happened. If anything, the opposite is the case: German culture was and still is dependent on the French, and necessarily so, "for up to the present day there has never been an original German culture" (1.164/10). Nietzsche quotes Goethe, the authority par excellence in matters of German culture, to support his surprising assertion: The real problem of German culture is that it hardly even exists at this point.[8] This claim opens up two questions: First, what a culture is; and second, if Germans *don't* have a culture, what is "this thing that in Germany calls itself culture" (1.160/6) that according to public opinion prevailed over the French culture?

Nietzsche defines culture as "a unity of artistic style that manifests itself throughout all the vital self-expressions of a people," and its opposite, barbarism, as "absence of style" or "the chaotic hodgepodge of all styles" (1.163/9). Since culture is so pervasive in the life of a people (and of individuals), its presence or absence is easy to notice: everything—from fashions through furniture or architecture, to people's manners and gestures—testifies to the kind of culture they possess. In the case of Germans, all these testify to their barbarism. Far from possessing any internal unifying principle, the contemporary German "culture" is rather a chaotic mixture of all kinds of styles and principles. The closest approximation of such a principle it has is actually its very opposite, namely "a phlegmatic insensibility to culture" (1.163/9). German culture doesn't just lack an organizing principle at its core—it doesn't even care about acquiring one. What the public opinion considers to be German culture and education, *Bildung*, is in fact merely *Gebildetheit*, scholarly learnedness that has no relation whatsoever to other spheres of human life.[9] As learned as the Germans may be, their learning is of no use "wherever it is a question not of knowledge but of capability, not of information but of artistry" (1.162/8). Their learning is not the unifying principle of a productive culture, but merely a kind of *Fachidiotismus*. What is even worse, the pride of the bearers of German learnedness blinds them against any critical consideration of the merits of their "culture." In fact, they believe that "that their own education is the ripest and finest that was

---

8. Cf. Eckermann, 2011, pp. 611–12 (conversation from 3 May 1827). A few years later, Nietzsche would call Eckermann's *Conversations with Goethe* "the best German book there is" (*WS* 109).

9. Neymeyr (2020, 1.77) points out that Wager had used the same distinction in his 1869 essay *On Conducting*. In the following pages she documents the ubiquity of this distinction in other early writings of Nietzsche.

ever produced by this or any other age" (1.162/8), that their learnedness is the peak of human cultural achievements so far.

The problem with this learnedness is not just that it exists, but that it can cause a most serious damage to Germany, in the worst case even the "*extirpation of the German spirit*" (1.160/5). What is at stake here is how the powerful German nature will be cultivated—for the original, ancient meaning of the word "culture," which is taken up by Nietzsche,[10] is a cultivation of *nature* (L. Strauss, 1995, p. 3)—or rather, whether it will be cultivated at all or not. Either the natural German bravery will be given a new direction and its energy will be used in education and in developing a genuine culture for the Germans—or the public opinion, which has no use for this bravery, will prevail and do whatever it can to placate and neutralize the power inherent in it.[11] The first chapter of *DS* shows us that Nietzsche's cultural critique will not target any foreign influences, but problems inherent to the German culture itself.[12] In the first place, it will be a negative effort to turn the courageous German souls "against their own inner enemy" (1.160/6), against the pseudo-culture of mere learnedness. Ultimately it will be a positive struggle to win these promising young souls for the course of genuine education and to teach them how to cultivate themselves, and so to contribute to the making of a productive German culture.[13]

But again, only very few see the glaring contrast between what a culture proper would be and what the present-day German learnedness actually is. No such contrast exists for the public opinion because no such contrast exists for those who form the public opinion. These are the *Bildungsphilister*, the "cultivated philistines." Like all philistines, they are "the opposite of the

---

10. This is well visible in the second definition of culture in the *UC*, culture as "new and improved *physis*," which we find at the end of *HL* (1.334/167). Cf. Hutter (2006, pp. 18–22) on the interrelation of individual (self-)cultivation and culture at large.

11. I don't believe Brooks (2018, p. 26) is correct in reading Nietzsche as claiming that "warlike nations inevitably descend into barbarism"; the question is rather how the warlike energies and qualities should be directed.

12. Nietzsche here quietly turns away from the view that German cultural renewal would mean the victory over French culture, expressed in Wagner's *Beethoven* (Wagner, 1983, 9.109/2014, p. 193) as well as in *BT* (1.149/111).

13. As Gadamer (2004, p. 10) notes, "the Latin equivalent for *Bildung* is *formatio*," and we should keep in mind this relation it has to *forming* or *shaping* together with its relation to image [*Bild*], which is frequently emphasized by Brooks (2018, pp. 27, 139, 145–152). The connotations of forming and shaping seem to be more important to Nietzsche himself: cf. the note 19 [307], 7.513.

22 | The Young Nietzsche's Education

son of the muses, the artist, the genuinely cultured person" (1.165/11), and in addition to this basic characteristic, the cultivated philistines are also unaware of being philistines. Nietzsche says that a philistine like this "fancies himself to be a son of the muses and a cultured person" (1.165/11).[14] The philistines are then distinguished from genuinely cultured humans by a threefold lack: First, they lack culture; second, they lack the knowledge of what culture is; and third, they lack the awareness of the first two lacks, that is, they lack self-knowledge. The first lack makes them philistines in general, the two other lacks combined make them cultivated philistines.[15]

What does it mean to lack culture, that is, to be a barbarian? As culture—of a people as well as of the individuals who constitute a cultured people—is distinguished by possessing a unifying principle on which all the expression of their life are based, the barbarian (in our case the philistine) lacks a *principle* that would order and guide their life. In the absence of such a principle, the philistine's life, and their soul, are directed by the bodily needs that are present to each of us throughout our lives and always demand satisfaction.[16] These demands constitute their "seriousness of life," defined as "profession and business, together with wife and child" (1.170/16).[17] They are serious about making money and providing themselves and their family with a comfortable bourgeois existence. Moreover, the barbarian also desires to be acknowledged as good by others like them: Their views are thus extremely susceptible to public opinion. And conversely, it is from the existence of a great mass of such susceptible people, who are anxious to present the "correct" opinions in society in order to appear "fashionable," to have their learnedness validated,[18] that public opinion gets its power to

---

14. Nietzsche follows Schopenhauer in his definition of the philistine: cf. Neymeyr, 2020, 1.89–90.

15. In what follows, I render *Bildungsphilister* simply as "philistine," since Nietzsche too tends to use these terms interchangeably in *DS*.

16. More precisely, they follow whichever of them happens to be the strongest at the given moment; their soul is chaotic or shapeless already in this basic sense.

17. Nietzsche made a similar point already in *BT* Foreword with the phrase "seriousness of existence" (1.24/*BT* 14). Goethe's comment to Eckermann from 22 March 1831 (Eckermann, 2011, p. 473)—"for wherein does barbarism consist other than in not acknowledging the excellent!"—is likewise relevant here.

18. Since learnedness has no bearing on one's practical life, it can exist in a barbaric soul without any friction.

compel conformity among the barbarians.[19] The content of these opinions is more or less irrelevant to them—they have no higher principle to which the opinions should conform—as long as these don't pose a challenge to their comfortable life. Anything that falls outside of these two overriding demands, for example, art or philosophy, is automatically stripped of seriousness and relegated into the role of mere fun or entertainment, or better yet: *divertissement*.[20]

The opposite of the barbarian, the cultured human being, is defined not so much by (fully) possessing an organizing principle of one's soul and of one's life, but by ceaselessly *searching* for such a principle.[21] Or rather, their life is organized around this search for a principle that could give their soul an ever-fuller internal unity and consistency. In effect, the life of culture consists in a tireless effort to answer the question that has been central to philosophy at least since Socrates: *pos bioteon? How to live?*, and in a tireless effort to actually *live* according to the answer one has found, that is, to order one's life in all its expressions and activities according to one's chosen principle.[22] This is an exceedingly difficult effort in two ways. First, intellectually: If one is to know what their best life is, one must *know oneself*, that is, one's capacities, desires, natural tendencies, and the possibilities of their satisfaction and perfection. This is a long and difficult process that requires a powerful motivation: If one lacks such a motivation, as the self-satisfied philistines do, one will hardly attain much self-knowledge and will likely fall into self-aggrandizing delusions, such as the philistines' belief in being the peak of humanity (1.162, 167/8, 13). And second, it is difficult in terms of the self-discipline required to carry it out: Hence Nietzsche speaks of

---

19. In *SE* 6, Nietzsche will succinctly express this aspect of barbarism by declaring its bearers to be "the tortured slaves of the three M's, Moment, Majority Opinion, and Modishness" (1.392/222–223). Braatz (1988, p. 23) remarks that for Nietzsche, the cultured way of existing in a public space integrates individuals into society not via conformism, but via *agon*.

20. Later on (1.203/47), Nietzsche will directly reference Pascal's idea of *divertissement*, meaning both "entertainment" and "distraction," i.e., entertaining activities whose purpose is to prevent us from confronting the question of the meaning of our existence, or more precisely the lack thereof. Cf. Pascal, *Pensées* §§ 165–171 (Pascal, 1995, pp. 44–49).

21. Related to this is also their searching for the truth, which Neymeyr (2020, 1.96–97) highlights in relation to Lessing as he figures in *DS*.

22. This is the second, higher sense in which the philistine is "deformed" (1.162/7): Their soul lacks a determinate form or shape that would order all its activities. Cf. the related parable of "the land of the hunchbacks" (1.223/65).

24 | The Young Nietzsche's Education

"the tyranny of true cultural demands" (1.169/15) that the philistines hate, since such demands implicitly but firmly belie their claim to be the peak of humanity.[23] Insofar as a cultured human being strives to live according to their own principles, they have no use and no respect for public opinion. *Their* seriousness of life is oriented not on breadwinning and comfort, but on their search for the best way to live and on the activities that are conducive to that search, such as art, philosophy, or philology.

Nietzsche believes that philistinism was originally a somewhat healthy reaction to the culture-endangering excesses of Romanticism. The Romantics and the idealist philosophers introduced a "carnival of all gods and myths" (1.168/14) into the still young German culture and thereby threw it into a chaos—and thus limiting the introduction of novelties was a good countermeasure.[24] However, the self-satisfied philistines, proud of their petty-bourgeois lives and limited horizons, absolutized this countermeasure into another culture-hostile extreme—namely into a rejection of seeking at all, that is, of the very principle of culture. *Their* principle is that "we should seek no further" (1.168/14), for everything worth looking for had already been found and is personified in the philistines themselves. This principle entails a thoroughgoing perversion of the meaning of culture, and according to Nietzsche that is precisely what the philistines accomplished. They perverted the character of the cultured human beings themselves: They are understood not as seekers [*Suchende*], that is, as those who seek the good life, but as finders [*Findende*], that is, as producers of the works of art that the philistines consume as after-work entertainment and of public opinions (i.e., readily quotable authoritative statements that lend the quoting philistine an air of sophistication).[25] They perverted the proper way of honoring them—namely striving to follow in their footsteps and

---

23. Goethe's words to Eckermann from 14 March 1830 (Eckermann, 2011, p. 709), quoted (and abridged) at 1.167/13, give us an example of the kind of (self-)tyranny in question. In the following sentence Goethe adds: "When everyone can say the same about themselves, it will all be well for us." The "tyranny" of culture is, then, not just personal, but a universal demand that sets up the cultured human being as exemplary to all. Goethe is in effect asking, if *he* could devote his life to the pursuit of true culture, what is *your* excuse for not doing the same?

24. Here Nietzsche touches upon the main problem of *HL*; cf. 1.250/89. Also cf. Neymeyr (2020, 1.97–99) for the historical context.

25. Braatz (1988, p. 36) notes in this context that the public opinion serves as the philistine "equivalent" of education; the philistines use this "education" not for self-cultivation, but to provide an appearance thereof, or "for the sake of deceiving themselves and others."

becoming a cultured human being oneself—into the consumption of their works as entertainment. They perverted the works of younger artists from being their own efforts to become more cultured into mere imitations of the earlier classics, into works of an alleged "age of epigones" (1.169/15). And finally, they neutralized the academic disciplines that can contribute to culture, such as philosophy or philology (insofar as it presents Classical Antiquity as exemplary) into purely historical disciplines that raise no claims about human excellence.

All these characteristic efforts of the philistines, together with their similarity to each other that arises from their susceptibility to public opinion,[26] ultimately amount to "a system of nonculture" (1.166/12). This system is a conglomerate of philistines who are everywhere "cast from the same mold" (1.165/11) and recognize themselves in each other, but this shared "form" (actually: shared *formlessness*—an amorphous mass as opposed to an articulated unity) decidedly does not constitute a culture in Nietzsche's sense. The philistine system is permissive as long as what one does has no bearing on practical life and the philistine supremacy in it ("with the proviso that for heaven's sake everything had yet to remain as it was"—1.170/15). However, those works and acts that are conducive to culture—such as "all the artistically productive forms and demands of a true style" (1.166/12)—and thereby pose a challenge to the philistine system of non-culture are met only with systematic negation and exclusion from public discussion and consideration. This is how the philistines rule Germany (1.165, 173/10, 18)—by producing and propagating a public opinion, a *doxa*, that is conducive to their comfortable existence and deleterious to all striving for culture proper. And their rule is so strong, says Nietzsche, that they even openly admit some of their weaknesses that they are aware of. They admit that cultured human beings are stronger than they are in terms of willpower (1.172/18), and that it is precisely their willpower that drives people like Hölderlin to strive for culture. They, being weak, have no such strength, no such drive, and no such striving. But, in a final perverse move, they see this weakness as an advantage. They are happy with their comfortable lives even without culture, and they intend to maintain the conditions in which they rule and their lives are considered the best. In other words, their "cultural" goal is a "barbarism built to last" (1.166/12). That strong souls like Hölderlin, desiring of a better life, of a life of culture, may perish of such conditions is of no great concern to them.

---

26. In contrast to this, it is the cultured human beings who are actually *individuals*.

26 | The Young Nietzsche's Education

The philistines and their barbaric, culture-hostile rule over Germany are the main target of Nietzsche's cultural critique in *DS*. In the remainder of this work he focuses on a particular target: the latest book of David Friedrich Strauss, *The Old Faith and the New: A Confession*. Nietzsche has several reasons for this procedure. First, this book had been immensely popular among the philistines—it went through six editions in little more than a year (1.201/45)—and because of this it stands out as an exemplary compendium of the current philistine "public opinions." Second, the book's author is superior to other philistines in his courage, which makes him their leader, as it were, and a peak example of the philistine type (1.208/51–52). Third, this book presents by far the most ambitious project the philistine "culture" has come up with yet—namely founding a new religion. Strauss's book is a "confession" in a twofold sense: not just by the beliefs Strauss voices in it, but also by the very fact that he finds his beliefs worthy of being published and widely read—that he considers his beliefs to be *authoritative*.[27] Thus it is ideally suited for Nietzsche to show us D. F. Strauss, this "peak of humanity" and the peak of the philistine "culture," as he really is, without the cover of his self-presentation and self-delusions. It is the possibility of laying bare the deformed philistine soul that moves Nietzsche to engage with Strauss and his book of confessions; neither he nor his book is worthy of consideration on their own merits (cf. *EH* Wise 7).

I.3. *DS* 4–12: The Portrait of the Cultivated Philistine

David Friedrich Strauss (1808–1874) was a Protestant theologian who made his name in 1835–36 with the publication of *The Life of Jesus, Critically Examined*. This book, a pioneer in the search for the "historical Jesus," aimed to purify our image of Jesus from the mythological baggage added to it by the Gospel writers. Instead, it depicted Jesus as a mere human being whose alleged "miracles" were fictions made up by his disciples to make him look like the Messiah foretold in the Old Testament, and it scandalized contemporary Europe. Nietzsche had read *The Life of Jesus* in 1864, and it apparently contributed to his break with Christianity and to the decision to abandon his theological studies and concentrate on philology (van Tongeren, 2000, pp. 21–22; also cf. Golder, 1990, p. 7). *The Old Faith and the New*,

---

27. It is significant that the criterion of a book's worth is its usefulness to the *thinker* (1.174/19).

David Strauss the Confessor and the Writer | 27

Strauss's last major book, appeared in 1872. Unlike its predecessors, it was not a work of serious scholarship, but rather his "confession of faith," or a summary of his beliefs and opinions.

This book is a manifesto of the progressive, intellectual middle classes (Strauss, 1872, p. 294/1874, II.119–120).[28] There is a crucial premise Strauss shares with Nietzsche: the conviction that "God is dead," or that "that the belief in the Christian God has become unbelievable" (*GS* 343), and that it needs to be replaced in its role as a lynchpin of culture with something better. Strauss's program is, in effect, generic secular humanism that claims to progress beyond Christianity and aims to replace it with natural science and hard work, which make the world an ever-better place to live;[29] he furthermore believes this process is already happening. This program of spreading science and enlightenment is based on the (implicitly Christian) premise that "the truth will set you free," that an increased rationalization of life will lead to greater happiness for all. In the terms of *HL*, this amounts to thinking that science should rule life.

The book itself is rather banal; Strauss is at his most courageous when discussing art. He manages to dismiss *Faust II* (Strauss, 1872, pp. 308/1874, II.139)—which Goethe considered to be the completion of his life's work (Eckermann, 2011, p. 490, conversation from 6 June 1831)—and Beethoven's programmatic symphonies (Strauss, 1872, pp. 359/1874, II.206) as subpar works with just a couple of sentences.

The biggest surprise concerning the "new faith" is how little ethics it gives us. Strauss claims to want no major social changes, nor to establish any new practices. It is a faith without any form of worship or structured activities it would require from its believers. Nor does it ask its faithful to change their lives in any way—they are to go on as before, to persevere in

---

28. Two notes on the texts of *The Old Faith and the New* I am using:

1) The page numbers to this book refer first to the 1872 German edition (which is the edition Nietzsche is quoting in *DS*), then to the 1874 English edition, which is arbitrarily divided into two volumes. An advantage of quoting by page numbers rather than by chapters is that on four occasions, a pair of chapters has been fused into a single chapter in the English edition, resulting in 108 chapters as opposed to the original 112 chapters; most chapters thus have a different number in English than in German.

2) I am citing according to the 1874 English edition rather than from the 1999 one. The translation in both editions is identical, but the 1999 edition is missing both appendices and the two concluding chapters (chs. 85–108 of the 1874 edition), as well as the table of contents.

29. Pinker, 2019, is a contemporary version of this ideology.

28 | The Young Nietzsche's Education

their work and in patriotic citizenship, and to be happy as the world gets slowly but steadily better. Furthermore, Strauss has a very limited idea of human greatness: "he who doesn't inflate himself is well aware of the humble measure of his capacities" (Strauss, 1872, p. 128/1874, I.149). We see what is *the* best way of life here, the life "truly moral, and because moral, happy" (Strauss, 1872, p. 12/1874, I.12): namely the regular life of a 19th-century bourgeois who does little besides what their job requires of them, but who nevertheless is the peak of human development simply by the virtue of existing at its currently latest point, or (to put it more pompously) of being the end result of the progress of the Cosmos so far.

In the first paragraph of *DS* 4, Nietzsche announces that his reading of D. F. Strauss's book and of its "new faith" will be organized around three questions: "First: How does the new believer conceive his heaven? Second: What is the extent of the courage with which these new beliefs provide him? And third: How does he write his books?" (1.177/23). These questions structure the remainder of *DS*: chapters 4–5 answer the question of the philistine heaven, that is, his idea of the good life. Chapters 6–7 examine his courage, that is, how is he able to deal with difficulties on the path toward his "heaven" or with challenges to it. Chapters 8–12 deal with the style of Strauss's book. Since Nietzsche earlier defined culture as the unity of style, the style of the book will most directly reveal us how (un)cultured Strauss is: His style will *demonstrate* the level of his internal culture. "*Style* is the physiognomy of the spirit," as Schopenhauer put it (*PP* II, p. 515/*Werke* V.605). All three questions are, then, in effect asking about the philistines' idea of the good life: how they practice it now, what they want to become in the future, and how they want to attain this goal.[30] Both their internal and external culture is included in the questioning. Nietzsche is reviewing Strauss's book from the perspective of cultivation of the human soul.

PHILISTINE "HEAVEN"

The "heaven" of the philistines, the best life they can imagine, turns out to be simply *the life they are already living*. They cannot imagine anything

---

30. Contrary to Church's (2019, p. 38) view, the three questions of *DS* 4 that are answered in the remainder of *DS* are not just "three features of Strauss's argument," but they form a synoptic account thereof. The critique of Strauss's style is integral to Nietzsche's argument; I thus disagree with Brooks (2018, p. 56), who believes that "these literary criticisms are not as important for demonstrating the unity of the *Untimely Meditations* as their theoretical counterparts" and judges *DS* 8–12 to be "five tendentious sections."

better—and that is why nothing else should be sought. This life is, as Strauss describes it (Strauss, 1872, p. 294/1874, II.119–120),[31] a middle-class life centered on one's profession. Despite the centrality of one's profession to this life, there are no high standards by which to judge the profession one should choose: The believers of the "new faith" are not just artists or scholars, but also civil servants, soldiers, or even merchants. And it is *besides* their profession, as Strauss says, that they occupy themselves with what Strauss calls "all the higher interests of humanity," that is, with political discussion, popular science, literature and music. It is clear that, despite Strauss's claims to the contrary, the philistines do not see the arts and sciences as *higher* interests—for if they did, they would devote their lives to what is higher rather than to their ostensibly "lower" professions. In fact, the "higher" interests are at best secondary for the philistines, and Nietzsche drives this point home by imagining their "self-cultivation" as visits to the beer hall or the zoo, or as newspaper reading (1.179/24).[32]

Nietzsche is particularly interested in the role of art in the philistines' lives, since here the philistine type appears in its purity, as Strauss says (1.180/25). Again, it is only used for entertainment or *divertissement* from the "crude reality" (1.180/25) in which the *actual*, serious life takes place.[33] Strauss has a lot to say about the German poets and composers, but it is of little value. His approach to them is "critical" in the worst sense of the word. Although he cannot compare at all to someone like Goethe in terms of artistic output, he is quick to pass sweeping judgments on him—judgments that often are not even the fruit of his own understanding, but simply borrowed from someone else (in one case, Strauss quotes Gervinus to "prove" Goethe had no dramatic talent—1.181/26). Conspicuously missing from Strauss's chapters on the German artists is any personal engagement with their works. It doesn't seem as if there was anything that, say, Goethe's *Faust* or Schiller's *Wallenstein* could teach the philistine, or as if they could lead them to a serious reflection on their own life. Instead, Strauss provides his readers with some piece of textual criticism that is likely meant to be "objective," as opposed to the "subjective" opinions that a personal engagement with a

---

31. Nietzsche quotes this passage in full at 1.178–179/23–24.

32. This association of newspaper reading with philistinism was made already by Goethe in *Wilhelm Meister's Journeyman Years* I.4 (*Werke* VIII.39).

33. The use of *divertissement* also protects from solitude and from the fundamental questions that tend to occur to us when we're not occupied by worldly pursuits. The consumption of culture as *divertissement* thus also shields the philistine from questioning their self-complacency.

30 | The Young Nietzsche's Education

work would produce. In this manner, the philistine's understanding of art is based in the preexisting public opinions and results in the production of several new opinions that are added to this supposedly authoritative body of opinion (cf. 1.205–206/49–50). This is a typical philistine procedure, of which Goethe had complained to Eckermann on 16 December 1828 (Eckermann, 2011, pp. 292–293): "The Germans, [Goethe] said, cannot get rid of philistinism.—They are now squabbling and arguing about some verses that are printed both in Schiller's works and mine, and think it is important to ascertain which really belong to Schiller and which to me. As if it mattered at all, as if anything could be gained by such an investigation, and as if the existence of those verses were not enough!" This kind of textual criticism or *Quellenforschung* is by itself pointless, says Goethe, because it misses the main thing—the *person* who was able to write the work in question. It is the person that matters rather than their spiritual nourishment, for we are all nourished in one way or another, but what we do with the strength derived from the nourishment is our own accomplishment: "one might just as well ask a well-fed man about the oxen, sheep, and swine which he has eaten and which have given him strength" (Eckermann, 2011, p. 293). Goethe concludes that "what matters is to have a soul that loves the truth and receives it wherever it finds it" (ibid.). The philistines then clearly miss the main benefit art offers us, namely its potential as a means for the cultivation of our soul.

The same superficial interest is the rule of the philistine's engagement with music. Nietzsche reserves particular contempt for Strauss's treatment of Beethoven (whom, it should be remembered, Wagner understood as the trailblazer for his own artistic project). Strauss dismisses his Sixth and Ninth Symphonies as inferior works with great ease. What is even worse, in doing so he implies his own superiority in matters of art over Beethoven, who—unlike Strauss—apparently didn't have the good fortune of being accompanied by the Muses throughout his life and works (1.186/31).[34] To conclude this section, Nietzsche likens Strauss's approach to art to worshiping idols with a sacrificial fire: The idols are those artists and works that conform to his opinions, and those that don't conform are cast into the (figurative) fire to "keep the master's image pure" (1.187/31).[35] Ultimately

---

34. Nietzsche is quick to point to us the comic value of a scene in which "a wholly inartistic minimaestro sits in judgment on Beethoven" (1.187/32).

35. Nietzsche doesn't doubt that if Strauss had the chance to actually burn the "problematic" symphonies and thus to "improve" the image of Beethoven, he would do it (1.187/31).

this is because the philistine believes they have nothing to learn, since the best is already known to them and nothing more should be sought. Works of art can therefore be either a confirmation of their views (and celebrated as such) or fall short of this standard (and thereby be deficient). For in the philistine's eyes it is they and their own views who are the measure of all things: Their worldview in effect amounts to saying " 'I myself am the only person I know who is always right' " (1.187/32).

So *this* is the philistine heaven: entertaining oneself with consumption and superficial discussion of those works of art that fit the philistine's prejudices—"that odious need for rest and relaxation and that casual, only half-attentive deference to philosophy and culture and especially to all the seriousness of existence" (1.204/47–48)—as a means of recovering from life in the "crude reality" in which their daily toils take place, of appearing "cultured" to other philistines, and as a means of *divertissement*, of preventing any disconcerting thoughts from occurring to them.

Philistine "Courage"

Strauss prides himself on his courage to live without the comforting fictions of Christianity, such as the immortality of the soul and divine providence. Nietzsche doesn't deny this requires courage; he rather asks how far Strauss's courage to live in a godless world extends. Schopenhauer and Eduard von Hartmann offered us a clear and bleak picture of such a world as senseless suffering, and they concluded it would be better if no life (Schopenhauer) or even no cosmos at all (von Hartmann) had existed. Strauss quotes these arguments in his book (Strauss, 1872, p. 142/1874, I.166). But instead of engaging with their conclusions, Strauss quickly dispatches pessimism with a sophism: if the world is a bad thing, the thinking that came to this conclusion is also a bad thing, and hence it invalidates itself.[36] The point of this sophism is to persuade his "faithful" that pessimism is intellectually worthless by pretending as if it were "but a trifling matter to refute Schopenhauer" (1.192/36).

Pessimism had apparently been refuted by the "new faith's" belief in the rationality of the Cosmos that leads to an ever-greater perfection of the beings within it, especially of human beings. But this belief turns out to

---

36. Strauss's conclusion obviously does not follow: Even if the world is "bad" (i.e., full of senseless suffering), this doesn't make the thinking that comes to this conclusion "bad" (i.e., faulty reasoning).

32 | The Young Nietzsche's Education

have shaky foundations. Nietzsche points out that the Cosmos is not just the source of all life, reason, and goodness, but also of their opposites—of decay, unreason, and evil (1.196/41). Strauss responds to this kind of criticism by portraying his Cosmos as being not rational *stricto sensu*, but as a process of developing ever-greater rationality through the struggle of various forces. But such a claim is not grounded in what modern science teaches us about the world and can be only accepted on *faith* (Zuckert, 1970, p. 31). The "rationality" of the Cosmos that is supposed to be a solace to the believers of the "new faith" turns out to be a metaphysical trick—a reinsertion of providence into a godless world that has no ground for it—that Strauss employs because he cannot reveal to them the extent to which the Cosmos is cold and careless. Strauss's entire *cosmodicea* amounts to an "*idolatry of success*," of whatever comes to pass, as the supposed rational necessity governing the universe (1.197/41). Considered from the perspective of Schopenhauerian courage, this is nothing but "a bitter mockery of the nameless sufferings of humankind" (1.192/37; quoting *WWR* I, § 59, p. 326/*Werke* I.447): this faith simply ignores the omnipresent reality of suffering and always looks on the bright side of life instead.

This is the limit of Strauss's "courage": it goes further than that of the average philistine, but nowhere near far enough to actually confront the realities of a godless world. Nietzsche then shows us a similar problem in Strauss's ethics. Despite extolling Darwin as a great benefactor of humanity and spending a large portion of the third part of his book by explaining Darwinian evolution, he fails to derive his ethics from a Darwinian understanding of the human being. That would namely mean to "boldly deduce from the *bellum omnium contra omnes* and the privileged right of the strong a moral code for life," and to try to derive the (actually existing) "phenomena of human kindness, compassion, love, and self-denial" from these naturalistic premises—but that would scare off his philistine audience (1.194–195/39–40). Instead, he derives his ethics from the idea of providential progress. Apart from that, grounding morality is extremely difficult, just as preaching it is easy—and to confirm this observation of Schopenhauer,[37] Strauss makes no such effort and instead proceeds to preach. His preaching is again at odds with his avowed Darwinism. He defines morality as "the self-determination of the individual according to the idea of the species" (Strauss, 1872, p. 236/1874, II.51). However, species are in flux according to Darwin, and it

---

37. The sentence comes from Schopenhauer's *On the Will in Nature* (*Werke* III.472); he later adopted it as the motto of his *On the Basis of Morality* (*Werke* III.629).

is the *differences* among the various individuals and groups who struggle for survival in competition with others *of the same species* that drive the evolution of that species. This diversity is particularly visible in humans, who have developed countless ways of life, and Strauss's definition of morality is so empty as to provide no reasons for choosing any one of them. Nietzsche thus paraphrases Strauss's moral imperative as "live like a human being and not like an ape or a seal" (1.195/39). But the real question remains unanswered: *What kind* of human being should we live like?

Strauss does provide an answer of sorts to this question: He says we should treat everyone as an equal, as having "the same needs and rights as thyself" (Strauss, 1872, pp. 238–239/1874, II.54). But this is decidedly not a Darwinist answer: a Darwinist knows that we have developed from lower animality to the heights of humanity by prioritizing our own needs over those of others, that is, precisely by *forgetting* that others have "the same rights" as oneself (1.196/40).[38] Had he been honest with himself and his "faithful," Strauss would have to admit that "an answer to the question of morality had to be found within scientific Darwinism" (Johnson, 2001, p. 72). Instead, he covertly reinserts a basic principle of Christian morality—the equality of all humans—into his ethics to easily get to the conclusion his readers, who after all live the best imaginable life, are expecting. But he isn't reverting back to Christian morality; he rather believes to progress beyond it. This notion of a ceaseless progress is a general feature of Strauss's thinking, a kind of corrupt Hegelianism. This quasi-providential progress allows Strauss to ignore Kant's critical philosophy and its implications for the notion of science he is operating with (1.191/35), to imbue his Darwinism with "an implied notion of improvement, higher morality, or progressively superior forms" (Johnson, 2001, p. 71), and to keep a central tenet of Christian morality despite having disavowed the premises on which this tenet depends.

Besides these two instances of cowardice in the face of a godless world, Zuckert (1970, pp. 37–39) also brings out the implications of Strauss's facile progressivism for his fear of socialism that Nietzsche points out (1.199/43). Socialists share with the philistines the idea that the seriousness of life consists in providing for one's livelihood, or more widely in economic activity. They also share their "heaven": There is no substantial difference between

---

38. Survival of the fittest means that the evolutionarily fit exemplars of a given species survive and reproduce at the expense of the less fit exemplars of *the same species*. Again, this does not mean that Nietzsche regards phenomena such as love or self-denial as unreal—but it means their origin is left unaccounted for by Strauss.

34 | The Young Nietzsche's Education

the philistine's cycle of work and consumption of cultural goods after it, and Marx's hunting in the morning, fishing in the afternoon, rearing cattle in the evening, and criticizing after dinner (cf. Tucker, 1978, p. 160). They also share the maxim that "nothing more should be sought" than their respective accounts of the good life. Finally, they both believe their "heaven" can be attained by force: the philistines had already attained their heaven with the establishment of the German Empire, while socialists plan to attain it by revolution. The socialists merely plan to extend the middle-class philistine "heaven" into a universal one.[39] And because the philistines also share the socialist belief in fundamental human equality, they have no intellectual resources to defend their "heaven" against the socialist push to democratize it; they can only defend against socialism by force (which is a good reason for them to glorify it). An intellectual defense against socialism would require a new, non-egalitarian account of human excellence—one in which a certain kind of human being stands higher than others and therefore is exemplary. Nietzsche hints at such an account in proposing a counter-imperative to Strauss's empty "live like a human being"—namely "live like a genius, that is, as nothing other than the ideal expression of the human species" (1.195/39).

We have seen that Strauss's courage, although marginally greater than that of his followers, exists in fact solely in the realm of words (1.194/38). He can face the challenges of pessimism, Darwinism, and socialism only by mockery, or by reverting to religious prejudices he supposedly surpassed, such as (Cosmic) providence, or by force. His religion turns out to be "religious" in the worst possible sense—as an irrational superstition.

Philistine "Style"

We enter the question of the style of Strauss's writing through an examination of the intended audience of his "religion." Nietzsche says that on the basis of the excited reception it had had among the educated Germans—six editions within a single year—the book is supposed to be "a *Bible for scholars*" (1.201/45); it should show the life of the scholar as exemplary. But this would mean that scholars, the products of the famed German gymnasia and universities, the pride of German culture and education, somehow fall together with the philistines, who were until now described by Nietzsche as

---

39. As Carl Schmitt (1996, p. 13) remarked, "the big industrialist has no other ideal than that of Lenin—an 'electrified Earth'. They disagree essentially only on the correct method of electrification."

Strauss's primary audience. The blossoms of contemporary German culture, the thorough and methodical scientific spirits, would turn out to lack culture and to be a force deleterious to culture proper. How is this possible?

Nietzsche believes it is a consequence of their being scientific spirits, that is, of the way in which they pursue the science in which they specialize. There is namely a paradox "in the essence of the scholarly person": The scholars study their specialized fields as if they had no need to think about their own lives and their meaning, about questions "Why and to what purpose? Whither am I going? Whence do I come?" (1.202/46). They share the philistine self-satisfaction with their middle-class existence. Their science has no bearing on who there are, they pursue it as if science were "a factory," and they live as if they were factory workers or even slaves (1.202/46; cf. 1.300/136). Their lives take on the structure of the philistine life with its cycle of labor and relax, labor being understood chiefly as means for making a livelihood and relax as after-work consumption of culture as entertainment or *divertissement*. Their knowledge—be it of physics, philology, or anything else—is as much a work tool for them as a hammer is for the worker, and decidedly not a means of self-cultivation. Just as it was the case with the ordinary philistines, their "culture" is mere learnedness. German education had degenerated from a serious effort to form cultured human beings into a mass production of spiritual laborers: That is Nietzsche's diagnosis of contemporary scholarship.[40]

Like the philistines, the scholars are proud of their "education" and believe nothing else should be sought. This is why they appreciate Strauss's book so much: it validates their self-satisfaction and their feelings of superiority over everyone else. It likewise fits their understanding of engaging with culture as the production of an "ever-growing compendium of scholarly opinions about art, literature, and philosophy" (1.205/49). Thus, although they may disagree with Strauss's opinions on one or another subject (especially on theological matters), in general they see *The Old Faith and the New* as the "ideal of a book" (1.207/51). But such criteria do not belong to culture proper. Since culture is a unity of style, Nietzsche begins his

---

40. Nietzsche would later say that the main subject of *DS* was German education (*EH* UC 1). The core of his critique in this respect is showcasing the reduction of education to learnedness and the integration of this degenerated form of education into the philistine system of public opinion. In the passage currently discussed he adds that this is not merely a problem of the intellectually mediocre philistines, but that this problem is all-pervasive in German education and affects even the greatest scholars—that this is an essential problem of the celebrated German educational system.

36 | The Young Nietzsche's Education

examination of Strauss's writing style by asking about "the architecture of a book" (1.209/52): Does his book form a unified whole? Is there a structuring principle—logical or artistic—that orders its composition?

Nietzsche does not see a logical order in the four parts of Strauss's book (1.209–213/52–56). The first question—Are We Still Christians?—gives the rest of the book an unpleasant theological hue; it is also unrelated to the other three questions, as not being a Christian implies very little about one's positive beliefs. The question "What Is Our Conception of the Universe?" has nothing in common with the question "Have We Still a Religion?": The intellectual honesty of a scientist shows itself precisely by *not* taking their faith into account in their scientific research. Strauss's confusion here is due to the fact that his "new faith" has little to do with religious faith and for the most part coincides with modern science (1.211/54). But science cannot provide Strauss's "faith" with any of the comforts of the old, Christian faith; he could establish these only by fraudulently reinserting metaphysical progress and providence into his worldview. Strauss's "new faith" is likewise unrelated to the question "What Is Our Rule of Life?"—the philistines have no need of this faith, as their lives were the same self-satisfied cycle of work and relax already before Strauss published his book, and they won't change even if they accept the tenets of the "new faith." Finally, also the question "What Is Our Conception of the Universe?" has no bearing on "What Is Our Rule of Life?"—we have seen how little Strauss's avowed Darwinism bears on his ethics, and it bears even less on his discussion of subjects such as divorce or the death penalty. Strauss's book turns out not to be a logical whole, but rather a product of the typical scholarly procedure of "assembling a book out of bits and pieces" (1.209/53).

Doesn't the book form at least a rhetorical or artistic whole, then? It does—but the purpose of this whole, ridiculed by Nietzsche as a "garden house" (1.214–216/58–59), is in the first place to show what a cultured man and great writer Strauss is. To this effect he strives to imitate his two models, Lessing and Voltaire, and he has even grasped that a main feature of a genius' writing is *"simplicity of style"* (1.217/60). Unfortunately for Strauss, the genius is also marked by an understanding of the profundity of the problems of human existence and of the good life, problems that are "serious and horrible, and [. . .] for millennia sages have treated them as such" (1.217/60). But, as had been amply demonstrated by this point, Strauss has no such understanding: In taking his scholarly-philistine life as the peak of human development, the good life ceased being a question at all to him, and he doesn't even try particularly hard to demonstrate the excellence of his own life.[41] As a consequence, the simplicity of his style serves only to underline the shallowness of his understanding. In Nietzsche's metaphor, Strauss attempted to imitate the naked goddess Truth, but failed to convey any truths and managed only to publicly strip himself naked. After this big reveal, Nietzsche offers us his diagnosis of D. F. Strauss: He used to be a great scholar who did valuable work in his field (namely *The Life of Jesus*), but he abandoned this work for the sake of becoming a leading figure of the philistine "culture." And in doing this he ruined his proper, scholarly genius, and became merely a bad actor and "an utterly abominable stylist" (1.219–220/62–63).

The last sentence refers to Strauss's style in the narrow, literary sense, and in this respect he is once again symptomatic of the philistine pseudo-culture.[42] This pseudo-culture does not cultivate its German—spoken or written—and the worst offenders are those who disseminate public opinion: the newspaper writers. In the absence of a simple and grammatically correct style, the philistines produce all kinds of strange innovations: metaphors that seem new by their use of modern technology, the use of short sentences for persuasion and long sentences for didactic purposes, and even grammatical "innovations" that are actually just bad German.[43] All of these innovations—which do not belong to a style in the proper sense, but are its corruptions—are amply used by Strauss, as Nietzsche documents in *DS* 11 and 12. The use of such "innovations" serves the needs of the philistine "culture": the philistines are tired after their work, and so they need such powerful stimuli to react at all and to be excited and entertained.

This language-corrupting industry of public opinion is moreover a part of the system of non-culture that Nietzsche analyzed in *DS* 2. It is supportive of everything similar to already existing opinions, and actively celebrates new "classics" who fall into this mold, but it consistently rejects

---

41. The closest Strauss came to recognizing the good life as a problem was in his glossing over the most difficult consequences of his faith in the godless Cosmos. However, it is unclear whether he did this intentionally—to hide the difficult truths from his audience—or whether he simply was unable to face these truths himself.

42. Nietzsche's analysis of the forces corrupting the German language draws heavily on Schopenhauer's essay *On Authorship and Style* (*Werke* V.589–650/*PP* II, pp. 501–553), as well as on his posthumous essay *Materials for a Treatise About the Terrible Mischief Done Nowadays to the German Language* (Nietzsche quotes the latter directly at 1.227/69; cf. Neymeyr, 2020, 1.224–225).

43. Nietzsche catalogues these under the heading "Solecisms, Mixed Metaphors, Obscure Abbreviations, Tastelessness, and Stilted Language" (1.225/68).

38 | The Young Nietzsche's Education

and marginalizes anything that falls outside of it or challenges its premises. But, Nietzsche urges us, *"everything that is truly productive is offensive"* (1.222/64)—that is, offensive to the philistines, because to actually be a cultural effort, it *must* challenge the philistine system and thereby become offensive to it (and not just "in tone," as Church, 2019, p. 52, writes). This system also has deleterious consequences on those who strive to cultivate themselves, who find themselves alone and in contradiction to seemingly everyone, that is, to the masses who listen to the public opinion. The lack of support and the uniformly dismissive general view of their efforts thus form another artificial obstacle on the already difficult path of self-cultivation. Besides the above-mentioned Hölderlin, Nietzsche also uses the example of Lessing to show the practical consequences of this system of non-culture (1.182–184/27–29). D. F. Strauss praises Lessing's "universality," his ceaseless polemical interventions in all kinds of public debates, without realizing that this polemical activity was in fact a heavy burden for Lessing. Nietzsche invokes the authority of Goethe to convey that Lessing's polemics were a result of the pitiful level of culture of his time (cf. Eckermann, 2011, pp. 234–235; conversation from 7 Feb. 1827). It is actually *despite* the philistines and with the added burden of polemics against them that great spirits like Lessing composed their works: and how much more could they have done without that unnecessary burden![44]

Nietzsche's examination of David Friedrich Strauss's soul has now been completed. It is a soul utterly unconcerned with what the genuine good is, and fully satisfied with its current—comfortable but miserable—way of life. It uses the great works of German culture not to cultivate and unify itself, but only to relax after the petty everyday concerns that constitute its "seriousness of life" and as *divertissement* from the actually serious questions. Moreover, despite being completely unartistic, it considers itself better than the great cultural figures who lived earlier simply because they lived earlier, which makes them "less cultured" in its eyes. Its courage exists only in speech: Even if it avows some difficult truths, such as the nonexistence of God, it cannot face the consequences such truths have for their lives and uses metaphysical tricks to avoid these consequences and to live as complacently as before. This soul has no unity of its own; its "style" consists in indiscriminate imitation of popular models in an effort to win a similar

---

44. This closing passage of *DS* 4 (1.183, line 14–1.184, line 5/p. 28, line 12–p. 29, line 1) is taken almost verbatim from *FEI* IV (1.724–725). The comments about Schiller in this passage are likely a reference to Goethe's words from 18 January 1827 (Eckermann 2011, pp. 213–214).

popularity for itself. This "style" is in fact mere subservience to public opinion, that is, a chaotic mix of popular views whose only "principle" is the systematic exclusion of a unifying principle, of real style and culture. It is fully integrated into the system of public opinion, supports it and draws its strength from it. The soul of D. F. Strauss is, then, completely barbaric—and it takes itself to be the peak of human development so far. And *this* exemplar of barbarism is supposed to be the leader of German youth and the author of a "catechism for strong spirits" (1.201/45)! They would never become cultured under such a leadership; they would either be destroyed by the continual frustration of their desire for culture in a society that systematically suppresses it, or simply join the ranks of the philistines. This is the goal of *DS*, and the central purpose of its unflattering portrait of D. F. Strauss: to show its (yet-unspecified) audience the contemptible philistine soul in its full misery, and to drive them away from its pernicious influence by ridiculing this pitiful exemplar.

The final paragraph of *DS* characterizes the essay as *Nietzsche's* confession (1.241/81). Leo Strauss has commented that "one writes as one reads" (1988, p. 230), that is, that the method a thinker uses to read other books is also instructive for how their own books should be read. Let us therefore ask Nietzsche's three questions from *DS* 4 about *DS* itself to see what it will tell us about Nietzsche and his project in the *UC*.[45] Nietzsche's *heaven* seems to be the life of culture, both internally—as the cultivating of one's own soul—and externally, as the establishment of a national (and even supra-national) culture that promotes, aids, and honors this self-cultivation. But we know very little yet about the finer details of either internal or external culture. Nietzsche hints at his intellectual *courage* to face squarely the consequences of a godless world by criticizing Strauss for failing to do so, but we have yet to see how he will do it. He has also shown his practical courage in standing up against the philistine culture despite being just a single man against many (1.242/81). Thereby he identifies himself as one of the few "struggling cultured individuals,"[46] whose dedication to

---

45. Church (2019, p. 51) makes a similar point about the form of the *UC*.
46. As Brooks (2018, pp. 4–9) suggests, this may be a polemical reference to Bismarck's *Kulturkampf*. Cf. Neymeyr (2020, 2.430) on Nietzsche's "rhetorics of struggle aimed at culture" more generally.

40 | The Young Nietzsche's Education

culture in a culture-hostile society forces them to live in a perpetual contradiction with the world (1.206/50). But he clearly believes that his goal is attainable and that the sacrifices he makes in the struggle for it are worth it. His method in this struggle is to speak the truth—as opposed to the false, but comfortable and comforting public opinions—and this is what makes him *untimely*. By extension—and with the awareness that Nietzsche will characterize the term "untimely" also in other ways throughout the *UC*[47]—we may say that every cultured individual living in a barbaric period is untimely as well, and that one of the meanings of this term is to express the contradiction in which they find themselves. Nietzsche's *style* shows us that he looks up to his cultural superiors (of whom Goethe and Schopenhauer figure prominently in *DS*), but he is not imitating them like Strauss imitates Lessing and Voltaire. For Nietzsche they rather are *examples* from whom he can learn the ways of self-cultivation. Nietzsche has also shown himself to be a fluent user of satire and ridicule. Finally, he seems to feel an affinity with Lessing as understood by Goethe, with Lessing the productive spirit who got mired in various polemics against his will. In the letter to Carl von Gersdorff from 1 April 1874, he says that he seeks the freedom to be truly productive, and to this end, "I defend myself and revolt against the many, unspeakably many unfree things that cling to me" (KGB II.3, p. 214). And in the letter to Malwida von Meysenbug from 25 October 1874, he explicitly ascribes to the *UC* the purpose of having eventually "excreted everything negative and rebellious that is stuck in me" (KGB II.3, p. 268).

David Friedrich Strauss believed that his worldview based on modern science can replace the declining Christianity as a basis of culture. But Nietzsche has found his book to be merely a "catechism 'of modern ideas' " (1.175/20) and utterly ineffective as a religious book.[48] Moreover, Strauss's worldview turned out to be the opposite of genuine culture. Nietzsche's "assassination attempt" (*EH* UC 2) on Strauss thus opens up a set of larger questions that will be the central topics of the remaining three *UC*.[49] The first of these questions is why Strauss failed in his effort to replace Christianity despite the power the philistines have in Germany. Is there perhaps a single cause for their social power and their cultural impotence? Is modern

---

47. At 1.246–247/87, 1.346/179, 1.362/194, and 1.432/260.

48. It is not so much that Strauss wants to found a religion that draws Nietzsche's criticism, as Church (2019, p. 38) thinks, but rather his complete failure at this.

49. Thus it indeed is an example of Nietzsche's "practice of war," as he claims in *EH* Wise 7.

science, on which Strauss relied so much, self-defeating in relation to the needs of human life? Is Strauss a symptom of some deficiency of modern science? These questions will be the subject of *HL*. Second, we need to know what worldview *can* replace Christianity as a basis of culture at this world-historical juncture. We need to ask what culture proper is, a culture that responds to the natural human needs and channels natural human powers. This leads us to a set of interrelated questions: What is the human being and its proper excellence, or its "genius"; how can one achieve the level of one's genius, or what are the inner workings of an individual's education;[50] and how can a society contribute to this process, or what does a genuine external culture look like? In short, the second set of questions asks about Nietzsche's *project* in the *UC*, both internal (the project of cultivating the souls of the individual readers, of those who despise philistinism and yearn for genuine culture like Nietzsche does) and external (the project of establishing new institutions that would support genuine culture and that could become the basis for a large-scale cultural reform). Third, we need to know who Nietzsche's audience is. They appear to be young Germans who would be otherwise attracted or at least influenced by Strauss's worldview, but this is far from a satisfactory answer. So far we can only say that his intended audience appears to be young and brave, but we don't know why precisely these, and not some other, qualities matter to Nietzsche. The third set of questions then is asking about who Nietzsche's audience is, and what makes them his intended audience. The latter two sets of questions will be answered in *SE* and *WB*.

---

50. In this respect, Zuckert (1970, p. 48) highlights the apparent paradox that culture consists in seeking an organizing principle rather than in possessing it. This seems to imply that self-cultivation in the current sense would cease to be possible once a principle is found—or that it can *never* be found, which would make self-cultivation a fundamentally futile effort.

II

On the Utility and Liability of History for Life

The Human Soul and Its Modern Deformation

> I decided that I must be careful not to suffer the misfortune which happens to people who look at the sun and watch it during an eclipse. For some of them ruin their eyes unless they look at its image in water or something of the sort. I thought of that danger, and I was afraid my soul would be blinded if I looked at things with my eyes and tried to grasp them with any of my senses.[1]

The overt subject of *HL* is, as announced in the *Foreword,* a critical examination of modern scientific history and of the historical education that is based on it. Contemporary Germany is proud of this historical education, and "justifiably" so (1.246/86), according to Nietzsche. It is a great achievement in the search for truth about the past. But knowledge is not the highest good for Nietzsche of the *UC.* Human life should not serve knowledge, but the other way around—and knowledge is not indiscriminately beneficial, as we learn from Goethe's words that open *HL.* There is knowledge that is beneficial in the sense of increasing one's will and capacity to act, but there is also "knowledge that inhibits activity" (1.245/85), or even outright deadly knowledge. The question thus opens up of how the knowledge produced by modern scientific history, and inculcated into the young by modern historical education, affects the lives of the knowers. In other words, what is its worth for "life," that is, for the good life as Nietzsche understands

---

1. Plato, *Phaedo* 99d–e.

44 | The Young Nietzsche's Education

it? Does scientific history serve life or stifle it? And more broadly, what is the relation of life and truth in general, of which the problem of scientific history is just one manifestation?

HL will argue that scientific history indeed contradicts the needs of life. Active life requires certain necessary conditions to grow, and scientific history does not provide these. Thus it can be at best an inessential luxury to education proper, to the cultivation of life. But the situation is even worse: The pursuit of scientific history has become excessive and feverish. The inessential kind of cultivation has taken the place of the essential; and the inessential kind of cultivation, if not preceded by the essential kind, is actively harmful to the development of those capacities of the soul that are necessary for active, growing life. Nietzsche learned this from two sources: first, from his self-examination, from his own feelings of being stifled by his historical knowledge and consequently being unable to act. And second, from his own "historical" education—from his studies of Ancient Greek thought and culture. This is our first direct indication that history can be beneficial to life if used correctly.

To properly develop the arguments outlined in the *Foreword*, *HL* will first discuss the nature of the human soul: What does it consist of, and what does it mean for it to "grow" in the light of its structure? This articulation of the human soul will be of central importance to the entire *UC*. On its basis, the proper ways of cultivating the soul can be discerned. It will also become possible precisely to articulate the ways in which scientific history and historical education are damaging to the soul, or to "life." Finally, Nietzsche will outline some suggestions to counteract the damage caused to the young souls by historical education.

II.1. *HL* 1: The Erotic-Historic Soul

The first chapter of *HL* opens with the image of a grazing herd of animals. These animals are said to live "unhistorically": They are construed as having no memory and no awareness of time. The animal lives absorbed in the present moment, it "appears in each and every moment as exactly what it is" (1.249/88); the animal needs not "become what it is," for it always already is what it is. The "unhistorical" is, however, a negative designation of this mode of perception: If the animals don't perceive "historically," how *do* they perceive? Following Zuckert (1976, p. 57), we can take our bearing on this question from 1.253/91–92, where Nietzsche tells us that the

On the Utility and Liability of History for Life | 45

force underlying the unhistorical mode of perception is passion, or more generally: *desiring*. The animal is then constructed as a pure immediacy of desiring with no memory, and the horizon of its perception is as if reduced to the single point of its present desire. The life of an animal consists in following and satisfying its momentary desire, which in their case is rather easy to satisfy, and this ease of satisfaction makes them happy. Desiring is the fundamental faculty of all living beings, including humans—and the fact that we all are desiring beings is one of the main reasons why there is no *cardinal* difference between man and animal (1.319/153):[2] All living beings have needs and desires, and the striving to satisfy these is the motive force behind all their actions.

However, the human mode of desiring is in an important way different from the simple unhistoricity of the animal. The source of this difference is the other basic faculty of the human soul, acquired during the long millennia of our becoming-human: *memory*. Memory, the "historical" force within us, means at the most basic level our awareness of time and its passing, of the "it was"; and by the same token it also opens up the dimension of the future to us. This awareness has far-reaching consequences for the human way of being, and in this sense it constitutes our specific difference from other animals. Nietzsche brings up first the kinds of suffering this brings: We suffer because we cannot change what already happened, because of our impotence vis-à-vis the past; we suffer because we see the changeable and perishable character of all things; and most importantly, we suffer from our own changeability or subjectedness to the flux of becoming. Our memory reveals to us "what [our] existence basically is—a never to be perfected imperfect" (1.249/88). We cannot live simply as "what we are" (as the animals do), because we are always already different than we used to be and because all our striving to become something concrete will necessarily be frustrated by the impermanence of all things, ourselves included.[3] Whatever we may want to become, our strivings will never be fulfilled, and our desires will never be fully satisfied. Hence, human life cannot be completed or perfected; it can only be—and it inevitably will be—terminated by death.

---

2. Other important reasons include the facts that we have a natural history just as other animals do, and that we have evolved from "lower" species. The latter is also an example of "the fluidity of all concepts, types, and species" (1.319/153), another of the "deadly truths."

3. Cf. Nietzsche's example of the person who would remember everything (1.250/89), and Jensen's (2016, p. 49) helpful illustration of such a person's problems.

46 | The Young Nietzsche's Education

This is what we realize (to a varying degree) when we are submerged in the "historical" mode of perception, and hence we as humans, as "historical" beings, suffer from the past.[4]

The second significant consequence of having memory is the way it transforms our desiring. When our perception of external things is combined with the capacity to remember, we become aware of a lot more than is strictly necessary for the satisfaction of our momentary desires, and thus our minds get burdened with all sorts of unnecessary information. To clean up this mental clutter, we possess the capacity of *active* forgetting (as in *GM* II.1). Active forgetting is possible and necessary only for beings capable of remembering in the first place, and thereby it is distinct from the animal lack of memory.[5] Forgetting is a part of the "unhistorical," which means that the principle on the basis of which we select what to remember and what to forget is the needs of our dominant passion, which is to say the needs of "life" (since desiring is the basic characteristic of all living beings).[6] Forgetting occurs in two modalities: First, on a more immediate level, one temporarily forgets the passage of time and its consequences, and thereby becomes capable of acting. "All action requires forgetting" (1.250/89), says Nietzsche: Only by setting aside our historicity and imperfective nature can we become absorbed in our passions and act on them. On this account, accomplishing any goal we may have requires that we assign to it a (fictitious) permanence and importance—which would not pass the scrutiny of the historically perceiving mind—and acting on this temporary fiction.

---

4. Lemm (2007a, p. 175) argues that suffering from the past is merely "the result of a particular conception of the past: one that ignores the ways in which the human animal needs forgetfulness." I believe this fails to consider just how deeply our suffering from the past is bound up with having memory at all, regardless of what conception of the past one may hold: I take it to be a constitutive limitation of the human animal.
I also believe that my reading of these passages belies Jensen's (2016, p. 46) claim that, "as with many of his theses in *HL*, there is no real argument [that humans indeed suffer from the past] that Nietzsche presents for our evaluation, but an insight surrounded by illustrations and examples that he leaves up to his reader to accept or reject."

5. The animal who is asked about its happiness in the first paragraph of *HL* 1 is said to "forget" its answer, but this forgetting is as rhetorical as its willingness to answer to us. It "forgets" in the sense that it is construed as incapable of forming memories at all. The active capacity of forgetting presupposes memory, and so is unique to humans.

6. Nietzsche considers the capacity to perceive unhistorically, i.e., to be governed by our desiring, to be "more significant and more originary" than the "historical" mode of perception (1.252/91). These characteristics of it arise from desiring being the fundamental force of all living beings.

Second, on a more "global" level, forgetting is instrumental in the forming of horizons that limit our worlds. These horizons are fundamentally erotic in that they are formed on the basis of the passion or desire that rules within us—be it passion "for a woman or for a great idea" (1.253/91), or for anything else.[7] This desire forms (or re-forms) how we see the world: In the grip of a powerful, ruling passion, all our (previous) valuations are "changed and devalued" (1.253/92), and the goal of this ruling passion becomes our new highest "value," so to speak. As such, this goal also becomes the criterion of significance for everything we perceive or learn: If it is conducive to our goal, that is, if it is significant, it remains in our memory; if it is insignificant, it will be forgotten. Our horizons are, fundamentally, horizons of *meaning*. These horizons delimit the world in which a given human being lives in that they enclose everything one considers important to one's life, and exclude whatever is not relevant to it. They are maintained by the power of active forgetting that selects what is to be included within it and what not. Within such a horizon lies our world, the contents of which are ordered in terms of their meaning for our life, for what we strive for. In this manner, our ruling desire is the "unhistorical" force that determines the structure and the limits of our world. Nietzsche stresses that being in the grip of a ruling desire is "the most unjust condition in the world" (1.253/92), that is, that our desires don't consider things[8] as they are, but solely as what good they can be to *us* and to our goals. Yet this fundamental injustice of the human

---

7. Contrary to Taylor (1997, p. 74), the horizons of significance are not merely an "assumption" of Nietzsche's psychology, but an integral part thereof, and they are not exclusively or necessarily mythical. Dannhauser (1990, p. 78) believes these horizons are "constituted by [one's] fundamental set of assumptions about all things, by what [one] takes, or mistakes, for the absolute truth which cannot be questioned." However, it makes more sense to conceive of the horizons as formed not by indifferent truths, but rather as beliefs (taken to be true, of course) about what is meaningful, significant, and valuable in one's life on the basis of one's ruling passion—to conceive of them as erotic. Such a reading can answer one of Dannhauser's own objections against the notion of a horizon (ibid., p. 83): "if horizons are the subjective creations of human beings, why do we not—why can't we—find, in principle at least, as many horizons as there are human beings?" On my reading, there *are* as many horizons, and worlds bounded by those horizons, as there are human beings. Which of course does not mean that many people's worlds can't be quite similar to each other—whether because of the influence of external forces such as upbringing in the same culture, or (more significantly) because of the similarity of their respective ruling passions.

8. I understand "things" in the sense of the Greek *pragmata* or of the Latin *res*—as objects of our actions, of our *prattein*, and not exclusively as physical objects.

48 | The Young Nietzsche's Education

way of being is the mother of *every* deed, and hence also of any *humanly possible* kind of justice: It is "not only the womb of the unjust deed, but of every just deed as well" (1.253/92).

The third crucial consequence of being endowed with memory is that this makes us truly human, that is, capable of what is highest in man. In an earlier version of *HL* 1 (note 30 [2], 7.726), Nietzsche suggests that our memory is praiseworthy "precisely because the past cannot die in us and tirelessly drives us farther like an inoculated drop of foreign blood, up the entire ladder of all those things that human beings call great, amazing, immortal, divine." There is a similar statement in the published version of *HL* 1 (1.252–253/91): "only when the human being, by thinking, reflecting, comparing, analyzing, and synthesizing, limits that ahistorical element, only when a bright, flashing, iridescent light is generated within that enveloping cloud of mist—that is, only by means of the power to utilize the past for life [. . .]—does the human being become a human being." By enlarging our horizons beyond the present moment, beyond the point that constitutes the horizon of an animal, our memory makes it possible for us to hold the past in mind together with the present and to *compare* them.[9] Comparing is an operation of measuring, and measuring requires a measure, a standard according to which the compared objects are judged: Comparing the past with the present is thus the original form of evaluation, of valuing. This comparing allows us not just to find more suitable means for our goals, but also to evaluate our goals themselves by comparing them with those of other people, or with our own past goals. But, contrary to Church (2019, p. 64), this doesn't mean that Nietzsche thinks of memory "in normative terms." While memory enables our "normative" capacities to exist by providing things to compare, the *criterion* by which we compare them is supplied by our ruling desire. Given that desire as desire is constituted by a lack—we desire something we don't have and perceive as necessary or good for us—in Nietzsche as well as in Plato (*Symposium* 200e), I describe our desiring with the Platonic word *erotic*.

Thus, the comparing of goals is the source of our capacity to grow, to overcome ourselves as we are now, and to extend the range of our possibilities

---

9. Cf. note 29 [29], 7.636: "All remembering is comparing, i.e., equating. Every concept tells this to us; it is the primordial 'historical' phenomenon." As Salaquarda (1984, p. 18) points out, and as Nietzsche himself says in his discussion of monumental history (1.261/99), all such comparisons are necessarily inaccurate and therefore strictly speaking untrue. But they are nevertheless necessary for the growth and extension of one's life.

On the Utility and Liability of History for Life | 49

(and so, in the limit case, the range of the possibilities of humanity as a whole), which is precisely the kind of life Nietzsche wants to foster in his readers (cf. 1.259, 1.317, 1.319/97, 151, 153). This growth and extension of our powers, perspectives, and possibilities is more than a simple change of goals over time, which occurs already in animals (who need now to eat, then to drink, then to sleep), and more than simple projecting on the basis of a fixed and unchanging goal (a farmer in archaic Greece may well spend his life in the belief that farming is his lot in this life, assigned to him by Zeus). It is a manifestation of the fact that humans are the *"yet undetermined animal"* (*BGE* 62). Here lies the true human privilege over other animals, our true humanity: namely in the potential for reaching the yet-unreached heights of life, for doing and making great, amazing, or even divine things.[10]

What we thus find in *HL* 1 is a conception of the human soul as arising from the two basic parts of desiring and memory; desiring is understood as a manifold of desires that vie for rule over the others (otherwise there could be no *ruling* desire); the desires then express themselves through memory-based structures such as evaluating or conscience in ways more complex than a simple drive for immediate satisfaction—a conception I call *erotic-historic* after its two constituent parts. Its chief experiential correlative is that we naturally find ourselves within worlds ordered by our ruling passion, expanded beyond the limits of the present desire by our capacity to remember, and bounded by erotic horizons—and in this way we experience our lives as meaningful. This conception is the root of what the later Nietzsche will call "perspectivism" (cf. *BGE* Preface).[11] At the center of these worlds are

---

10. While I appreciate James Conant's (2014, pp. 351–356) distinction between "the layer-cake conception of human spiritual capacities" and "the transformative conception" thereof, on the basis of my reading I cannot agree with his claim that "the layer-cake conception is [. . .] very deeply-seated in Nietzsche's early thinking" (2014, p. 353). On the contrary, I believe that my account of how memory transforms human desiring into a specifically *human* capacity shows *HL* 1 to be a fine example of Conant's "transformative conception."

11. Goethe is an important forerunner of this conception, as is evident from his aphorism *Observations in the Sense of the Wanderers* 155 from *Wilhelm Meister's Journeyman Years* (*Werke* VIII.306). Nietzsche was an avid reader of Goethe, and there is a piece of indirect evidence that he had the *Journeyman Years* in mind while writing *HL*: his paraphrase of Goethe at 1.301/137 to the effect that sciences, being by their nature "esoteric," should contribute to public life "only by means of an *enhanced praxis*." The source of this statement is *From Makarie's Archive* 78 (*Werke* VIII.471)—and not the other collection of aphorisms in the *Journeyman Years*, *Observations in the Sense of the Wanderers*, as is mistakenly indicated at 14.70. However, this aphorism is also reprinted in *Maxims and*

50 | The Young Nietzsche's Education

our ruling passions and their desiderata, in terms of which everything else is considered (or ignored).[12] We strive to attain these, and thus we conceive of our lives in terms of future-oriented projects that we hope to accomplish (and having *hope* is a sign of having such a project that underlies it). Our ruling desires, and the projects arising out of them, are consequently the basis of the manifold human ways of life, that is, ways of ordering our lives toward the goals that we, as individuals or as communities, seek to attain. A world thus understood is here a universal structure correlative to human subjectivity, an integral part of "human nature":[13] It is not just a feature of pre-modern humanity, as Church (2019, pp. 100, 111, 117, 134 and elsewhere) claims. For Nietzsche, there cannot be such a fundamental break between pre-modern and modern cultures, as all cultures cater to humans with the same basic psychic structure. A "universal horizon," claimed by Church to be a particular achievement of modern culture (2019, p. 159), may for Nietzsche be at best an aspiration, and only for an individual (cf. the *hypothetical* "most powerful, most mighty nature" at 1.251/90; also cf. *BGE* 39) as opposed to an entire culture; the mistaken striving for (something like) it will turn out to be the root of the "historical sickness."

A world, ordered and bounded by a horizon as it may be, is not a closed system. On the one hand, things within our worlds change and pass away, and on the other hand, new things come into being or enter our worlds from outside. One's world thus is constantly changing, and there is always a wealth of phenomena in it that have not yet been ordered within its structure. This ceaseless process of ordering the external things (which

---

Reflections 474 (*Werke* XII.430). A full consideration of Goethe's influence on Nietzsche's conception of the world and/or perspectivism is beyond the scope of this study.

Graham Parkes discusses the notion of productive imagination in Nietzsche's predecessors (1994, pp. 256–267); in *BT* (ibid., p. 66); in *On Truth and Lies in an Extra-Moral Sense* (ibid., p. 97); and in Nietzsche's later works (ibid., pp. 289–305). Cf. Kuchtová (2024, pp. 33–37).

12. Our worlds are of human making in the sense that they result from the activity of our soul, not in the sense that they would be arbitrary fabrications that we could make and unmake as we please. This also does not mean that one's world and its horizons must be entirely or chiefly of one's own "making"—a tradition forms a significant part of one's horizon, and tradition is by definition not of one's own making.

13. Here lies my main disagreement with Brooks's reading of *HL*, which culminates in the claim that human nature is almost completely malleable and "as 'historical' as history itself" (Brooks, 2018, p. 108). There is a lot the yet-undetermined animal can change about itself and its way of being, but certainly not these basic psychic structures, which constitute human nature in an eminent sense.

On the Utility and Liability of History for Life | 51

include our knowledge of the past), or "incorporation" [*Einverleiben*], is, however, a demanding activity, and one can incorporate only as much of the external things as their "*plastic force*" (1.251/89) is capable of processing. This notion of plastic force serves as an index of the strength of one's nature: the more we can incorporate into our world, the better we are equipped to pursue our goals.[14] It also determines the optimal size of the horizon of one's world—normally, our worlds are only as large as we can "stomach," and the capacity of active forgetting is a mechanism of psychic excretion of superfluous knowledge. However, if the horizon of our world comes to encompass more than we are able to incorporate, the structures that order our world begin to break down, and our world turns into chaos in which we are unable to proceed with action—just as our digestive system is unable to do its work when we suffer from dyspeptic states.

This conception of the world ordered in terms of meaningfulness is clearly visible in the "historical humans," who live in the hopes of accomplishing their projects in the future, yet their projects are fundamentally unhistorical (i.e., erotic) even if they are not aware of it: "they have no idea how unhistorically they think and act despite all their history" (1.255/93). It is more difficult to see how the "suprahistorical human beings" fit into this framework: After all, they are said to see history as "the omnipresence of imperishable types" (1.256/94) and, because they see human beings as determined in this way, to have no hopes to accomplish anything beyond the already given human possibilities. However, as Zuckert already has pointed out, the suprahistorical humans also are motivated by a powerful passion (and hence unhistorically).[15] In their case it is the passion for justice—and this passion had been frustrated so much by their awareness of the necessary "blindness and injustice dwelling in the soul of those who act" (1.254/93) that they have no hope left for attaining it. In this situation—which is a case of suffering from the "it was," from their impotence to change the world according to their desires—they find solace in some kind of moralistic or

---

14. Compare the idea of the "superabundance of formative, curative, molding, and restorative forces which is precisely the sign of *great* health" in *HA* I Preface 4. Friedrich Schiller and Jacob Burckhardt are likely sources for Nietzsche's usage of this term (Neymeyr, 2020, 1.417–418).

15. Zuckert (1976, p. 57n4); also cf. Ansell-Pearson (2013, p. 245). Here it is important to note that, unlike the "unhistorical" and the "historical," the "suprahistorical" does *not* refer to a "part" of our soul, but rather to human cultural productions like art and religion (1.330/163). In other words, the "suprahistorical" exists on a different order of being than the "unhistorical" and the "historical."

52 | The Young Nietzsche's Education

ascetic doctrine. These doctrines teach "happiness or resignation, virtue or atonement" (1.256/94), as opposed to action, as the purpose of human existence.[16] However, this description shows the key problem of these doctrines: They are ignorant of the nature of human life insofar as they pretend it is possible not to act "unjustly," without a motivating passion (and they are blind to *their own* motivating passion).[17] As a consequence, they ask us to live "justly," that is, in ways that make genuine action impossible. We may therefore call this justice deadening, or, to use the later Nietzsche's word, life-denying. This tension between life on the one hand and truth and justice on the other pervades not just *HL*, but the *UC* as a whole, and to my knowledge is not resolved in them.[18] Nietzsche certainly leaves this issue unresolved at the end of *HL* 1 and turns instead to the three useful kinds of history, to three ways in which knowledge of the past can be conducive to our growth and self-overcoming.

II.2. *HL* 2–3: *Historia Magistra Vitae*

Life is in need of history so that it may form ever higher goals and pursue them ever more competently, and the three useful kinds of history are "useful" insofar as they "serve life," that is, fulfill this need. The "life" in

---

16. The Buddhist Four Noble Truths seem like a good example of what Nietzsche has in mind here: They describe life as essentially suffering and offer ascetic practices as one's only chance for release from it.

17. Church (2015, p. 65; 2019, p. 76) suggests that Nietzsche's own perspective, his "untimeliness," should be identified with the suprahistorical standpoint. This seems unlikely to me because of the implied but powerful critique of the suprahistorical perspective at the end of *HL* 1.

18. Thus I cannot agree with Church (2019, p. 73) that justice is a constitutive human need and that "Nietzsche does not simply enjoin cultures to embrace illusion [. . .] all such illusions are unjust, and [. . .] we must provide a new [and truthful] justification for modern culture." The basis of this claim is his thesis that in the *UC*, "Nietzsche portrays the modern exemplar as categorically distinct from pre-modern individuals in virtue of the modern achievement of transcending all historical horizons" (ibid., p. 235), for which I find no textual basis in the *UC*. *All* human life—and indeed all life in general—is fundamentally unjust, for all humans share the same fundamental psychic structures, and there is no suggestion in the *UC* that modern human beings are somehow different in this crucial respect. Besides, if this were the case, how could the *ancient* Greeks have suffered from the same problem as the *modern* Germans and be a model for overcoming it (1.333/166–167)?

On the Utility and Liability of History for Life | 53

question is defined as an insatiable appetite for more, it is "that dark, driving, insatiable power that lusts after itself" (1.269/106).[19] In other words, it is life not simply as the perpetuation of one's existence, but life as the capacity to grow, expand, and overcome itself, whose specifically human form is the capacity to compare various goals and to set ever-higher goals for ourselves. Taking stock from Vanessa Lemm's (2011, p. 170) suggestion that plastic force is "at the core of each of the three forms of history in the service of life," we may conversely understand the three useful kinds of history as ways of artificially or consciously aiding our plastic force in its task of incorporating the past into our ordered view of the world. In other words, the useful kinds of history are ways of making the facts about the past meaningful in such a way that we remain oriented toward, and capable of, further growth.

History as the study of the past is given this privileged position in our world because history as the past is the realm constituted by human action. History as the study of the past is then in effect the study of human action, its ends, and its consequences. This makes it eminently suited for the tasks of our self-orientation in the vast world our memory opens up to us (both as being oriented within a certain space: Where do I stand in relation to others?—and as being directed at a goal: Whither am I trying to get, and whence?), and for deliberation about *our own* actions and ends. History can help us deliberate about what consequences our planned actions are likely to have, how to act to make accomplishing our goals as likely as possible, and what goals to accomplish in the first place. It is the accumulated experience of the past generations of human beings that is our best source of guidance for life. This is why history, and the ways in which we approach it, is of such eminent importance for our lives—for good or for bad—and why it matters not just for how we incorporate the events of the past, but also for how we deal with external things here and now, and how we conduct ourselves in general.[20] The three useful kinds of history are in

---

19. Jensen (2016, p. 43) must have overlooked this characterization of life when he wrote that "what Nietzsche means by 'life' is not clear in *HL*." Brooks (2018, pp. 72–73) likewise doesn't see this as a "robust prerequisite account of what 'life' is," and later on goes so far as to claim that Nietzsche "seems explicitly to abandon the power of rational proofs on the very first page of the foreword [to *HL*]" (2018, p. 78). Taylor (1997, p. 14n32) too speaks disapprovingly of Nietzsche's alleged "tendency to substitute assertion for argument."

20. In this regard Nietzsche's attitude to history is characteristic of modern philosophy more generally, as described by Leo Strauss (1963, p. 95): "[the] special subject [of history]

54 | The Young Nietzsche's Education

effect Nietzsche's way of taking the ancient wisdom that *historia* is *magistra vitae* and explicating what it means in terms of the erotic-historic soul that needs to process and incorporate the past and the foreign.[21]

From the above follows that conceptions such as those of Most (2002, p. 32), Emden,[22] Large (2012, p. 93), Jensen,[23] or Brooks (2018, p. 72), which see Nietzsche's *Historie* as roughly identical with academic historiography, offer far too narrow a view of the scope of Nietzsche's argument in *HL*. We get a more accurate picture from the note 30 [2], 7.730, where *die Historie* is defined as "every occupation with the past [*Geschichte*]." The three useful kinds of history are not just kinds of historiography, but ways in which an individual (or a group) may perceive and incorporate facts about the past in a fruitful manner. Nietzsche's *Historie* is more akin to the Ancient Greek *historia*, "inquiry," than to modern notions of history that mean exclusively the study of past events (which can be conceived as

---

is the study of aims and projects. By the distinction between good (i.e., successful) and bad (i.e., unsuccessful) aims, it makes possible a knowledge of the norms for human action." However, philosophy in the *UC* is not limited to practical matters (in a broad sense), unlike in Hobbes or Bacon (as discussed by Strauss, 1963); therefore, unlike them, Nietzsche doesn't tend to "replace philosophy by history" (ibid.).

21. This sentence from Cicero's *De Oratore* II.36 has its precedent in Polybius I.1. Nietzsche paraphrases the original sentence at 1.258/96: "Polybius [. . .] called political history the proper preparation for governing a state and the best teacher." This paraphrase takes place in the context of monumental history, but, as I show below, the other useful kinds of history are just as much teachers of life—just of different kinds of human life. But cf. Neymeyr (2020, 1.432–435) on the different thrust of Nietzsche's and Polybius's understanding of history.

22. Emden's understanding of the three useful kinds of history is interesting, but it relies on examples that go beyond Nietzsche's text and are contrary to Nietzsche's own examples. To give two salient cases: Nietzsche's monumental history is oriented on *individuals*, not nations, the chief example being the men of the Renaissance rather than something like Emden's Valhalla temple (2006, p. 14); and antiquarian history is oriented on *one's own* past, such as the history of one's city or people, not at a foreign past, as philology, Emden's chief example (ibid., pp. 18–22). This results in his understanding of critical history as "impossible" (ibid., p. 23), and his consequent evaluation of *HL* as an "inconclusive and transitional work" (ibid., p. 30).

23. Jensen (2016, pp. 68–78) interprets monumental, antiquarian, and critical history rather narrowly, as modes of historiography that stem from the fixed personal biases of the historiographer. As a consequence, he doesn't find much of interest in them. To explain how history can be useful to life, he comes up with a new concept—"affirmative history," which consists in such a combination of monumental, antiquarian, and critical history as is actually conducive for life and growth (2016, pp. 146–148). This category does the work that, on my reading, the three useful kinds of history already do by themselves.

a subset of *historia*). And this expansive understanding of *Historie* is not just a peculiarity of *HL*. When we consider later passages that deal with the "historical sense," such as *HA* 274, *AOM* 223, or *BGE* 224, we see that in all these aphorisms it refers to a general capacity to understand humans and entire cultures that are external and foreign to us, be they external to us in time (such as a culture from the past) or in space (such as a culture from a different present-day corner of the Earth). Despite the somewhat misleading name, "historical sense" for Nietzsche is not necessarily connected with understanding of humans of the past (although those are its frequent objects): It is rather a sense for how to inquire into the conditions, values, and lives of those who don't live like we do, who are *other* than us (the object of historical inquiry must be at least to some degree foreign to us; that which is familiar and known to us, that which strikes us as "self-evident," does not call for a "historical" way of approaching).

The useful kinds of history are not mutually exclusive: A single person may use different kinds of history even regarding the same events, according to their present need. By this I do not mean that we can arbitrarily choose which kind to use in any given situation, but rather that our psychic growth may necessitate a "revaluation" of an event, which in the framework of *HL* would mean approaching it with a different kind of history. Nietzsche himself presents the Renaissance Italians in quick succession both as exemplars of monumental history (1.260–261/98) and as models of antiquarian history (1.266/103), implying that their original antiquarianism reawakened "the ancient Italian genius" within them, which subsequently enabled them to pursue further endeavors of monumental character. The useful kinds of history remember and forget selectively—they do not aim at the truth at any cost, but serve life, that is, the goals of our ruling passion—and so the past "suffers" (i.e., is falsified to a certain extent) under each of them. They are kinds of "poetic" or "artistic" rather than "theoretic" or "scientific" history: They are creative interpretations that necessarily make a certain selection of the available facts and interpret them from a certain perspective,[24] this perspective being (in the ideal case) determined by the needs of the interpreter

---

24. Jensen (2016, p. 92) explains that the historian qua historian necessarily performs two kinds of mental construction on the past. First, he introduces "generalizing concepts that abbreviate the welter of experience into intellectually manageable units," and second, he provides "the 'links,' so to say, between events, times, places, and agents that take an account of the past from pure chronicle to a genuine history imbued with narrative structure." Such falsifications are necessary features of *any* history, and so they do not constitute a particular shortcoming of the three useful kinds of history, contrary to Jenkins's (2014, p. 173) and Church's (2019, pp. 72–73) views.

56 | The Young Nietzsche's Education

in question. These interpretations involve not just constructing narratives of events, but also (re)evaluating events particularly important to oneself.

The proper use of the useful kinds of history is such that contributes to the growth of the user's horizons and capacity for action; the improper uses, their "disadvantages," are such that undermine this function in one way or another.[25] Insofar as they are used in the latter way, Nietzsche calls such "service" "degeneration" (1.268/106). The useful kinds of history correspond to three different kinds of needs or desires that shape particular kinds of human life: monumental history serves to "one who acts and strives" (1.258/96) or to one who "wants to create something great" (1.264/102); antiquarian history serves to "one who preserves and venerates" (1.258/96) or to one who wants "to remain within the realm of the habitual and the time-honored" (1.264/102); and critical history to "one who suffers and is in need of liberation" (1.258/96) or to one who wants "to throw off the burden at all costs" (1.264/102). All these uses are different modalities of the single overarching need of life to grow beyond what it currently is. With this in mind, the unity of the three useful kinds of history can be expressed as follows. Monumental history is a means to *produce* the conditions of growth of a certain (namely the interpreter's) kind of life; antiquarian history is a means to *preserve* such conditions; and critical history is a means to *destroy* the conditions that prevent us from growth.[26] I thus disagree with Heidegger's interpretation of monumental history as corresponding to the future, antiquarian history to the past, and critical history to the present. They all are rather interpretations of the past (or of the foreign), in the present (situation), for the sake of the future (growth or action).[27]

---

25. Nietzsche recognizes two basic kinds of improper uses of each of the useful kinds of history. The first arises from inexpert application of the given kind of history, e.g., when an attempt at a monumental history results in a mythic fiction (1.262/100). The second is using history as a weapon to hinder the growth of others rather than as a tool for one's own growth, as the philistines tend to use it (1.263/100–101).

26. Cf. the note 29 [115], 7.683 with the following scheme:

The human being wants to create	monumental
to remain in the habitual	antiquarian
to free oneself from a distress	critical.

27. Heidegger (1962, pp. 448–449). Heidegger's lectures on *HL* (2016, § 39) give fundamentally the same account thereof as *Being and Time*. Zuckert (1976, p. 64n26) has criticized this account by noting that the three useful kinds of history "seem, however, actually to describe three different pursuits of knowledge which different men have undertaken at different times." Geisenhanslüke (1999, p. 134) also argues that

MONUMENTAL HISTORY

From Nietzsche's perspective, history belongs "above all" (1.258/96) to the active humans who strive to accomplish great things, to those who *make* history.[28] They aim to bring forth "some kind of happiness" (1.259/97), but they think it on a grand scale: it is not merely their own, private happiness, but the happiness of their nation or even of humanity as a whole. In return for these great benefactions they expect glory, or what Heraclitus (B 29) called *kleos aenaon thneton*, "eternal glory among the mortals": they wish to be remembered and celebrated for their benefactions and in this way to attain a humanly possible immortality.[29] The "meaning" (1.258/96) of history for them—that is, the use of history for their ruling passion—is that it helps them to accomplish their deeds, and monumental history serves them to make their lives meaningful by facilitating such accomplishments. The past is to provide them with examples of people who have already accomplished similar great things, and in these they find "inspiration to emulate and to improve" (1.258/96). These examples then serve them to improve their own efforts, to attain "a higher form of praxis" (1.263/101).

Those who appropriate the past monumentally in effect act out what was described above as our true humanity: Their actions bring out new, yet-unseen human possibilities, and thus drive the development of the human species. Hence, Nietzsche speaks of their great deeds as of expressions of "the fundamental thought in the belief in humanity" (1.259/97), of a "Nietzschean humanism," as it were.[30] It is thanks to them that ever-new human potential first becomes visible and eventually becomes a reality. He also interprets the principle on which they act as the appropriation and actualization of qualities and capacities that are "capable of extending the

---

Heidegger's account is a "forced interpretation" and points out that "each of the three kinds of history encompasses all three modes of time." However, his claim that they are oriented on the present rather than on the future (ibid.) isn't consistent with the fact that the activity or "life" of the human soul, as it was developed in *HL* 1, is fundamentally a future-oriented projecting of goals to be attained.

28. Cf. Goethe, *Observations in the Sense of the Wanderers* 56 (*Werke* VIII.292).

29. Church (2019, p. 81) puzzlingly claims that since "we will not be around to experience our own immortal fame," this "cannot be a matter of self-love." I believe—and it has been believed at least since Heraclitus and Plato (*Symposium* 208c)—that the desire for immortal fame is one of the main ways in which our self-love is able to project itself beyond our inevitable death.

30. Neymeyr (2020, 1.439) mentions Schiller as a precursor of this idea.

58 | The Young Nietzsche's Education

concept of 'the human being' and of giving it a more beautiful substance"
(1.259/97): *interprets*, for they themselves need not, and for the most part
do not, think that the purpose of their actions is to extend the range of
human possibilities. This is a formal principle that admits of various kinds
of content, of various kinds of cultivation of the human soul, and of various
kinds of deeds. Machiavelli provides an illustration of this use of history for
life and action when he recommends that "a prince should read histories
and consider in them the actions of excellent men," and that "Above all he
should do as some excellent man has done in the past who found someone
to imitate who had been praised and glorified before him, whose exploits
and action he always kept beside himself, as they say Alexander the Great
imitated Achilles; Caesar, Alexander; Scipio, Cyrus."[31] The main use of
monumental history is, then, that it provides one with examples to imitate
(as much as the different circumstances permit it), and so in the best case
with a way to attain greatness of one's own.

However, the monumental mode of appropriating the past is highly
selective and inaccurate. When we look for examples to imitate, "the individuality of what is past must be forced into a general form" (1.261/99),
and in doing so we ignore that in fact there are no truly identical actions
or persons. But it is only by ignoring or falsifying this uniqueness of each
event that monumental history can provide lessons for the present. As a
consequence, the exemplary individuals of monumental history begin to
appear as "effects in themselves" (1.261/99), or as isolated singular events
that stand apart from the otherwise irrelevant stream of becoming. In the
extreme case, monumental history can turn into a "mythical fiction," which
surely is *subjectively* meaningful, but, unlike history proper, cannot provide
any concrete guidance for action (cf. 1.262/100). This disadvantage is particularly obvious when the incompetent use monumental history in their
attempts at great actions, resulting in wars, murders, revolutions, and other
upheavals, which, despite involving lots of human beings and shedding lots
of blood, fail to accomplish their intended goals, and in that sense often
are meaningless (at least as far as their authors are concerned).

---

31. Machiavelli (1998, p. 60). Cf. the note 29 [87], 7.669, where (although using a
different conceptual framework than in the published version of *HL*) Machiavelli is grouped
together with Livy and Tacitus—historians whose works are well suited for monumental
appropriation. I believe this passage from the *Prince* is a better reflection of Nietzsche's
conception of monumental history than the passage from Machiavelli's famous letter to
Vettori quoted by Jenkins (2014, p. 172). Nietzsche had read Machiavelli's *Prince* as
early as 1862 (Brobjer, 2008, p. 44).

Another disadvantage of monumental history is that in striving to become great themselves, the ambitious are faced with the opposition of the many who don't have a sense for any higher goals than simply "to live at all costs" (1.259/97). This kind of life is, in effect, animal life: There is nothing that would distinguish it from mere animal existence apart from more intricate ways of ensuring one's survival. Those who want to appropriate history monumentally must be aware of this danger and find ways to deal with it—but monumental history itself does not provide help with this task, and this help must be sought elsewhere. Even worse, those who want simply to live can (ab)use monumental history against the "monumental historians." By painting the greatness of the past monumental individuals in vivid colors they can show the (current) smallness of the present-day would-be monumental individuals, and thereby dissuade them from attempting to grow (1.264/101–102). This is the philistines' preferred method of dealing with artists and with anyone who strives to cultivate themselves in general, as we saw in *DS* (1.167–169/13–15).

Antiquarian History

Antiquarian appropriation of the past is essentially the history of one's own,[32] of the tradition one has been raised in and finds familiar and comfortable, of one's "home." This tradition is recognized as the origin that made us what we are—as a *good* origin for which we are grateful. This distinguishes it both from monumental history, which tends to draw its examples from more foreign sources and strives to imitate their deeds rather than conserve what they accomplished, and from critical history, whose attitude to its objects is the opposite of the antiquarian veneration. The objects of antiquarian history are then chronicled and catalogued so they may be preserved as fully as possible even despite the inevitable decay of all things. Its scope is very limited—it cares only about its particular object—but within this limited scope it strives to preserve everything, no matter how small or insignificant it otherwise would seem, as faithfully as possible. As such, this is the

---

32. On this cf. the note 29 [178], 7.705, which quotes Aristotle's *Politics* 1262b22 ff. (cf. Huang, 2017). The passage from the *Politics* discusses a thing's being "one's own" and its rarity as the two main sources of attachment to it, and Nietzsche goes on to discuss antiquarian history with reference to it. Cf. Patočka's (1989, p. 251) analysis of how the natural world of human existence is "in its very being" divided into the familiar [i.e., one's own] and the alien or foreign. Freud (2016, p. 48) remarks that people enjoy even the smell of their own farts.

60 | The Young Nietzsche's Education

principle of all kinds of local and national historiographies, which engage in precisely this kind of cataloguing the past of "one's own"—they preserve the memory of all rulers, events, and poets that belong to one's country, region, or city, regardless of how uninteresting they may be to an external observer who would compare them with events or poets from other places. For the antiquarian historian of Slovakia, a Martin Kukučín is infinitely more important than Shakespeare or Goethe for the simple reason that Kukučín was Slovak and the latter two poets were not. Given this character of antiquarian history, Nietzsche says that its greatest value lies in "binding even less-favored generations and populations to their native land and native customs" (1.266/104), that it gives the common people an elementary satisfaction with their hard and unexciting life and teaches them to think of themselves as parts of a greater, more glorious whole, from which they can derive a certain pride and satisfaction. At its core, antiquarian history creates *traditions*: narratives that bind a people or a group of people together as parts of a shared project established by a great founder[33] in the past. Thus it is essential for the creation of communities of unequals, in which the lesser individuals can find a meaningful way of participating in the projects devised by the greater ones.[34]

It is, however, only of limited immediate use for the great individuals themselves. While it can preserve and perpetuate the conditions of greatness—as Nietzsche says the Renaissance Italians recovered ancient poetry that spurs to great deeds (1.266/103)—it cannot *make* such conditions. This leads to two distinct disadvantages of antiquarian history. First, it can lead to a mummification of life by overly focusing on the past glories and/or injustices,[35] without these having any clear beneficial effect for the future. Second, the antiquarian preference for piously preserving the old and the

---

33. I.e., by a monumental person (Zuckert, 1976, p. 60). Zuckert (ibid., p. 64) also notes that antiquarian history is instrumental for preserving the achievements of the past great individuals (or at least knowledge thereof) for the following generations, and so allows the posterity to build and expand upon them.

34. Emden (2006, pp. 13–18) is correct that national histories, especially those of larger and imperially minded nations, often have significant monumental traits. However, even these national histories exhort in the first place to preserving and continuing the glories of the past rather than to establishing something radically new, and thus also they are fundamentally antiquarian.

35. Hungarian national history, with its memories of nine hundred years of kingdom and of the Treaty of Trianon, which broke this kingdom apart after World War I, is a good example of such a mummification of the past.

On the Utility and Liability of History for Life | 61

traditional "lames the person of action" (1.268/106): In effect it asks the would-be innovator, "who are *you* to challenge the ways our great ancestors have established?" It is in this sense that *"everything that is truly productive is offensive,"* as Nietzsche said in *DS* (1.222/64). Whoever wants to act, to make something new, to make history, must be ready to offend those who revere the status quo, and the antiquarian mode of history is always on the side of the status quo.

CRITICAL HISTORY

The purpose of the critical mode of appropriating the past is destroying the conditions that are unsuitable for one's growth.[36] This takes place by exposing the given piece of the past as unjust and unworthy of being preserved and revered and so breaking its hold over one's mind. A past condemned in this manner then ceases to be an obstacle for one's growth, for one's project. Even though justice (and lack thereof) is the ostensible criterion by which the critically appropriated cast is condemned, such condemnations in fact do not occur for the sake of justice. Critical history operates with the self-contradictory conception of justice we saw in action among the suprahistorical individuals in *HL* 1—according to this conception, all life is essentially unjust, and therefore worthy of condemnation.[37] Critical history uses this conception of justice selectively—namely only on those pieces of the past that are hindering to the practitioner of critical history—and in this manner it serves their life, as defined at 1.269/106. By being just selectively, critical history is unjust according to its own criterion of justice.

For if it were to apply its justice universally, it would have to also condemn its own practitioners, who too are "products of earlier generations" (1.270/107), and thus carry at least traces of the condemned past within themselves. The most extreme example of such a universal application of justice is the suprahistorical individuals, who are aware of the injustice inherent in all action, including their own actions, and thus they are unable to

---

36. Heidegger (2016, § 31) points out that critical history is not just liberation from something, but also liberation *for* the pursuit of a particular goal. In this sense it is connected and ministerial to monumental history. However, I do not find his larger claim—that *"critical history* is *philosophical reflection"* (ibid., § 49)—to be supported by Nietzsche's text.

37. Neymeyr (2020, 1.462–3) remarks that this conception is actually Schopenhauer's. Nietzsche's distancing from it is thus a sign of his distance from Schopenhauer's doctrines already at this point.

62 | The Young Nietzsche's Education

act and have to seek refuge in life-denying moralistic doctrines (1.256/94, 1.269/107). In this way they demonstrate one of the chief dangers of critical history: "too frequently we stop at knowing what is good without actually doing it, because we also know what is better [in this case, the good of their alleged justice] without being capable of doing it" (1.270/107–108). This kind of "justice" is also readily visible in one of the most obvious examples of critical history, namely in the way revolutionary movements treat their respective ancien régime: All that belongs to the past is treated with suspicion and removed to make room for the new, revolutionary, just order. However, the new, just order inevitably fails to materialize, for the good that had been accomplished by the revolution always pales in comparison with the ideal that animates the revolution, the perfect but humanly unattainable justice. As this failure of the revolution becomes evident, ever more and more of the past is being condemned—the revolution begins to eat its own children, with the consequences we know from the history of the French or the Russian revolutions.

However, if done properly, critical history remains unaware of its injustice.[38] Its real aim is to serve life by condemning what hinders it, not to bring about universal justice of the life-denying kind. This service at its best consists in breaking up old habits and traditions for the sake of establishing new ones that are suitable to the needs of the practitioner's life: "we cultivate a new habit, a new instinct, a second nature, so that the first nature withers away" (1.270/107). Plato's ruthless critique of the traditional Greek poetry and of the habits and attitudes this poetry instills in its audience (*Republic* 376e–398b) would in Nietzsche's view be a prime example of such critical practice for the sake of establishing something yet unseen.[39] If all goes well, this second nature will over time become a new "first nature":[40] It will open up the mental space for new traditions and for new endeavors to the humans of the present.

---

38. It is not a "premise" (Lemm, 2007a, p. 186) of critical history that "every past is worthy of being condemned" (1.269/107), but rather its unstated *implication*.

39. Cf. Acampora (2013, p. 48): "Nietzsche regards Platonic Socratic philosophy as fundamentally organized in terms of contesting Homer." Zinn (2015) is another good example of critical history.

40. The "nature" Nietzsche means here is the ruling passion within one's soul, and by extension the order of one's soul. In other words, the perspective from which critical history conducts its critique will over time become the perspective which guides one's overall actions and strivings.

II.3. *HL* 4–9: The Problem of Scientific History

If the useful kinds of history represent the "natural relation" (1.271/108) to the past and the foreign by virtue of allowing us to incorporate their objects into our structured worlds, the opposite is true of the currently dominant scientific history.[41] Scientific history claims to strive to discover the full, undistorted truth about the past: It presents itself as one of the peaks of modern truthfulness. The past is to be known "as it actually happened," in Leopold von Ranke's famous words, and so it will no longer "suffer," as it does under each of the three useful kinds of history. In being more truthful than the past generations, scientific history also promises to make us more just, to do justice to the past in a way that was previously impossible. It is then unsurprising that contemporary German scholars see scientific history as a great achievement and that modern education has become identical with "historical education," in which the proper education of a young person is believed to hinge upon attaining a wide overview of world history according to the best current scientific knowledge. Furthermore, even those who suffer from scientific history—who feel on themselves its deadening influence on life, analyzed by Nietzsche in these chapters—are so enchanted by its promises that they are unwilling to abandon it. They believe "in the *necessity* of this type of education" (1.326/160) because their suffering appears negligible in contrast with the promise of scientific history to make us wiser and thereby more just—in effect, to make us better human beings. Seen in this light, their suffering may be just a kind of growing pains. Abandoning the path to wisdom and justice for the sake of something as petty as personal comfort appears to them positively base and cowardly.

Nietzsche's analysis of scientific history aims at dispelling this ideology. He will show that the promises of scientific history are false: Its "justice" is far removed from justice proper, and it will not make better human

---

41. Church takes the three useful kinds of history to be "ancient or pre-modern" (2019, pp. 77, 91), as opposed to the "modern" scientific history, and claims that Nietzsche is trying to "dialectically synthesise" them (ibid., p. 57). I disagree with this conception for the reasons given in fn. 18 above, and also because Nietzsche given us ample modern examples of the useful kinds of history, such as the Renaissance Italians (1.261/98, 1.266/103) or Goethe's antiquarian appreciation of Gothic architecture (1.266/103; cf. Goethe, *Werke* XII.7–15). I would say the useful kinds of history are natural in the phenomenological sense, in the sense in which Jan Patočka talks of the "natural world" (1989) or of "the *natural* human stance" (2002, p. 36); and scientific history is a derivative modification of this natural stance (cf. Heidegger, 1962, § 13).

64 | The Young Nietzsche's Education

beings out of its practitioners. In fact, the opposite is true: The changed constellation of life and history that pursues the truth at any cost carries the cost of destroying its practitioners' life as growing or ascending life. This *"historical sickness"* (1.329/163) weakens those who practice scientific history in manifold ways that Nietzsche will describe in these chapters. The suffering from scientific history is, then, no growing pain, but a sign of real damage being done to one's soul. In terms of the psychology of *HL*, this damage can be described as follows. Scientific history—understood as the disinterested pursuit of knowledge for its own sake, without regard for the practitioner himself—is *unnatural*, it is the opposite of the above-mentioned "natural relation" to the past, because its effects on its practitioners are the opposite of healthy incorporation. Insofar as it posits the indiscriminate pursuit of knowledge about various ways of life as an unquestionable good, it effectively hijacks our structures of meaningfulness and turns them against themselves. Those who accept this "good" as their own good, who accept the limitless pursuit of knowledge as their ruling passion, are led to learn more and more, without regard for the limits of their plastic force—and thus they will eventually cease to be able to incorporate what they learn and to order their worlds. Their soul becomes dyspeptic. Nietzsche recognizes two broad classes of psychic damage caused by scientific history. The first of these is the damage to our plastic force and so to our *capacity* for growth, which is treated in *HL* 4–5. The second is the destruction of the hopes and illusions that are (at least for the vast majority of humans) necessary for growth and action, whereby it destroys our *will* to strive for growth at all—the topic of *HL* 7–9.[42]

HL 4–5: THE EXCESS OF HISTORY

Nietzsche focuses first on the issue that historical education burdens its pupils with an overload of facts that are of no particular use to them. This is a burden on our plastic force, which strives to order the new knowledge into our preexisting structures of desiring, but this proves impossible for two reasons. First, because of the sheer amount one is expected to learn and know (and consequently to incorporate); and second, because the new

---

42. The problem here is physiological and not just that we "lose sight of the sublime," as Ansell-Pearson (2013, p. 244) thinks. Contrary to Brooks (2018, pp. 75, 94–103), scientific history is not a degenerated form of antiquarian history, but a different beast altogether; cf. 1.267/104–105 with 1.271/108–109.

On the Utility and Liability of History for Life | 65

knowledge is not organized according to any of the three useful kinds of history (if it were, it could foster a tendency beneficial to life in one's soul). The various parts of the newly acquired knowledge are "involved in a struggle with one another" (1.272/109), pointing the knower in a variety of different directions, and thereby canceling out each other's potentially beneficial effects—no useful lessons can be learned from this unordered and contradictory manifold of knowledge. One eventually learns how to live in these conditions and develops a "second nature" (1.272/109), a new order of the soul oriented on knowing as much as possible, on becoming "walking encyclopedias" (1.274/110–111). What this weaker and sicker second nature amounts to is a dissolution of order in one's world: The horizons that used to bound one's world have been pushed back "as far back as infinity" (1.272/109) in all directions, and one thereby loses track of what is the meaning of the possibilities in one's life. What before seemed clearly desirable and important now becomes simply one possibility among many others, and this chaos cannot be ordered into a new, larger whole because one cannot encompass the whole any longer. This is what happens when one's historical knowledge exceeds the limits of one's "plastic force," or power of incorporation.

This condition, that is, this (dis)order of the soul, has now become commonplace thanks to historical education of the young. Historical education has transformed education from the process of formation, ordering, and strengthening of one's soul into "only a kind of knowledge about education" (1.273/110), into a catalogue of how people in other times and places have lived that has no bearing on how one should live oneself. Thus emerges a disorder peculiar to modern humans, namely their split personality, or "the remarkable antithesis between an interior that corresponds to no exterior and an exterior that corresponds to no interior" (1.272/109). Such a person suffers from a "split" of one's personality into ineffectual knowledge and unreflective practical life. This split of the inner and the outer actually means the weakening of one's "instinct," of one's ruling or motivating passion, which is now no longer capable of shaping one's life in its entirety. The sufferer of the historical sickness no longer feels capable of that, they become "hesitant and uncertain and can no longer believe in [themselves]" (1.280/117). According to the definition of culture as a unity of style, this means they become uncultured, that is, barbarians in the sense of *DS*. More precisely, they lose their *capacity* for self-cultivation. Historical education is then not identical with education, as the moderns believe (despite the Greeks providing evidence to the contrary—1.273/110,

66 | The Young Nietzsche's Education

1.307/142), and already this negative consequence shows that actually it works contrary to education proper.

In practical life, this manifests itself by the false opposition of "form" and "content," which sees formalism in external action as an empty convention and believes that by abandoning such conventions one will become more "natural." This view misses how important form is for making the content of one's mind effectual in practical life. Its consequence, especially for modern, historically educated people, is "comfort and the smallest possible measure of self-overcoming" (1.275/112). In the absence of any higher ordering principle and even of a form of behavior, all that remains to guide one's actions are the basic bodily desires that can be summed up as the desire for comfortable life. The freedom these modern barbarians have won for themselves by abandoning the stifling conventions is not a freedom that would drive them to great deeds or works, but the false freedom of simply doing "whatever feels good." This results in a life of bourgeois conformity, in which individuality and cultivation thereof is feared and replaced by the inhabiting of socially determined roles (professional, class, etc.). Since "historical education and the universal bourgeois cloak rule simultaneously" (1.281/117), the "content" of such people's mind, says Nietzsche, is most apparent in their books (1.276/113). This is the reason why *DS* was a review of D. F. Strauss's book. This review showed us that even one of the most celebrated German scholars of his time has next to nothing to offer in terms of culture, and now we learn why.

This issue of the split, weakened character and its consequences is manifest in the contemporary approach to philosophy. In the Antiquity, philosophy was a *way of life*, a way of forming one's soul in accordance with the philosophic doctrines of the school to which one subscribed, so that it may attain what was thought to be its proper good, and this effort informed everything the philosophizing person did or undertook. As Pierre Hadot (1995, 265) describes it, "philosophy was a mode of existing-in-the-world, which had to be practiced at each instant, and the goal of which was to transform the whole of the individual's life." The ancient philosophers understood philosophy not as a set of any given doctrines, but rather as an agreement of one's life with those doctrines that is outwardly visible in one's conduct of life. It was a way of ordering one's goals and values according to a single principle, so that this principle shines forth in everything one does, from great deeds to the smallest everyday activities: a way of shaping one's soul and one's entire existence. Wagner's leading of Nietzsche to live according to Schopenhauerian principles, which we have seen in Chapter I.1, was at least in the direction to a way of life thus understood. Philosophy as a way of life understood in *this* sense—which, as we will see in Chapter V.2, is quite different from the

On the Utility and Liability of History for Life | 67

philosophic life as the mature Nietzsche understood it—is a type of moral practice, a shaping of one's self according to externally given standards that are publicly known, and the results of this practice are publicly visible.

However, things are very different in modern times. Hadot (2002, pp. 258–261) explains that philosophy has ever since the Middle Ages been reduced to a purely theoretical or speculative activity, while its practical moment was usurped by Christian monasticism. Observing the results of this development, Nietzsche comments that "no one lives philosophically" anymore in the contemporary world (1.282/118), and that philosophy is for the most part reduced to idle academic chatter, whose authors live the same kind of bourgeois life as any other middle-class person. Philosophy was thereby stripped of almost all its value for the individual existence. Nietzsche expresses this quite pointedly in the note 31 [4] (7.749): "I believe that the vegetarians, with their prescription to eat less and more simply, have been more beneficial than all the more recent moral systems taken together."[43] Despite this, or rather *because* of this, philosophy is more popular than ever before: "for philosophy doesn't torment people anymore, many are in fact entertained by it, and anyone may open their mouth and blather on without any danger" (note 31 [5], 7.750). And if a genuine philosopher, one who strives to live as their philosophy teaches them, appears by any chance in these conditions, they will necessarily become a "solitary walker" whose wisdom will be their alone because (almost) no one else cares for it. Kant, whom Nietzsche singles out in *SE* as an emblem of this degradation of philosophy to mere speculation (1.351/184, 1.414/243) and in this sense the opposite of Schopenhauer, was in fact painfully aware of this issue, but considered it impossible to live philosophically in the modern times (Kant, 1980, p. 12; cf. Hadot, 2002, p. 267): "Plato asked an old man who told him that he was listening to lectures on virtue: "When are you finally going to start *living* virtuously?" The point is not always to speculate; ultimately, we must think of actual practice. Nowadays, however, he who lives in a way which conforms with what he teaches is taken to be a dreamer [*Schwärmer*]."[44] The issue at stake between Kant and Schopenhauer or Nietzsche is then not so much the awareness of the degraded character

---

43. The significance of this remark becomes more apparent when we recall that Nietzsche was no friend of vegetarianism: cf. Chapter I, fn. 3 and context.

44. To fully appreciate the force of this comment, we need to realize that *Schwärmerei*—as distinguished from *Enthusiasmus*—is Kant's term for *fanaticism*, his strong condemnation of various irrational but highly passionate human attachments (cf. Banham, Schulting, & Hems, 2012, p. 191).

68 | The Young Nietzsche's Education

of modern philosophy, but rather the *courage* to do something about it—or lack thereof.[45] And the weakening of modern character effected by historical education is not helping in this respect.

Having put forward all this evidence of the negative physiological consequences of excessive exposure to history, Nietzsche concludes that "*history can be endured only by strong personalities; it completely extinguishes weak ones*" (1.283/119). The majority of the historically educated turn into "eunuchs"—that is, people incapable of any passion, of any higher desiring, and therefore impotent in the sense of being incapable of ruling over themselves. Their lives are shaped exclusively by the external circumstances they find themselves in. Such people are incapable not just of making history, but also of properly understanding those historical figures they presume to study: they have no access to what was central to their achievements—to the motivating passion that led the great individuals of the past to accomplish them—because they have no experience of a similar ruling passion in themselves. Thus their accounts of the people and works of the past, for example, in the form of their historical or philological works, will necessarily fail to give a faithful account of their topics—their "objectivity" stems from their authors' "subjectlessness" (1.284/120), from their lack of passionate investment that is a necessary prerequisite for any non-superficial understanding of a subject. Their works will consequently never have any real effect on others' life, they will never move anyone to change their life, as, for example, Plutarch's works can do (1.295/131; cf. KGW II.5, pp. 266–267: "even with an average talent"). Their only effect is others' production of critiques of their work—but "everything remains as it was" (1.285/121; cf. 1.170/15) in their life, in their uniform bourgeois existence.

HL 7–9: The Sapping of the Will to Growth

The second group of negative consequences of overexposure to scientific history is destructive of our will to grow itself. That is, while the previously discussed problem is the damage it causes to one's capacity to order one's life in accordance with one's ruling passion, this problem is the destruction of the will to order one's life in this way at all, or the destruction of the ruling passion itself. This happens because for a motivating desire to be truly motivating, the object of our desire must be "in the shadow of the

---

45. This is not to say that Kant lacked courage altogether: cf. Neymeyr (2020, 2.264–269) on various instances of his civic courage.

On the Utility and Liability of History for Life | 69

illusion of love" (1.296/131). In other words, for a desire to be as strong as to allow us to order the entirety of our life according to it, we must first possess "the unconditional belief in perfection and justness" of the desideratum (1.296/131): We must believe that we are truly striving for the best possible thing there is, that we are striving for genuine happiness and a genuine good. This is in most cases an illusion, as scientific history correctly teaches us: What past generations considered to be "perfect and just" is for later generations often just a result of folly and ignorance, and Nietzsche himself thinks the vast majority of human efforts amount to little more than meaningless suffering (cf. 1.377–278/209–210). Here Nietzsche shows us this effect on the example of Christianity, which, after being subjected to scientific history, was cleansed of so many follies and injustices (which in the past were seen through the illusions of love and considered essential parts of the faith) that what remained of it has assumed a "scarcely visible form" (1.297/132), that is, has almost ceased to exist. And Nietzsche worries that a similar fate may befall other great objects of human desire, especially the belief in "the revolutionary and reforming healing power of German music" (1.297–298/133)—the belief in the capacity of Wagner's art to work toward establishing a genuine culture in Germany, which will play a major role in *WB*.

However, despite the falsity of "the unconditional belief in perfection and justness" of our desiderata, that is, despite this belief being (almost necessarily) an illusion, it is indispensable to possess such a belief in order to begin to grow, or to form a project at all, in the first place. One may outgrow such illusions eventually, but one will never reach that stage if one doesn't begin supported by an illusion of this kind. Goethe provides us with a fitting example of such a salutary illusion from his own life (Eckermann, 2010, p. 174, conversation from 16 Feb. 1826; Nietzsche wrote down this quotation in the note 29 [77], 7.663): "But had I known [when I was young] as clearly as now how many excellent things have already been here for centuries and millennia, I wouldn't have written a single line, but done something else instead." Even the greatest German poet needed to believe in the absolute value of his youthful efforts. The reality of their limited value in comparison to other great works of the human spirit had to wait until he grew strong enough for it.[46] However, if a young person is by their

---

46. I thus do not consider this aspect of Nietzsche's argument to come close to a "sacrificium intellectus," as Neymeyr (2020, 1.399) does; nor do I think that "illusion" is a kind of "mysterious fluid" (ibid., 1.515).

70 | The Young Nietzsche's Education

education bereft of such illusions, they become "homeless" and "skeptical of all customs and concepts" (1.299/135), of those that guided the lives of past generations as well as those they were themselves taught to believe in. The question arises: If everything the past generations believed in has been shown to belong to a ceaseless and meaningless line of follies, by what right do *we* think ourselves exempt from this universal rule?—and no satisfactory answer may appear. In such a case, one is bound to conclude that "in every age things were different, it does not matter what you are" (1.300/135). This attitude—that nothing one may strive for truly matters, for eventually it will all be revealed as a folly, just as everything people of the past believed in—is the core of what Nietzsche calls "an *ironic* existence" (1.302/137).

The excess of scientific history may also promote an ironic existence by instilling the belief in the old age of humanity (1.303/138). This belief amounts to thinking that any new major project or goal one may set for themselves is ultimately meaningless because everything truly important had already been accomplished. This is originally a Christian belief: For the Christian, the decisive events in history were the life, death, and resurrection of Jesus, from which we should derive the rules for our life; and the only great event to come is the Last Judgment, in which we will be judged on how obedient to those rules we had been. Christianity is therefore hostile to every culture—to every kind of self-cultivation—"that incites people to go on striving" (1.305/140), that is, striving for anything radically new and thereby challenges the Christian claim to complete truth. For Christianity, any such culture "seduces to existence" and thereby "lies about the value of existence" (1.304/139): Christianity is for Nietzsche not just hostile to any new growth and striving, but more radically it sees this-worldly existence as worthless in itself, and of worth only insofar as it prepares us for the true life after death. Christianity is therefore life-denying.[47] As we saw above (cf.

---

47. In *SE* (1.389/220), Nietzsche will claim that "Christianity is certainly one of the purest manifestations of that drive for culture." How it is possible for Christianity to be both life-denying and one of the purest forms of culture, of what Nietzsche is trying to promote? I believe that insofar as culture is unity of style, Christianity may well be considered a life-denying unity of style. The sentence from *SE* would then be an expression of admiration for the manifold ingenious *methods* of self-discipline and self-cultivation that Christianity has developed (for example, the Christian focus on the individual and their soul, and the concomitant shunning of worldly success—cf. 1.321/155), but not for the *ends* these methods aim to produce. In other words, Christianity can produce a genuine culture, but only a Christian culture, and Nietzsche is striving for a culture that would develop all kinds of human genius. Cf. Hutter (2009, pp. 212–213) for a more detailed account.

On the Utility and Liability of History for Life | 71

1.297/132), the Christian God may be dead now; however, the belief in the old age of humanity, the belief that everything meaningful had already been done, persists as one of his "shadows" (in the language of *GS* 108). It has reappeared in a stream of contemporary thinking about history (represented here by Wackernagel) that sees the contemporary humanity simply as epigones of the ancient world. It can also be a consequence of believing one lives after the "absolute moment" postulated by Hegel's philosophy. But regardless of the reason why, if one takes themselves to be an epigone, they will live ironically, for all their efforts will never go beyond the shadow of their great predecessors.

The belief in the old age of humanity also takes another form, which Nietzsche dubs "cynicism." Cynicism is a particularly self-satisfied interpretation of Hegel's philosophy of history. Hegel (1988, p. 20) writes that "the essence of spirit is its freedom," and that history of the world is the progressive realization [*Verwirklichung*] of this freedom. This realization proceeds in three major stages, the first of which was represented by the oriental nations, the second by the Classical Antiquity, and the third by the Germanic world (Hegel, 1988, p. 21):

> In the world of the ancient Orient, people do not yet know that the Spirit—the human as such—is free. Because they do not know this, they are not free. They know only that *one* person is free; but for this very reason such freedom is mere arbitrariness, savagery, stupefied passion; or even a softness or tameness of passion, which is itself a mere accident of nature and therefore quite arbitrary. This *one* person is therefore only a despot, not a free man. It was among the Greeks that the consciousness of freedom first arose, and thanks to that consciousness they were free. But they, and the Romans as well, knew only that *some* persons are free, not the human as such. Even Plato and Aristotle did not know this. [. . .] It was first the Germanic peoples, through Christianity, who came to the awareness that every human is free by virtue of being human, and that the freedom of spirit comprises our most human nature.

The Germanic nations, under the influence of Christianity, have realized that the human being as such is free, and thereby attained the self-consciousness of freedom. This is the "absolute moment" of world history, the moment in which the development of the spirit is completed or perfected, the moment toward which the entire world process was leading: "the *final goal of the world*" is "Spirit's consciousness of its freedom, and hence also the actualization

72 | The Young Nietzsche's Education

of that very freedom" (ibid., p. 22). All that is left to do now is fully to realize this self-consciousness of freedom, "to introduce this principle into worldly reality [. . .] so that it permeates the worldly situation" (ibid., p. 21). The substantial self-consciousness of freedom had been attained with the appearance of Hegel's philosophy; and so Nietzsche glosses that "for Hegel the apex and culmination of the world process coincided with his own existence in Berlin" (1.308/143).

The cynics appropriate Hegel's thought of the world process as the progressive and now accomplished development of the self-consciousness of freedom, and conclude from it that they, the modern Europeans, are the necessary peak of human development: that "we are the goal [of the world process], we are nature perfected" (1.313/147)—and this exalted status requires no effort or achievements of one's own, it is attained simply by being born at the right period of history. Such a debased form of the belief in the end of history conveniently absolves the philistines from any need to form projects (at least any projects that go beyond the maintenance of a comfortable bourgeois existence) and cultivate their souls: They are already perfect as they are. The concomitant view of the past events amounts to "the idolatry of the factual" (1.309/143), to a worship of whichever force managed to prevail over other competing forces, for every such victorious force must have been a necessary contribution to the historical process. But all human greatness stems from the will to resist that which already is, to pursue one's own project rather than to be a cog in someone else's project; it resides in those who rebel "against that blind power of facts, against the tyranny of the real" (1.311/145). No such will is to be found in the self-satisfied cynic. Cynicism is the form the historical sickness takes in the philistines, as is evident not just from the similarity of the preceding description to the account of the philistine "culture" in DS 1–3, but also more directly from the fact that D. F. Strauss's book was described as "cynical" in precisely this sense in DS (1.173/19, cf. 1.197/41).

This fetishizing of the world process reaches its peak in the work of Eduard von Hartmann, who surpasses Strauss in arguing that the present-day state of humanity completes and justifies the existence of humanity as such "not only on the basis of the past, *ex causis efficientibus*, but also on the basis of the future, *ex causa finali*" (1.314/149). Nietzsche presents von Hartmann's doctrine as taking the premises of the world-process-thinking *ad absurdum*:[48] He shows us the modern humans in their misery and pettiness,

---

48. Cf. note 29 [52], 7.648: "Hartmann is important because he kills the thought of the world process by being consequential with it." A more detailed account of the

On the Utility and Liability of History for Life | 73

the bourgeois philistines who strive for nothing beyond their own comfortable existence (cf. 1.315/149), as the peaks and conclusions of the world process, and thus exposes what is for Nietzsche the central contradiction of this line of thinking. The only step remaining to be taken, according to von Hartmann, is the widespread realization of the meaninglessness of human existence, and the consequent collective suicide.[49]

~

We have seen that scientific history is destructive of our motivating or ruling passion in three distinct ways: It may show all human goals to be valuable only relatively to their age and therefore ultimately meaningless; it may show all *new* goals—all goals one may pursue oneself—as radically inferior to what had already been attained; or it may make us believe that we are already as perfect as humanly possible, and so sap the desire to make a serious effort to lead and order our lives. All these three disadvantages take away the possibility to meaningfully compare ourselves with humans of the past and stem from a single root: from the realization, brought about by scientific history, of the radically transitory character of all things—not just of material things but of human beliefs, valuations, and desiderata as well. Nietzsche therefore dubs scientific history "the science of universal becoming" (1.272/109): It shows us all that has ever occurred as a part of a ceaseless chaotic stream of generation, change, and destruction.[50] This idea that nothing is actually permanent, that there is no stable being, is the core insight of the "deadly truths" (1.319/153): "The doctrines of sovereign becoming, of the fluidity of all concepts, types, and species, of the lack of any cardinal difference between human and animal—doctrines I hold to be true, but also deadly." I take the most important reason why these truths are "deadly" to be that they (insofar one knows these truths) remove any

---

importance of von Hartmann to *HL* can be found in Salaquarda 1984 (esp. pp. 41–45). Since the function of the discussion of von Hartmann's thought in *HL* is quite clear, I cannot agree with Jensen's (2016, p. 123) view that "Nietzsche treats Hartmann in a singularly bizarre fashion."

49. Cf. Salaquarda's (1984, p. 40) summary of this final stage of von Hartmann's world process: "then it may happen that the great majority of humanity decides to end the ill-fated striving and to go out into nothingness." Also cf. Neymeyr, 2020, 1.542. Contrary to Pearson's (2018, p. 6) opinion, this is certainly not a "whiggish conviction."

50. It also makes us much more aware of the uniqueness of each historical event, and thus of its incommensurability with any other, earlier or later, event.

74 | The Young Nietzsche's Education

kind of transhistorical support to our desiderata and make them all appear historically conditioned.[51] Thereby they discredit any possible belief in the *unconditional* goodness of our desiderata, which is necessary for our motivating passion to rule and order our life. They also cause the useful kinds of history—the purpose of which is precisely aiding our ruling passion in attaining its ends—to be viewed as falsifications of history (1.296/132), and thus they become useless. The deadly truths are deadly because they destroy the psychic conditions that are essential to life in the sense of growing or expanding life, of the truly human and not merely animal life. The lack of any eternal support of our understanding leads to a nihilistic groundlessness and irresponsibility in our actions and overall conduct of life (cf. Patočka, 2002, p. 90).

Nietzsche extrapolates from this that the widespread exposure to deadly truths, and to scientific history more widely, effects a thorough anti-cultural transformation of society. A historically educated people will lose its sense of unity that stems from antiquarian history and ceases "to be a people at all" (1.319/153), and historically educated individuals will no longer be able or even willing to grow. The effort to grow will then be replaced by the effort to secure a comfortable existence, and society will be transformed so as to facilitate this new, low goal: It will become a collection of "systems of individual egoisms" (1.319/153). The only constraint is that these petty egoisms are to be "prudent," that is, such that do not (visibly) harm anyone else. The state is only to provide a legal framework securing the peaceful coexistence of these egoisms: "it is supposed to become the patron of all prudent egoisms" (1.322/156). This is in effect the liberal-capitalist state, which is why Nietzsche had called liberalism the "actually anti-cultural doctrine" in a longer, unpublished version of *Foreword to Richard Wagner* (note 11 [1], 7.355). The ultimate consequence of these trends would be what Catherine Zuckert (1970, p. 105; cf. Zuckert, 1976, p. 67) has called "an end of history" (as opposed to *the* end of history): a state of humanity

---

51. Nietzsche treats the deadly truths together with writing history "from the standpoint of the *masses*" (1.319/154) because he seems to think that all constructions of history as a meaningful process unduly privilege masses at the expense of the individuals, who can be considered "merely as the clearest expression" of the mass-driven historical process (1.320/154, cf. 1.317/151). A construction of history as a stream of becoming *against the run of which* a great individual may appear by their own effort would not read history from the standpoint of the masses, nor as a *meaningful* process; but it would still have to deal with the issue of *panta rhei*, of there not being anything stable or permanent.

On the Utility and Liability of History for Life | 75

in which no new great events would transpire—not because everything great had already been done, but because there would be no one capable of greatness anymore.[52]

II.4. Curing the Historical Sickness

After the preceding account of the dangers that scientific history, and truth itself, pose to life, we have to ask two major questions. First, are we as humans really condemned to live in untruth? Is the truth simply deadly and to be avoided? Is it even *possible* to willfully choose untruth over the truth, however painful or even "deadly" the truth may be? And second, how does Nietzsche propose to counteract the harmful influence of the "historical sickness" in its various forms?

JUSTICE, TRUTH, AND PHILOSOPHY

Justice and the various claims to it play an important, if somewhat under-stated role in *HL*. Already in *HL* 1 Nietzsche observed the "blindness and injustice dwelling in the soul of those who act" (1.254/93) that is a necessary condition for any human action at all, and how this injustice motivates the "suprahistorical humans" to devise life-denying doctrines that, if followed, would supposedly justify human existence. Furthermore, justice is also "the loftiest claim of the modern human being" (1.288/124): The contemporary humanity's claim to preeminence over the previous periods rests on the promise of scientific history that by knowing more of the truth, we will become more just than ever before. And Nietzsche claims himself in *HL* 6 that "only insofar as the truthful person has the unconditional will to be just is there anything great in that striving for truth that everywhere is so thoughtlessly glorified" (1.287/123), that truth is great and worthy of the

---

52. Nietzsche wonders out loud whether "there will even be *future ages* at all that can be understood to be cultured" (1.311/146)—whether, if these tendencies continue to exert their influence, there will be in the future anyone left capable of self-cultivation and thus also of making history. Hutter (2009, p. 216) has a more detailed treatment of liberalism's hostility toward genuine culture as a result of its "completely Mammonistic orientation" that is incapable of understanding and dealing with the *thymos* of the "young souls" (and other thymotic characters). Cf. Chapter III.1 below on the central role of *thymos* in Nietzsche's project in the *UC* of establishing a new, genuine culture.

76 | The Young Nietzsche's Education

suffering it carries with itself only in the service of justice. Nietzsche thus clearly sees justice—and truth, insofar it serves justice—to be of paramount importance to human life. But what *is* justice in the first place?

Nietzsche explains clearly enough what justice is *not*. First, it is not the disinterested "objectivity" (i.e., subjectlessness) of the scientific historians. Indeed, the highest form of "objectivity"—in which the artist (be it a painter, a historian, or a dramatist) as it were depicts the constellation of events as if it were purely reflected in him without any personal interest—is in fact a highly personal creative act, "the most powerful and most spontaneous creative moment in the inner being of the artist" (1.290/126), and not disinterested at all. Calling it "objectivity" misses precisely the *subjective* moment at the core of such depictions, the artist's motivating passion. The "subjectless" account of "objectivity" fails to see in the "objective" artist precisely the same thing it misses in the actors of the past.[53] Second, it is also not the life-denying justice of the suprahistorical humans, who (correctly) judge that all action is based on error and injustice, but fail to apply this judgment to themselves. If they did so, they would realize how their condemnation of humanity is based on their own, frustrated, passion for justice—and thus is itself unjust. They fail to understand the difficult knowledge that the unjust unhistorical passion is "not only the womb of the unjust deed, but of every just deed as well" (1.253/92), of any humanly possible goodness and justice (cf. Lemm, 2011, p. 172). The doctrines they develop for consolation are consequently life-denying.

Nietzsche presents his idea of justice proper in the second paragraph of *HL* 6. Becoming just is described as a movement of ascending from a preparatory stage: "from pardonable doubt to rigorous certainty, from tolerant clemency to the imperative "you must," from the rare virtue of generosity to the rarest of all virtues, justice" (1.286/122). I believe this is the same movement as that described in a famous passage from *WB* (1.445/272): "It seems to me that the most important question in all of philosophy is the extent to which things possess an unalterable nature and form, so that, once this question has been answered, we can with relentless courage set about the *improvement of the aspect of the world recognized as being alterable.*" What is described in these passages is first attaining as much knowledge about human beings and the world as is in one's powers. This knowledge is characterized by magnanimity—by an effort to take things as they are regardless of how much one may dislike them—and by doubt as to whether

---

53. Cf. Zuckert (1976, pp. 65–66) and Jensen (2016, pp. 98–104) for more thorough accounts of Nietzsche's critique of historical "objectivity."

On the Utility and Liability of History for Life | 77

one really knows things correctly and magnanimously enough. This knowing is marked by a particular attention to what is special about human beings, what in them makes them great and beautiful, and what kind of conditions are conducive to the thriving of such human qualities and of the humans who embody them. The second step is using this truth "as ordering and punishing judge" (1.286/122–123), as a basis for legislating such an order of the human things (and for the "appraisal of their importance"—note 29 [21], 7.633), for establishing such ways of individual and collective life that actually fulfill the needs of the growing or ascending life to the greatest possible extent. As Heidegger (2016, § 79) writes, this justice is "the *capacity* to an *originary act of judgment*, that is, legislation, and not the mere *application* of an already valid law."[54] What Nietzsche describes here is justice as the highest practical task of the philosopher, as the establishment of a social order that corresponds to the natural order of rank among humans and fosters the cultivation of the higher human types—justice as Nietzsche saw it in the works of Plato.[55] This is "truth, in a word, as Last Judgment [*Weltgericht*]" (1.287/123),[56] for no institution or organization in the world is exempt from this forensic examination as to whether it serves life or hinders it. But, unlike the suprahistorical "justice," this justice seeks to aid life rather than to condemn it: its judgments and its legislation serve not to suppress life, but to realize its potential as much as possible.[57]

---

54. Lampert (1993, pp. 289–291) made a similar suggestion before Heidegger's lectures on *HL* were published.

55. The young Nietzsche saw Plato as a political thinker of this kind. Cf. the note 14 [11], 7.379, where he claims that "*The organization of the state of geniuses—that is the true Platonic republic.*" Two later notes (both from 1873) describe Plato's ideal state as the peak of philosophy: "Plato's state as *suprahellenic*, as not impossible. Philosophy attains here its greatest height as the founder of a metaphysically ordered state." (29 [170], 7.701); and the note 29 [174], 7.704, describes Plato himself as in the first place a legislator of this kind: "Theory: Plato was mainly a legislator and reformer, and never a skeptic in this regard." Also cf. the accounts of Nietzsche's Platonic understanding of politics in Drochon (2016, pp. 40–46) and Lampert (2017, pp. 50–53).

56. The idiom of philosophy as *Weltgericht* would go on to enjoy a long presence in Nietzsche's thought. As late as in an unsent draft of a letter to Georg Brandes from early December 1888, *The Antichrist* is described as "truly a *Weltgericht*" (KGB II.5, p. 502).

57. Nietzsche emphasizes how essential knowledge is for the establishing of genuine justice by contrasting the philosophic legislator with a person who desires justice but lacks knowledge or "the power of judgment" [*Urtheilskraft*]: The latter is a *fanatic* rather than a genuine judge of human affairs, and "the most horrible afflictions have befallen humanity" because of the fanatics' desire to establish their fanciful and ungrounded notions of justice in the world (1.287/123).

78 | The Young Nietzsche's Education

Only this kind of striving for truth is beneficial to life—for, as we have seen, truth is deadly in almost all other cases—and only insofar as truth can in this way aid life "is there anything great in that striving for truth that everywhere is so thoughtlessly glorified" (1.287/123).[58] However, the deadening effect of truth can be avoided only by *concealing* the truth. The doubts of the thinker must be hidden behind the legislator's veneer of "certainty." The thinker's magnanimity, necessary for giving things their due, must be replaced by imperatives and by punishments for those who disobey them. In other words, the just legislator in this sense must act as if they had full certainty that their legislation is an expression of *the* truth, while in truth they cannot have any such certainty. But while this truth may—and in fact must—be concealed from the many, the legislator does not have this luxury. Being just in this sense means for them personally that "in every moment [they] must do penance for [their] own humanity and tragically consume [themselves] in pursuit of an impossible virtue" (1.286/122). The just individual has to bear the burden that their imperatives are justified by lies, even though they be lies in the name of one's "truth" about what is best for human beings (cf. *HA* 241). They may never publicly admit the doubts they, as a thinker, necessarily have. They have to live in awareness of the not-completely-attainable nature of the standards they set up for others. They must do without the comforting illusions that are helpful and even indispensable to the vast majority of humans. They are aware of the perishable nature of all things, including of whatever they may be able to establish. And finally, they suffer the greatest and most spiritual sufferings (cf. 1.451–452/278–279) that are beyond the comprehension of the many who live in the atmosphere of life-promoting illusions. In short, the philosophic legislator's soul becomes the site of the conflict between truth and life, and they must carry this conflict within themselves without having any hope of resolving it: That is their tragedy (cf. Lampert, 2017, pp. 63, 66). In *HL*, and in the *UC* as a whole, the conflict between truth and life is fundamental and insoluble; it can at best be concealed from others by the legislator.[59]

Thus, in the young Nietzsche's conception, the highest form of justice is inextricably bound up with philosophy in the proper sense of the word.

---

58. This is the reason why philosophy is "the most truthful of all sciences" (1.282/118).

59. One significant consequence of this idea is the emphasis Nietzsche places on belief, and even *unconditional* belief, in places such as 1.296/131. In contrast, the mature Nietzsche will consider "the taste for the unconditional" as "the worst of all tastes" in *BGE* 31.

On the Utility and Liability of History for Life | 79

In his lectures on the pre-Platonic philosophers, he says "a legislation of greatness, a naming, is bound up with philosophy: it says 'that is great' and thereby it elevates the human being" (KGW II.4, p. 218n8; cf. note 19 [83], 7.447–448). Such a legislation is the proper work of the philosophic legislators such as Pythagoras or Empedocles (1.758) or Plato. These thinkers legislate out of their *philanthropy*, out of their love for what is great in humans and their will to help it come to fruition, which Nietzsche calls "pity" [*Mitleid*] in *HL* (1.278/114; cf. 1.758).[60] In this sense, justice as legislation of greatness is the application of "the fundamental idea of *culture*" (1.382/213; cf. 1.756), the cultivation of the human soul toward yet-unseen greatness. Therefore, in *On the Pathos of Truth*, the philosophic legislators are described as "the most daring knights among these seekers of glory" (1.757) right after the passages that are used in *HL* 2 to describe the monumental individuals (cf. 1.755–757 with 1.259–260/96–97). The philosophic legislators are the greatest monumental individuals—they form "a kind of bridge over the turbulent stream of becoming" and live *above* the historical process, "timelessly and simultaneously," in a "republic of genius" (1.317/151)—for they deliberately strive to foster what the lesser monumental individuals do "instinctively." Consequently, they are hated by the many just like the monumental individuals are (1.259, 1.287/97, 123; 1.756). This conception of philosophy as the legislation of human greatness understands religion and art as inferior and ministerial to philosophy, rather than the other way around. In *HL*, these forces are called "true helpers" of the philosophic legislator in the task "to plant the seeds of a culture that answers to true needs" (1.281/118): they would be the providers of the "lies in the name of truth," of the salutary illusions that comprise the outward form of the philosophic legislation.

Nietzsche himself has the ambition to become a legislator of greatness for the Germans, as can be seen from the closing paragraph of *HL* 4 (1.277–278/114–115). However, he recognizes that such legislation cannot be simply proclaimed—it requires a people willing to receive such a legislation and able to fulfill its commandments. But the contemporary Germans are no such people: They are divided both internally, suffering from the "split personality," and externally, in that "the unity of national feeling is lost" (1.277/114) and the desire for true culture is now the privilege of only a small group. In these conditions, Nietzsche could at best legislate only to

---

60. Nietzsche will say in *WB* that it is because of hopes like these that philosophers have always been writing books and didn't keep their wisdom to themselves (1.445/272).

80 | The Young Nietzsche's Education

this small group, to a "sect." Thus, before he can proceed to the task of legislation, he must accomplish a preliminary destructive task: "as judge he can at least condemn what he, a vital and life-giving being, regards as destruction and degradation" (1.278/115), that is, to expose and condemn scientific history and historical education that caused the divisions within and between the Germans. In doing this, he "hopes to sow the seeds of a need" (1.278/115), of a powerful motivating desire for self-cultivation that would be able to restore the order within one's soul and guide one's life. And if this desire becomes widespread, if many people come to live as it were in a shared world with a shared ruling passion and a shared goal—then they will become *a people* again, and they will be ready to accept Nietzsche's legislation that will help them attain their goal. I take this, in broad terms, to be Nietzsche's goal in writing the *UC*; and more broadly, as his first programmatic statement of what he as a thinker and a practical man aims to accomplish—of *his project*.

NEGATIVE COUNTERMEASURES

The first step of this program is finding ways to fight the dangers of scientific history. For this it is essential to spell out these dangers in the first place, and that is why Nietzsche has given his readers a thorough account of the deleterious effects for life of the exposure to scientific history. However, history can have these effects on the young only because contemporary German education, to which they are subjected, is based on scientific history. This education is not education proper, it is only "a kind of knowledge about education" (1.273, 1.327/110, 160), education about how other peoples have been educated in the past that has no consequence for how we lead our lives.[61] This education takes no account of what it means to really cultivate a human being—its goal is rather to produce productive scholars as quickly as possible, and such scholars need not cultivate their souls, they need only to learn the knowledge and skills necessary to their profession (1.326/159–160). Being such a scholar is fully compatible with being a weak, split personality, as well as with being a philistine.

This account of the drawbacks of modern historical education is embedded into an argument about *why* the young are subjected to this education: namely to make science "more and more useful in the economic

_____

61. Cf. *D* 195 for a later statement of this problem with explicit reference to the German "classical education."

sense" (1.301/136). However, the fact that historical education aims at rearing economically productive workers belies its claims to seek the truth for its own sake. It shows us that it actually seeks such "truths," and educates such seekers of truth, as are conducive to the great modern goal of securing a comfortable life (1.300–301/135–136). Science is to yield results that increase wealth and "quality of life" measured in purely economic or material terms. A consequence of this orientation on comfortable life—of barbarism as the driving force behind modern science—is that real culture becomes superfluous at best. A society (or "culture") like this rather needs weak, docile humans who do not—who *cannot*—ask for more than the comfortable life it offers (1.319–323/153–157). Thus it makes perfect sense that although the declared goal of historical education is the production of scholars, its actual product is "the historically and aesthetically cultivated philistine" (1.326/160) and, consequently, the entire system of philistine "culture" that was the subject of *DS* 1–3. Nietzsche stresses that this education, together with its effects, are implemented with precisely the purpose of "uprooting the strongest instincts of youth" and thereby "cheating youth out of its most beautiful privilege, out of the power to plant, overflowing with faith, a great thought within itself and letting it grow into an even greater thought" (1.323/157). His final verdict is that the true purpose of historical education is rearing weaklings who will easily become a part of the barbaric capitalist-bourgeois system oriented on the comfortable life and nothing beyond it.

Nietzsche hereby enacts what he says is the solution to the problem of scientific history: "history itself *must* solve the problem of history, knowledge *must* turn its goad upon itself" (1.306/141). By showing what kind of human being is actually produced by scientific history and for whose benefit, he aims to break the illusions that sustain its power over the minds of the young—the illusions that it is the peak of modern truthfulness and that it makes its practitioners wiser and more just than anyone in the past. Instead, they learn that this kind of education is not necessary at all, and that it is "anti-natural" (1.326/160), that is, working contrary to the natural tendency of life to grow and expand. The critical-historical account of scientific history (and of present-day society in general) that is given in *HL* 4–9 enables the young to recognize and condemn it, and so free themselves from its pernicious influence—that is, to be honest with themselves and to realize the "necessary truth" (1.328/162) that they have no culture yet and that they are sick with history. The purpose of this realization is, as is the case with critical history in general, to sow "a second nature" (1.270/107):

82 | The Young Nietzsche's Education

to enable them to acquire a new ruling passion, which will be the basis for beginning to recover from historical sickness and for seeking genuine culture. In Nietzsche's words, this critique frees the young so that they may "educate [themselves]—educate [themselves], moreover, against [themselves]—[. . .] in order to acquire new habits and a new nature" (1.328/162).

However, it should be emphasized that the target of Nietzsche's critique is not so much academic historical science, but rather the proliferation of scientific history as the sole valid mode of relating to the past and the external. The tools of scientific history are a great contribution to the toolkit of the professional historian who knows why they need to study a particular people or historical period. The problem of scientific history arises only when scientific history doesn't remain "esoteric" in Goethe's sense (*Werke*, VIII.471; cf. Neymeyr, 2020, 1.522): that is, when it doesn't contribute to the given culture's way of life by suggesting particular improvements to it, or an "*enhanced praxis*" (1.301/137), but when it instead challenges that way of life by presenting appealing alternatives to it.[62] Thus, the real problem of scientific history is that it's being taught to every boy and girl these days, rather than remaining a preserve of qualified experts. We find an indication as to how Nietzsche would imagine the non-scientific-historical education of youth in the note 14 [25], 7.385: "The *teaching of children* is the duty of *parents* and *community*: preservation of the tradition is its main task." In other words, it would be education along the lines of antiquarian history. Elementary education would foster the children's attachment to "their own" and reinforce the acculturation they have already received from their parents. In contrast, the methods and results of scientific history would be available only to those who will actively show an interest in them, and only for the purposes of their research, the results of which would be known only to other experts.[63]

---

62. Insofar as scientific history strives to be "value-free," i.e., refuses to take the side of its culture's way of life, it challenges that way of life by presenting other ways of life as equally valid alternatives thereof.

63. Thus, contrary to Church's (2019, p. 97) opinion, modern culture does not have "a bottomless stomach for knowledge" (or it is sick insofar as it does), and Nietzsche wants to regulate and limit its presence in culture. Cf. the note 19 [11], 7.419, where Nietzsche compares the drive to knowledge to the sexual drive: "the *indiscriminate* drive to knowledge is equal to the indiscriminate sexual drive—signs *of vulgarity!*" Just as a person who would pursue sexual relations with anyone is enslaved by this passion, one who strives to know indiscriminately is in effect promoting (what should be) a means into an end, at the expense of the life to which knowledge as means ought to serve.

On the Utility and Liability of History for Life | 83

POSITIVE COUNTERMEASURES

Now that the readers know what they are suffering from, how do they heal their damaged souls and develop a "new nature" for themselves? We already know that the central conflict within the modern soul is between life and knowledge. Nietzsche now poses the question: Which of these two powers, "life" and "knowledge," is "higher and more decisive" (1.330/164)? In other words, which of the two basic functions of the human soul recognized ever since the Antiquity, the animating and the cognitive, is the higher and more important one? And he sides without a doubt with "life," with the animating function: He calls it "the higher, the ruling force" (1.330/164) on the basis of its more fundamental character. *Cogito, ergo sum* is replaced by *vivo, ergo cogito* (1.329/162). The more fundamental is at the same time the higher.

On the basis of this reflection, Nietzsche suggests that his readers establish "a *hygiene of life*" (1.331/164) to counteract the consequences of excessive exposure to history. The two main antidotes against history are the unhistorical (as the capacity to forget and to be at least temporarily satisfied within a closed horizon) and the suprahistorical.[64] The suprahistorical is characterized here as comprising art and religion, understood as "powers that divert one's gaze from what is in the process of becoming to what lends existence the character of something eternal and stable in meaning" (1.330/163). Nietzsche thus suggests than one should, insofar as one can, dwell within illusions that provide a stable horizon of meaning to one's world. This is of course a tricky proposition, for illusions can provide meaning only

---

64. The accounts of the suprahistorical in *HL* 1 (1.254–256/92–94) and *HL* 10 (1.330/163) look quite different from each other at the first sight, which led Jensen (2016, p. 17) to declare them "inconsistent" with each other, and to "suggest that [the concept of] überhistorical may have been offered at least partly out of a mind for symmetry rather than out of a clear and precise philosophical motivation." A few pages later (2016, p. 24) he speculates that this (alleged) inconsistency could be explained by the fact that *HL* 10 was written hastily and, unlike the rest of *HL*, wasn't edited by Carl von Gersdorff. However, I don't think we need to go so far as to accuse Nietzsche of sloppy writing in order to resolve this interpretive problem. Already Zuckert (1976, p. 57n4) offers the idea that in both *HL* 1 and *HL* 10 Nietzsche "is referring to the desire (fulfilled or frustrated) to give human life a meaning which extends beyond the temporal and other limitations of the individual." On this reading, the suprahistorical men of *HL* 1 would be a subset of the religious (and thus a subset of the suprahistorical humans rather than the sole suprahistorical humans), and while Nietzsche would hardly condone their doctrines, at least there is still passion behind them. In that sense they are less dangerous to life than the passion-destroying historical sickness.

84 | The Young Nietzsche's Education

when one actually believes in them, or as long as one does not take them to be illusions. However, we have seen that illusions are necessary for the psychic health and growth of most humans, and in this respect Nietzsche is consistent with his previous words. After the healing progresses, one may study history again, but now in the three useful ways, that is, as a means to support one's psychic growth. What exactly these rather formal pieces of advice would mean in practice depends on the particular needs and wounds of each individual trying to cure themselves—Nietzsche provides just general guidelines, and everyone interested has to "translate them by means of their own experience into a doctrine that is personally meaningful" (1.332/165).

The proper task of the young is learning to live (1.325/158), that is, finding or developing a way of life suitable for them and their ruling passion—one does not live by bread alone, and human life is much more than just providing the conditions for one's continued survival. This task requires more than just healing the damage caused by historical education—it also requires self-knowledge. Nietzsche explains this by means of a "parable" (1.332/165) that compares the present situation of the German youth with the situation faced by the Greeks once upon a time, effectively using the Greeks as a monumental example for his readers (as Most, 2002, p. 34, notes) and demonstrating how his own historical education can contribute to solving the problem of historical education (cf. 1.247/86). The Greeks also were in the danger "of perishing in a flood of things alien and past, of perishing of 'history'" (1.333/166),[65] and consequently their souls were disorganized and chaotic, that is, barbaric, in ways similar to those of the contemporary Germans. The Greeks managed to order this inner chaos by following Apollo's exhortation to "know thyself," which Nietzsche understands as the knowledge of one's "genuine needs" (1.333/166). On the basis of this knowledge of their needs they could cultivate their nature in the sense of ordering the chaos that is the "natural" (or basic) state of the human soul: They became able to satisfy their "true" needs at the expense of the "false" ones, and to subordinate the lower needs to the higher ones.[66] Such

---

65. Note that here *Historie* means not just the past, but explicitly both the past *and* the external or alien.

66. Thus it is not true that Nietzsche's readers are to reject all external influences save for the Greeks, as Most (2002, p. 35) believes. The issue is rather one of giving an order to the external influences: as Siemens (2001, p. 93) points out, the exemplarity of the Greeks' "unhistorical education" lies in their "capacity to deal with the historicity of human existence" and to incorporate what they learn for the benefit of their life.

On the Utility and Liability of History for Life | 85

an ordering of one's inner chaos into an organized whole is culture both in the sense of unity of style (as defined in *DS*) and in the Greek sense of "new and improved *physis*" (1.334/167)—as a new ordering of the needs or desires that constitute the driving forces of the soul, which allows one to grow and expand much higher than the previous chaotic state. *HL* thus gives us a fuller account of what culture is than *DS* that is consistent with *DS* and with its central opposition of genuine culture to barbarism. Nietzsche hopes that by using the same methods as the Greeks, "the first cultured people, and hence the model for all future cultured peoples" (1.333/167), the German youth may eventually attain a similar level of self-cultivation, and perhaps even agonistically overcome them (Siemens, 2001, pp. 104–106). From this position—that of epigones of classical Antiquity rather than of the decaying Hellenistic antiquity (1.307/141–142)—they themselves may then become the founders of a new, genuine culture (1.311, 1.333/146, 167). This is possible in part because Nietzsche thinks that a relatively small group—some hundred people—is sufficient to initiate such a cultural renewal (1.260, 1.295, 1.325/98, 131, 159; cf. the letter to Erwin Rohde after 21 Dec. 1871, KGB II.1, pp. 256–257). However, similarly as with the account of justice, this account of self-knowledge and its benefits is highly abstract, and Nietzsche does not elaborate here *how* to find out what one's "true needs" are. Thus, the entire project of cultural renewal is, at this stage, a sketch at best. We will see how this sketch will unfold in the following two *UC*.

~

HL turned out to be about much more than just its overt topic, the dangers of scientific history. One of its core subjects, the importance of which has been stressed especially by phenomenologists such as Heidegger (1962, pp. 448–449) or Fink (2003, pp. 28–29), is human historicity and the ways in which it shapes our existence. However, the account of human historicity is, on my reading, embedded into a wider account of the overall structure of the human soul. The soul is understood as essentially erotic, as containing various desires and passions that vie for dominance over each other and that may be ordered into more or less stable hierarchies with a ruling passion on top—or remain chaotic. Desiring ("the unhistorical") is together with memory ("the historical") one of the two basic faculties of the human soul, the combination of which shapes the specifically human way of being. It is the combination of desiring and memory (or, in other words, the way in

86 | The Young Nietzsche's Education

which our desiring is transformed by memory) that gives rise to the worlds in which we live, meaningful worlds bounded by erotically determined horizons of significance.

This account of the human soul sets the terms for the overt subject of *HL*, which is a diagnosis of the various ways in which an excess of "history" (or any other kind of knowledge) can damage the structures of a healthy soul. These kinds of psychic damage are widespread in contemporary society, and that is not an accident—it is fostered by the modern, bourgeois, liberal-capitalist society in the effort to raise docile subjects whose desires do not extend beyond the desire for comfortable life. Nietzsche then outlines his efforts to counteract the historical sickness and to promote growth and self-cultivation of the souls of the young and sketches a couple of methods for this. These efforts in turn flow from his ambition to effect a cultural reform, and ultimately from his conception of philosophy as entailing justice and legislation in the highest sense as its practical task. At the same time, the issue of the "historical sickness" brought to light the fundamental tension between truth and life, which also will play a major role in the remaining two *UC*.

But *HL* leaves a lot of its central themes without satisfactory elaboration. This is most visible in its account of philosophy and justice, which is so abstract as to say almost nothing about how it could be carried out. The methods of self-cultivation sketched in *HL* 10 are indeed only sketched, and many pointed questions can be asked about them, as Heidegger (2016, § 97) does. With regard to Nietzsche's demand that one recognize one's "genuine needs" (1.333/166), Heidegger asks, "how is the genuineness of needs determined, and what is artificial within them?" Answering on Nietzsche's behalf that "genuine" needs are those that heighten life, he asks, "in what does the *height* of 'life' consist? [. . .] *Who* determines what height is?" In this relation he also asks, "who decides which genius is to become the one setting the standard?" (Heidegger, 2016, § 97). And he is right that *HL* by itself does not offer satisfactory answers to these questions.[67] Finally, while we did learn a few things about the young, *HL* still does not tell us enough to know who precisely they are and why precisely *they* matter to Nietzsche so much. Perhaps this is why *SE* will open with another and much more precise address to the youth.

---

67. This is likely intentional. Nietzsche wrote to Erwin Rohde on 15 February 1874 (KGB II.3, p. 202) that "a certain generality was required because I had to have considerations for more specific expositions in the later *Untimelies*."

III

Schopenhauer as Educator

The Good Life According to the Young Nietzsche

No one knows what he is doing while he acts right; but we are always conscious of what is wrong.[1]

III.1. *SE* 1: Erotic-Historic Self-Knowledge

SE begins in the same way *HL* ended—with a direct address to the young souls. Nietzsche tells them that each of us is unique and unlike anyone else, that "every human being is a one-of-a-kind miracle" (1.337–338/171). He admits that this may not be apparent at first sight, as most humans—especially in the present day—"appear to be mass-produced commodities" (1.338/172).[2] But this appearance is not due to them actually being copies of each other. It is due to their laziness, that most common human quality,[3]

---

1. Goethe (*Wilhelm Meister's Apprenticeship* VII.9, *Werke* VII.496).

2. Already here Nietzsche obliquely criticizes Schopenhauer. For Nietzsche, the regular person only *appears* as a factory product, whereas Schopenhauer makes no such qualifications: "the common, ordinary human beings, that manufactured article of nature which she daily produces in thousands" (*WWR* I, § 36, p. 187/ *Werke* I.268; cf. Neymeyr, 2020, 1.180–181 for further references).

3. Neymeyr (2020, 2.55–56) remarks that the two possible causes of human mediocrity discussed in this paragraph—laziness and fearfulness—are quite similar to laziness and cowardice, the causes of human immaturity in Kant's essay *An Answer to the Question: What Is Enlightenment?* However, while Kant puts more emphasis on fearfulness (e.g., in the famous motto *sapere aude!*), Nietzsche presents laziness as the more important factor.

88 | The Young Nietzsche's Education

as the Odyssean figure of the traveler[4] tells us: Most humans prefer the easy imitation of established habits and modes of life, the following of public opinions, which are really "private lazinesses" (1.338/172),[5] and the focus on securing a comfortable life for themselves over the long and difficult effort of cultivating one's unique self (and we will soon see just *how* difficult it is). But even if most humans make no effort to cultivate their uniqueness, they are nevertheless unique; what is more, they *know* they are unique—for their conscience tells them so. The call of conscience is heard especially strongly by "every young soul," but even those who are too lazy to listen to it are aware of it at some level—and hide this call "like a bad conscience" (1.337/171).

According to Nietzsche, our conscience tells us, the young souls: "be yourself! You are none of those things that you now do, think, and desire" (1.338/172). This imperative is, taken by itself, vague and puzzling: Where does it come from? And how are we to "be ourselves" if all we are is apparently *not* ourselves? We can begin to make sense of these questions by noticing the aspirational character of the voice of conscience. Our conscience tells us not just that we are unique, but also that this uniqueness of ours is something yet to be attained; that our current deeds, opinions, and even desires are not yet truly ours; that what we truly are needs to be liberated from "chains of opinions and fear" (1.338/172). Our conscience demands that we get to know our uniqueness—that we get to *know ourselves*—and that we consequently live according to what we truly are, "according to our own standards and laws" (1.339/173). It tells us we have to lead our life as *our* life, be responsible for it, develop it, and cultivate it—cultivate, that is, the uniqueness that we are. In Kaufmann's (1978, p. 161) pointed phrase, Nietzsche takes our individuality, worth, and dignity to be not *gegeben* [given], but rather *aufgegeben* [assigned as a task] to us.

The call of conscience obtains its motivating force from the awareness of our mortality,[6] from the fact that "we possess nothing but this brief

---

4. As pointed out by Lampert (2017, p. 75). Cf. *Za* I On the Thousand and One Goals, and Meier 2017, p. 37n41. The figure of the traveler or foreigner has also appeared in *DS* (1.162/8) and in *HL* (1.276/113). Large (2012, p. 104n8) points out that this position may well apply also to Nietzsche himself.

5. Nietzsche repeated this dictum in *HA* 482: "*And to repeat.*—Public opinions—private lazinesses."

6. This is one of several points in which Nietzsche's discussion of "be yourself!" strikingly prefigures Heidegger's conception of authenticity in *Being and Time*; cf. § 53. Also cf.

today in which to show why and to what purpose we have come into being precisely at this moment" (1.339/173)—and thus, if we do listen to our conscience, we have no time to waste in lazy conformism. And to add to the power of this call, Nietzsche also claims that the imperative *be yourself* is of decisive importance for our lives: He promises the rewards of true happiness and true freedom to those striving to fulfill it, while shirking this supreme responsibility amounts to leading an inhuman, animal, and utterly forgettable life. The conscience is, then, oriented much more on the future than on the past or the present—just as a healthy soul is ordered around a ruling passion and its project, a goal that is to be attained. On the basis of this correspondence between the conscience and the ruling desire of the soul, we can understand conscience formally as a memory-based structure that is oriented on the future—more specifically, as structure that compares what one aims at, what one wants to be (and is not yet), with what one is now. It is in this sense (i.e., as compared with what we aim to be) that our very deeds, thoughts, and desires—the deeds, thoughts, and desires of our *present* selves—are not truly our own.[7]

This conscience does not issue from any transcendent source, from any "beyond"; it is rather a function of our psychological constitution. I need to highlight here another characteristic feature of conscience: Namely that it is a peculiarly *negative* capacity. Conscience is much more likely to protest against the wrong deeds (i.e., such as do not lead to, or hinder the attaining of, the goal of our ruling passion) we are about to do than to actively guide us toward the right ones. The same is true of conscience in the form of the imperative *be yourself*, which only tells us what our self is *not*. But how do we find out what we truly are if our present self is a completely inadequate guide in this respect? If even something as fundamental to us as our desires, which structure the very world we live in (as we have seen in Chapter II.1), does not belong to what we truly are? It would seem that if what we currently desire is not what we are, then whatever we think we know of ourselves is simply a projection of what our current ruling desire would like to make of us. Nietzsche poses the question of self-knowledge—of *how* to understand ourselves, and of *whether* we can understand ourselves at all as more than

---

§ 58 on the role of conscience, which is likewise analogous to the *UC*; and there is also the more general parallel of characterizing human existence in terms of future-oriented projecting. However, a thorough examination of the influence of the *UC* on *Being and Time* is beyond the scope of this study.

7. Conscience is understood in an analogous manner also in *GS* 270 and *BGE* 158.

90 | The Young Nietzsche's Education

whatever our current ruling desire tells us we are in the first place—with great sharpness. Are we more than our ruling desire? Can we transcend that which seems to govern the very structures of our meaningfulness?

Self-knowledge is the subject of the fourth paragraph of *SE* 1, where Nietzsche discusses two methods of getting to know oneself.[8] The first method consists in examining one's present self, one's inclinations, attributes, talents, and capacities, as one already possesses them. But this method doesn't lead to the desired goal: In the course of such self-examination, we learn that we are "a dark and veiled thing" (1.340/174) and that beneath each layer of our soul we painstakingly explore there lies yet another one, and another one, and so on, without any clear endpoint to this process. Rather than leading us to its purported goal, this method of self-knowledge is a kind of being led astray, or "erring" (cf. Heidegger, 2008, pp. 132–137; and 1962, p. 67, regarding *Dasein*'s "properties"). Furthermore, this method of self-examination carries the risk of damaging oneself so that no doctor can heal us, of permanently crippling our soul. I believe that such damage may easily issue from an excessive focus on various wild, dark passions[9] that are naturally found in every human soul, but which would have very troubling implications if taken as a key testimony to who oneself as an individual is (cf. *Republic* 571c–d). This psychic damage may take either the form of despair over who one is and consequent distrust in and forceful curtailing of one's passions (i.e., some form of asceticism to contain the hell one found within oneself), or conversely of defining oneself in terms of these wild desires and ordering one's life around them, around the strongest and loudest but also basest and most animal forces within our soul. In the first case, one can no longer use the force of one's passions for further growth; in the latter case, one loses the very sight of one's self as something yet to be attained. In both cases it means limiting our self-understanding only to the capacities we already possess, thereby foreclosing the possibilities of growth which we may have without yet being aware of them.

---

8. With the exceptions of Tracy Strong (2000, p. 78) and Jeffrey Church (2015, p. 148), no previous commentator I know of had pointed out that Nietzsche discusses *two* separate methods of self-knowledge here. Cf. Schacht (1995, p. 158), Breazeale (1998, p. 15), Lemm (2007b, p. 18), Franco (2018, p. 55), and Pearson (2018, p. 13).

9. "Dark" in the sense of being obscure, of lacking clarity. Cf. Patočka's (1996, pp. 98–101) description of "the dimension of the demonic and of passion" in which "we are *enraptured*" (ibid., p. 99), i.e., carried by a force stronger than ourselves over which we have little control or understanding. Patočka's two main examples of such experiences are the sacred and the sexual.

Nietzsche sees that this first method does not lead to a genuine, productive self-knowledge, and hence he goes back to the idea that everything we do, the way in which we act in things small and great, the way in which we order our lives, is a much better testimony and expression of who we are than whatever we can find by digging in the depths of our soul.[10] But not everything we do is of equal importance, and so Nietzsche advises the young souls to look toward the most important things they have been doing so far, to ask themselves "what have you up to now truly loved, what attracted your soul, what dominated it while simultaneously making it happy?" (1.340/174). After thinking back to what were their highest desiderata, the objects of their ruling passion(s), in their life so far, they are to order them in their temporal sequence (1.340–341/174):

> Place this series of revered objects before you, and perhaps their nature and their sequence will reveal to you a law, the fundamental law of your authentic self. Compare these objects, observe how one completes, expands, surpasses, transfigures the others, how they form a stepladder on which until now you have climbed up to yourself; for your true being does not lie deeply hidden within you, but rather immeasurably high above you, or at least above what you commonly take to be your self.

This meditation expressly engages our capacity to compare our goals with those of others (and with our own previous goals), and hence our true humanity, our character as the yet-undetermined animal. The self-knowledge we get from it unites the two basic faculties of our soul, our desiring and our memory—it is an erotic-historic self-knowledge—and thereby it understands our genuine self as a dynamic, growing being, as a living being that partakes in the basic character of all life (cf. 1.269/106). It strives to give us clarity about ourselves—at least partial or provisional clarity, which is nevertheless a better guide than other forms of self-knowledge—by considering our ruling passions so far not in isolation, but in their relation to each other: By seeing

---

10. This idea was referred to already in *DS* (1.163/9) and *HL* (1.264/102). I take it to be an early version of the famous dictum from *GM* I.13 that "the deed is everything," and I believe—together with Church (2019, p. 141)—that Pippin's (2010, ch. 4) interpretation of it as the doer being expressed in the deed can be applied also here. A theoretical basis for this view can be found in the note 19 [209] (7.483): "the first thing is the *deed*, which we then connect with a quality." This connecting is the error of those who try to find themselves in the qualities deep within their souls.

92 | The Young Nietzsche's Education

how our later highest goals expand on and supersede the earlier ones, we come to realize there is a certain directionality in their sequence, one that is likely to continue in the future.[11] It is a self-knowledge that matches the nature of the soul that is its subject: It takes the soul on the terms of its own being, on terms of desiring and temporality, unlike the first way of self-knowledge that forces the soul into static, atemporal categories that are alien to it.

This method of self-knowledge that is adequate to the nature of our self also acts as a guidance for ordering our passions and guiding our growth: It gives us a certain critical distance from our present highest goal, an awareness that in the course of our life and growth it will likely be superseded by another, greater goal, just as our previous highest goals were. This however doesn't make our strivings meaningless: Unlike the perspective of scientific history, which sees the history of human value systems as a sequence of so many errors, our past goals are seen here as integral parts of who we are, as stages of growth that were necessary (and whose overcoming was necessary) to arrive at who we are today and who we may become in the future. Thus, what we do, think, and desire today is not who we truly are, but these things are nevertheless crucial signposts to our true self that is immeasurably high above us. The true self is conceived as our genius, as "a productive uniqueness" which is the "kernel of [our] being" (1.359/192), but which is usually tied down by the chains of conventions and fear, and is unknown to us to begin with. The effect of following the imperative *be yourself*, of getting to know ourselves and following the path that the knowledge of ourselves and our highest desires so far indicates to us, is the ever-greater liberation (and hence expression) of our productive uniqueness, of the genius that lies dormant within us (1.358/190).[12] Where exactly this

---

11. Church (2019, p. 142) misses the temporal dimension of our fundamental law. Conant (2001, p. 203) expresses this well: Nietzsche "pictures each of us as a series of such [higher] selves, each in flight from, and yet each also representing a stepping stone toward, its own unique, exemplary successor." He also points out that it is the future, higher self "*for* whom [Nietzsche] is writing," but of necessity it is our present self "*to* whom [Nietzsche] writes" (ibid.). There is no notion of "essential self" in *SE*, contrary to Franco's (2018, p. 55) view: The only thing essential to a true self is that it is a genius, and the only thing essential to a genius is, as we will see below, some form of redeeming insight.

12. Cf. Goethe, *Observations in the Sense of the Wanderers* 30 (*Werke* VIII.287): "for not only what is born with us belongs to us, but also what we can acquire, and we are it." Also cf. William Arrowsmith's note on the connection between Nietzsche's usage of "genius" with the Greek *daimon* in the sense of individual destiny or fate (Nietzsche 1990, p. 163n1).

process of liberation and self-cultivation[13] will lead us is initially unknown to us—which is why our conscience can give us negative signs so much more easily than positive ones—we do not yet know who we truly are, what our genius will turn out to be; we only know what to do to get there, what path to follow: namely the path of the imperative *be yourself*. On any other path "you would pawn and lose yourself"; and on the contrary, "a man never rises higher than when he does not know where his path may lead him" (1.340/173–174).[14]

How is it possible to gain such a critical distance from one's current highest goal, from that in the light of which the rest of our world is seen? It is because if one is willing to use this method of self-knowledge, one had already accepted (or at least entertained) Nietzsche's claim that following the imperative *be yourself* is the path to the highest good, to the greatest humanly possible satisfaction. The striving to become oneself has become one's new highest goal, and it effected an expansion of one's world in which the previous highest good remains valid, but only provisionally so—only insofar it can still lead us further on the path to our true self. Becoming what we are thus requires a suspension of judgment with regard to the goodness of any concrete goal, similar to Socrates's recommendation in the *Second Alcibiades* (141c–3a). Such a doctrine—one that demands that one follow the imperative *be yourself* above everything else—requires a particular kind of audience. It requires people who have grown skeptical of the claims about the good life that are held up by their tradition or society (be it service to the state, a life of scholarship, or philistine "culture")—for whom the good life has already become a *question*. However, unlike the "cynics" and "ironical existences" of *HL*, these people had not become desperate yet, and they still possess the passion to search and strive for the good life. They are still capable of ordering and unifying of the manifold forces within their souls.

The "young souls" are precisely this kind of people. Their "youth" doesn't mean they are strictly identical to young people, and it means more

---

13. Contrary to Church (2019, pp. 139–140), this is not a neo-Kantian act of self-determining freedom that is opposed to nature as the realm of necessity. It is rather a process of self-cultivation: The relation of nature and culture is understood here on the ancient model, in which culture means a cultivation of our natural capacities and thus is continuous with nature rather than diametrically opposed to it. The nature in question here is our ruling desire in its temporal development, and the main means of its cultivation that Nietzsche recognizes in the *UC* are, as we have seen, the three useful kinds of history.

14. This picture of becoming-oneself in its basic principles agrees with that presented in Richardson (2015).

94 | The Young Nietzsche's Education

than just that their nature hasn't yet been fully denatured by the philistine culture. On the one hand, not every young person is necessarily a young soul; and on the other hand, some souls, such as Wagner's, become young only later in their life (1.436/264).[15] Cavell (1990, p. 52) says that for Emerson[16] and Nietzsche, "youth is not alone a phase of individual development but—like childhood for the earlier romantics—a dimension of human existence as such." The fundamental mark of the young souls is that they are particularly attuned to the voice of their conscience that stresses their responsibility for leading their own life—"every young soul hears this cry [i.e., "be yourself! . . ."] night and day and trembles" (1.338/172)—unlike the lazy many, who avoid this voice by distracting themselves with various *divertissements*. This connection between youth and conscience, this extraordinary power of conscience over the young soul, has a direct bearing on two more visible characteristics of the young souls—first, their skepticism of or even contempt for the established forms of "good life," for what is presented to them by their elders and authorities as the good life; and second, that they nevertheless harbor powerful hopes to lead a genuinely good and satisfying life one day—*hope*, a capacity that was stressed as proper to the young throughout *HL* (cf. 1.255/93, 1.277/114, 1.295–296/130–131, 1.307/142, 1.312/146, 1.332/165–166). In the unpublished words of my friend Garrett Allen, "everything depends on the future with such men—and thus they are young."[17] This combination of passion for the good life and dismissal of what is publicly presented as the good life, of hope and contempt, makes them akin to Glaucon and Adeimantus, the thymotic interlocutors of Socrates in the *Republic*, who despite being skeptical of the traditional accounts of why is it good to be just, nevertheless believe there is more to living well than amassing wealth, enjoying bodily pleasures, and prevailing over one's enemies by any means available. That is why they demand of

---

15. In the letter to Wagner from 20 May 1874 (KGB II.3, p. 230), congratulating to his 61st birthday, Nietzsche wishes him that he may preserve his "victorious courage and steadfastness and *youth*."

16. Cf. Conant (2001, pp. 233–236, and endnotes 111–13) on the silent presence of Emerson—as another of Nietzsche's educators—throughout *SE*. Lampert (2017, pp. 84–90) expands on this account: He argues that it was Emerson (and certainly not Schopenhauer) who educated Nietzsche on life-affirmation and on the overwhelming importance of philosophy for human life. He also discusses Nietzsche's later dissatisfaction with other aspects of Emerson's thought. Also cf. Parkes, 1994, pp. 35–42.

17. Cf. Large, 1994, on the general orientation of Nietzsche's thought on the future and how this makes it "untimely."

Socrates to explain to them "of what profit is justice in itself to the man who possesses it, and what harm does injustice do" (*Republic* 367d), to explain why being just is a genuine good, disregarding the good reputation that normally accompanies it and that seems to be the only reward of justice in the conventional accounts. Just as Plato's thymotic characters, the young souls desire the truly good life even without knowing what precisely it is. That is what their conscience leads them to: to reject the bad without knowing the good, to reject the conventional alleged goods for the sake of searching for the genuine but yet-unknown good.

The young souls are Nietzsche's intended audience; they are those to whom above all others the *UC* are addressed. Knowing this, we are now in position to see how the rhetoric of the *UC* is designed to appeal to them. The main purpose of the *UC* is to attract and motivate the young souls to the tasks of self-cultivation and of promoting genuine external culture, which alone, Nietzsche tells them, can make their lives truly meaningful and give them what they seek and cannot find elsewhere. In *DS*, Nietzsche ruthlessly criticized the philistine pseudo-culture through the person of D. F. Strauss, its most prominent representative, and in *HL* he provided an incisive analysis of the forces that gave rise to and foster this "culture" oriented on nothing beyond profit and the comfortable life. In doing so, he was speaking to the anger and contempt of the young souls who are dissatisfied with what this "culture" offers them and holds up as exemplary for them, even though they may not be able to articulate their dissatisfaction. His ruthless and (especially in *DS*) scathing criticisms of this "culture" in effect tell the young souls: You are right to be angry and dissatisfied, you are right to be contemptuous of Strauss, *and here is why*. Nietzsche presents himself as the ally of the young souls, as one who accepts and understands their anger, and by thus validating their anger he strives to channel the energy that fuels it. This energy is nothing else but the young souls' passionate concern for living a truly—and not just conventionally[18]—good life, which turned into anger because it is not listened to with the same seriousness with which they voice it.

---

18. Since the young souls reject the tradition they have been raised in, antiquarian appeals are of no interest to them—which is why Nietzsche systematically dismisses them in *SE* 1. The person who tells us that laziness is the most common human quality is a traveler, a person who knows many countries and peoples and so stands above their particularisms (1.337/171). Two pages later Nietzsche tells us in his own voice that "it is so provincial to bind oneself to views that already a few hundred miles away are no longer binding. Orient and Occident are chalk lines drawn before our eyes in order to mock our timidity." (1.339/173).

96 | The Young Nietzsche's Education

Nietzsche hopes that by listening to and validating the deepest concern of the young souls, by showing himself as their ally, they will give him a hearing in return. This explains the marked shift in tone between the two halves of the *UC* (noted by Gray, 1995, p. 410; Brooks, 2018, pp. 12–13; and Church, 2019, pp. 1–2), between *DS* and *HL* on the one hand, and *SE* and *WB* on the other. While in the first half he was getting the attention and friendship of the young souls, in the second half he will speak directly to the central concern that underlies their anger and contempt. He will appeal to their (self-)love and to their desire for the truly high, for what is truly worth living for. He will showcase two men who can serve as objects of the young souls' admiration and aspiration, who can serve as educating exemplars for them, two men who have attained their respective highest—Schopenhauer and Wagner, the philosopher and the artist. And he will lay out his own project of establishing a genuine cultural institution that is to be the core of transforming the German culture at large—a project in which he hopes to enlist the young souls. To summarize: The movement of the rhetoric of the *UC* is first to take up the anger of the young souls and channel it against the sources of their misery—against the unworthy pretenders for their devotion that populate modern "culture"—and then to direct their passion in a productive manner, productive of both a good life for them (as Nietzsche understands it at this point) and of a genuine culture in general. And it is to the young souls in particular that the imperative *be yourself*, as the path to the best possible life, is addressed. Nietzsche himself tells us this about the rhetoric of the *UC* in the note 37 [5] from 1885 (11.579):

> I don't write treatises; those are for dunces and newspaper readers. I don't write speeches either. I directed my *Untimely Considerations* as a young person at young people, whom I told of my experiences and my vows in order to lure them into my labyrinths—at German younglings [*Jünglinge*]: but I was persuaded to believe that German younglings have died out. Well then: I thus have no reason anymore to be "eloquent" in that earlier manner; today I perhaps couldn't even do it anymore.

III.2. *SE* 2–4: The Educator

The fourth paragraph of *SE* 1 transitions seamlessly from the erotic-historic method of self-knowledge to the importance of the figure of the educator

[Erzieher] to the process of becoming what we are. It thus appears that when Nietzsche exhorts the young souls to look upon what they have loved the most so far, the principal kind of desideratum he seems to have in mind is *people* that we want to be like—that our principal desire is for some particular way of life, for a type of existence. The educator is such a desideratum, a person whom we love and admire; and Nietzsche will later describe a devotee of an educator as a person "who has [their] heart set on a great human being" (1.385/216). The educator thus is not a living person, at least not in the first place, but rather a mental image one forms of the person. Our desire is not for the possession of the educator (for how one could *not* possess a mental image?), but rather to *be like them*. The educator is an aspirational example, a person who manifests our goals: They are an embodiment of who we want to become ourselves. Put differently, in loving and admiring our educator we see who *we* want to become as if reflected in them; they are a mirror of our highest desideratum. Nietzsche himself says in the note 34 [13] (7.795) that he doesn't believe to have understood Schopenhauer, "but I have only learned to understand myself a little better through Schopenhauer; that is why I owe him the greatest gratitude."[19] Implicit in this understanding of the role of the educator is the idea that what we can accomplish is inextricably bound up with who we are: Only a Caesar can accomplish the deeds of Caesar, and only a Plato can compose the works of Plato.[20] Thus, by loving and admiring the person who is our educator we are learning what we have to become to accomplish what our ruling passion asks of us: How should we lead our life, and how should we order and orient our souls? By being an aspirational example, they serve as a point of orientation for our growth and for the ordering of our soul according to our task, according to the needs of our ruling passion.

The role of the educator in the process of becoming what we are is, at the first sight, somewhat contradictory. The sentence that introduces this

---

19. As Conant (2001, pp. 231–232) writes, "you 'become who you are' by learning to cultivate a trust in your (higher) self as it appears reflected in what you admire." This idea can be traced back to the *Phaedrus* (255d–e), where the beloved sees himself reflected in his lover; the process is reversed here—we as lovers see our higher self reflected in whom we love, in our "beloved." In this regard it should be pointed out that this kind of erotic reflection is a mutual process for both Plato and Nietzsche.

20. The educator can thus be considered a kind of a monumental example to oneself, and the way they affect the ordering of our souls explains the importance of such examples to would-be monumental individuals. This is true even if the educator in question is not an actual, living person, but just a mental image or a fictional character; in this sense, Achilles was the educator of Alexander the Great (cf. Machiavelli, 1998, p. 60).

98 | The Young Nietzsche's Education

figure into the text tells us first that "your true educators and cultivators reveal to you the true primordial sense and basic stuff of your being," but it ends by a more modest claim: "your educators can be nothing other than your liberators" (1.341/174). The educator should tell us who we truly are despite being capable only of liberating us from the chains of fear and conventions; they should have insight into our true being that not even we ourselves know despite being concerned only with things external to our true self. This difficulty disappears when we keep in mind the status of the educator as an aspirational example. By manifesting what kind of person we want to become and what kind of life we want to lead, the educator helps us to recognize and develop our "root force" (1.342/176) and to align the peripheral forces of our soul in harmony with the root force so that they may contribute to (and not disturb) the strivings of our ruling passion. In Nietzsche's image, the example provided to us by our educator serves "to transform the entire human being into a solar and planetary system with its own life and motion and to discover the laws of its higher mechanics" (1.343/176).[21] The educator reveals to us what is "the true primordial sense and basic stuff of your being" by embodying what we have to become in order to accomplish our deepest desire (while keeping in mind that it is our deepest desire only for the time being). They accomplish their other task, being our "liberator," by helping us understand what is essential to our project and what is accidental to it—what is just conventional ballast that we need to get rid of if we are to reach what is immeasurably high above us. This is why Nietzsche uses the term *Erzieher* for the educator—their purpose in our self-cultivation is *er-ziehen* (translating the Latin *e-ducare*), that is, "drawing out" what is already present within us in some way, by the means of being an example for us to admire and to aspire to—and not *Lehrer*, that is, a teacher of some doctrine (cf. Schacht, 1990, p. 153).[22] But since the educator is in the end just a mental image, the work of education is fundamentally *self*-education, and self-cultivation means not

---

21. Cf. Neymeyr (2020, 2.66–70) on Schiller and Goethe as forerunners and influences of this idea.

22. Conant (2001, p. 220 and endnotes 83 and 86) traces this conception of the educator first to 18th-century German Classicism (Winckelmann, Wieland, Goethe, Schiller, Schlegel), and then further to Hellenistic thinkers like Epictetus or Plotinus. Strong (2000, esp. pp. 76–77) goes even further into the past, namely to the paiderastic educative relationships of Classical Antiquity, and particularly to the concerns about the relation of *eros* and knowledge that are articulated in Plato's *Protagoras*. Cf. the note 8 [73] (7.250), titled *philia and paideia*, where Nietzsche remarks, "Sappho as the starting point: erotics in connection with education."

Schopenhauer as Educator | 99

just the cultivation of our self, but also a cultivation that we have to do by and for ourselves and that cannot be delegated to anyone else.[23] The educator can provide invaluable help in this effort—but only help. *We* are responsible for the leading of our own life, and no one else can either take this responsibility away from us or relieve us of this burden (provided one refuses the philistine enjoyment of *divertissements*).

Nietzsche describes Schopenhauer as his own educator. Further underscoring the character of the educator as primarily a mental image, Nietzsche admits he never actually met Schopenhauer—he only read his books (1.350/183). Schopenhauer died when Nietzsche was fifteen years old: He never heard of Nietzsche and never said anything about him or to him. Nietzsche reports he discovered his books in a situation of loneliness and helplessness vis-à-vis an age that couldn't satisfy or even recognize his deepest need (1.346/179)—the same situation in which he expects the young souls to be when they discover the *UC*.[24] Schopenhauer is presented

---

23. Brooks (2018, ch. 4) doesn't understand this central point. He takes the issue of self-knowledge to mean simply the knowledge of whether we are a "superior" or an "inferior" self, these selves existing in a rigid hierarchical structure. He can thus say sentences like "when ordinary people live under the influence of a superior self like Schopenhauer" (ibid., p. 144); or think that self-knowledge is ultimately, for most people, a knowledge of their flaws and deficiencies, i.e., of the being an "inferior" self (ibid., pp. 153–154); or even misread the third paragraph of *SE* 5 to the effect that "the distance between ordinary human beings and the genius is so great" as to constitute a difference in kind between them (ibid., p. 177n93). The entire dimension of self-cultivation through the mental image of the educator whom we love and admire, and the notion of the higher self as *our own* higher self that lies immeasurably high above us, which are central to my reading of *SE* and which in my opinion make this essay supremely beautiful and fascinating, are absent from Brooks's interpretation. Cf. fn. 50 below.

24. Nietzsche's comments on his own rhetoric in *HL*—that in it he takes revenge on the suffering caused by his historical education by describing it (1.246/85), and his critique of "the immoderation of its criticism" and its "character of the weak personality" (1.324/158)—can be read not just as honest self-criticisms, but also as a way of highlighting his kinship with the young souls. These passages show Nietzsche as someone who was in the same position as the young souls are now, but who found a way out of it—and thus he can lead the young souls by both example and instruction. Unlike Gray (1995, p. 404), I find nothing "bitterly ironic" about this self-critique: It is the mark of a good writer to be aware of their weaknesses and to be willing to learn and improve. Neymeyr (2020, 1.295) reports that in the period of the *UC*, Nietzsche was purposefully studying and teaching rhetoricians, both ancient and modern, in order to improve his own writing style. For a full list of Nietzsche's teaching activities in this respect, cf. Most & Fries (1994, p. 17n1). For the text of the extant lectures, cf. KGW II.4, p. 363 ff.

100 | The Young Nietzsche's Education

as answering to precisely this need,[25] and that is why Nietzsche is so devoted to him: He claims that "my faith in him appeared immediately, and today it is just as complete as it was nine years ago" and, even more implausibly, that "I never discovered a paradox in Schopenhauer" (1.346/179–180).[26] Nietzsche tells us that "I attach importance to a philosopher only to the extent that he is capable of setting an example," which example must be set "in [the philosopher's] visible life" (1.350/183; cf. 1.417/246).[27] That is why Nietzsche sought to learn from Schopenhauer not so much his doctrines, but above all how to live, that is, how to order one's life according to one's thought—how to establish a philosophic way of life, the kind that ancient philosophers had led. Kant, having lived the conformist and conventional

---

25. The Goethe quotation Nietzsche uses to express his excitement upon discovering Schopenhauer at 1.349/182—"How magnificent and precious every living thing is! How suited to its condition, how true, how full of being!"—is rather cryptic. Goethe wrote ▪these words in the context of observing mussels and crabs on a beach in Venice during the ebb (*Italian Journey*, pp. 84–85/*Werke* XI.92–94). The crabs were attempting to hunt the mussels, but these always managed to hide in their shells. Goethe concludes that although he observed the animals "for hours," he didn't see a single crab succeed in the hunt. Is Schopenhauer compared here to an incompetent crab or to a careful mussel?

26. These and similar claims are clearly rhetorical. Nietzsche had been profoundly critical of central aspects of Schopenhauer's thought already in 1868 (Janaway, 2003, pp. 162–163), and certainly even more so when he was writing *SE* six years later. Indeed, in *HA* II Preface 1 (2.370), Nietzsche relates that at the time of writing *SE* he was "already deep in the midst of moral skepticism and destructive analysis [. . .] and already 'believed in nothing anymore,' as the people say, not even in Schopenhauer." And in the note 10 [B31] (9.418–419) he says that in *SE* he temporarily forgot "that for a long time already none of his dogmas could withstand my mistrust" in order to fully express his gratitude to Schopenhauer. The purpose of the claims about Schopenhauer in *SE* is to present him as an exemplary philosopher, a position to which Nietzsche, at the time a twenty-nine-year-old professor of philology, cannot at this point publicly pretend. The emphasis in *SE* is clearly on Schopenhauer the man rather than the thinker, on his exemplary character and courage to live in his own way. This favorable view of his character persists throughout Nietzsche's career: As late as in *GM* III.5, Schopenhauer the man is described as "a genuine *philosopher* [. . .], a genuinely independent spirit [. . .], a man and knight with a brazen glance, who has the courage to himself, who knows how to stand alone and does not first wait for front men and nods from on high." Also cf. the note 28 [11] (11.303) and Haar (1996, ch. 2).

27. Neymeyr (2020, 2.90, 2.272) shows this is a completely un-Schopenhauerian attitude. *D* 195 takes up this motive: "Was all reflection on morality not utterly lacking in our education—not to speak of the only possible critique of morality, a brave and rigorous attempt to *live* in this or that morality?"

Schopenhauer as Educator | 101

life of a university professor, offers no such example despite the profundity of his thought (1.351/184, 1.414/243); in this regard he is a case of the modern "split personality," for which the "content" of one's soul has no effect on the outwardly lived life. In contrast, Nietzsche learned from Schopenhauer "to be *simple* and *honest* in thought as in life—in short, to be untimely" (1.346/179). The simplicity means here living according to a single law of one's own; the honesty means, as the continuation of the quoted sentence shows, a kind of transparency to oneself that is impossible for the chaotic, uncultivated modern souls. And insofar this widespread lack of spiritual culture is a phenomenon peculiar to the present age, as Nietzsche's account tells us, it is untimely to pursue and attain even a certain degree of such culture. Schopenhauer is for Nietzsche an aspirational example of the philosophic genius, of the fulfilled imperative *be yourself* of a philosopher. Herein lies his greatness, which means simply "being free and entirely himself" (1.362/194).

Of particular interest to Nietzsche are Schopenhauer's three virtues, honesty, cheerfulness, and steadfastness, which enabled him to overcome the dangers inherent to being a philosopher (1.350/183). The first of these dangers is isolation, the solitude that is imposed on the philosopher (and on all "unusual human beings" in general—1.352/185) by the modern pseudo-culture that feels threatened by everyone and everything that challenges its sense of self-satisfied superiority. Schopenhauer suffered by being ignored and shunned by his contemporaries, by having the first edition of *The World as Will and Representation* pulped, and—worst of all, according to Nietzsche—by being mistaken for somebody he was not (1.354/187). He resisted all these sufferings thanks to his virtue of steadfastness, thanks to his ability to persevere in his work, which derived from his awareness of the importance of what he had to teach. His second danger was "despair of truth" (1.355/187), the post-Kantian doubt of whether we can get to know the truth at all. Schopenhauer was able to overcome this danger—by arguing that we do in fact have access to the thing-in-itself, and that it is the Will (cf. *WWR* I, § 21, pp. 110–111/*Werke* I.170)—and thus he was able to see and interpret the image of life as a whole. This interpretation of the whole of being allowed him to see it as meaningful, and to see his own life as a particular instance of the meaningful process of life. In Nietzsche's words, his philosophy tells us, as every great philosophy does, " 'this is the picture of life; learn from it the meaning of your life.' And conversely: 'Just read your life and decipher on the basis of it the hieroglyphs of life in general' "

102 | The Young Nietzsche's Education

(1.357/189).[28] Had Schopenhauer not conquered this danger, he would have become a "pure scientist" without any concern for the meaning of human life and how it should be lived (1.360/192); but because "his thought has conquered the most difficult thing" (1.350/183), he attained his second virtue, cheerfulness, the cheerfulness of one who knows themselves to live in accordance with the essence of life as such. From this root stems also Schopenhauer's own ambition to be an educator, to spread the knowledge of being as a whole and of life in accordance with it that he had attained; his aim in this respect was (1.357/190) "attaining power in order to come to the aid of the *physis* and provide a meager corrective for its stupidities and ineptitudes. At first, of course, only for oneself; but through oneself, ultimately for all." Schopenhauer educates others out of his philanthropy, out of his love for humans and especially for the most promising humans, whom he wants to help live the life of genius they are most capable of. Thus he, like other philosophers, is one of those who, "because they have thought the most profound things, cannot help but love what is most alive," as Nietzsche tells us in paraphrasing Hölderlin's poem *Socrates and Alcibiades* (1.349/182). Schopenhauer's third danger was "moral or intellectual hardening" (1.360/192)—the danger of recognizing the limitations of one's self (in Schopenhauer's case, that he wasn't able to become a saint) and of subsequently becoming desperate and "feeble or useless where culture is concerned" (1.360/192), no longer striving to produce the various forms of genius within and without oneself. Schopenhauer overcame this danger thanks to his virtue of honesty: He was able to see his limitations clearly and to accept himself as he was, including his limits. In sum, Schopenhauer's three virtues mark him as a knower of the whole, as a knower of himself, and as a practical man who strives to spread his knowledge and enrich others with it.

Besides the services an educator can provide to an individual, they can also play a more general role within the culture at large. The present age lacks "moral exemplars and people of distinction, visible embodiments of all creative morality in this age" (1.344/178). This role is especially needed now because of the weakness of present-day culture, in which there are no longer institutions that would provide a young soul with a basis for

---

28. Indeed, for Schopenhauer, the Will, which is the thing-in-itself and the essence of the world, is at the same time "what is known immediately to everyone" (*WWR* I, § 18, p. 100/*Werke* I.157). Thus the understanding of the essence of things goes hand in hand with the understanding of the meaning of one's own life.

self-cultivation such as education in speaking and writing (1.343/177) and with a like-minded community of peers. The contemporary grammar schools [*Gymnasia*] and private teachers fall short of this task in Nietzsche's view, as does the scientific education at the universities, whose deleterious consequences for the health of one's soul were discussed at length in *HL*. In the absence of such exemplary individuals and of genuine cultural institutions, the contemporary Germans turn to other forces that pretend to tell them how to lead their life, such as the "dogma that has of late been preached from all the rooftops, a dogma that asserts that the state is the highest aim of humanity" (1.365/197; cf. Hegel 1988, 41–42).[29] The sciences are "pursued without moderation and with an attitude of blind laissez-faire," and the ever more influential "monetary economy" seeks to gain money by catering to every human desire, no matter how low or base (1.366/198).

The root cause of this cultural crisis is what Nietzsche will later call the death of God. Christianity had surpassed the ancient ethical teachings by "the loftiness of its ideal" (1.345/178), the ideal of a virtue so great that a human being can attain it only by God's grace. But the Christian hold on culture has gradually weakened, and it has survived the Reformation only by declaring many fields of human activity to be *adiaphora*, that is, "domains in which religion should not hold sway" (1.367/200).[30] Christianity has ultimately weakened to the point of no longer being believable, but its critique of ancient ethics made it impossible to return to the latter. This crisis is an instance of the problem inherent to critical history, as is evident from the phrase used to characterize it: "when better and loftier things could still be recognized, although no longer attained, we could no longer return to the good and lofty, to the virtues of antiquity" (1.345/178; cf. 1.270/107–108). The two greatest cultural systems of the past have vacated the field and there is nothing to replace them, apart from idols such as the state or modern science. These, however, not only cannot provide genuine culture, but they also cannot contain "wild, primal, and completely pitiless forces" within the human soul—at best they can give them direction occasionally, say, into a war—and thus, Nietzsche says, "for a century now we have been

---

29. Cf. Stewart (2021, ch. 6) and Lipták (2023) on the legacy of this idea in Marx's thought.

30. Nietzsche thinks that already the victory of Christianity over "the far more religious world of antiquity" (1.368/200) was won only at the price of declaring some fields of human activity *adiaphora*; he seems to have in mind a conception of ancient religiosity similar to that of Fustel de Coulanges (1980).

104 | The Young Nietzsche's Education

anticipating fundamental upheavals" (1.367/199). The most likely of these is what Nietzsche calls "atomistic revolution" here (1.368/200): the victory of the moneymakers and of the market over all other social structures, the pursuit of ever greater profit by feeding any and every human desire and selling some satisfaction to it, and the consequent dissolution of society into individuals (or, in keeping with Nietzsche's metaphor, nuclear families at best). In sum, "never has the world been more worldly, never has it been poorer in love and goodness" (1.366/198).

Nietzsche is not the first to notice these tendencies of cultural decay, nor is he the first who attempts to counteract them. He discusses three previous attempts to provide a new model for human self-cultivation, a new "*image of the human being*" (1.368/200): Rousseau's, Goethe's, and Schopenhauer's. Rousseau's human being is a passionate rebel against the modern society with its inequality and corruption, and as such he is the inspiring force behind socialist revolutions.[31] He strives for a "return to nature," which he cannot attain—but hereby "he despises himself and yearns to transcend himself" (1.369/201), and so contributes to the growth and expansion of humanity. Nietzsche says that Goethe's "Faust was the supreme and boldest likeness of Rousseau's human being" (1.370/201–202);[32] but this image fails to properly promote culture because of its denial of any limits to human malleability, which gave rise to the culture-hostile socialism (Zuckert, 1970, p. 118).[33]

The image of the human being provided by Goethe's own life is much calmer: It is "the contemplative human being in the grand style" (1.370/202) who finds their joy in examining the greatest achievements of humanity so far, be it in art, science, or political action. However, in striving to avoid

---

31. His kinship with revolutions shows that he doesn't correspond most closely to monumental history, as Zuckert (1976, p. 75) and Church (2019, p. 160) believe, but rather to critical history. Goethe's human being then (roughly) corresponds to antiquarian history, and Schopenhauer's human being to monumental history. But in a deeper sense, all these images of the human being are "monumental" exemplars—not for action, but rather for self-cultivation.

32. Zuckert (1976, pp. 74–75) and Brooks (2018, p. 149) misread the text as saying that Faust is *Goethe's* image of the human being. While this can be in a limited sense said of Faust from *Faust II*, Goethe himself is a better embodiment of that image.

33. Culture is the cultivation of nature, while socialism wishes to radically transform the human being as we know it for the sake of an alleged future state of full human perfection and happiness. Human nature as we know it now—and as we *are* it now—is of no interest to this project: It is conceived of as either irrelevant to the human spirit or as corrupted by the oppressive conditions under which present-day humans live.

the excesses of Rousseau's revolutionary, they ended up being ineffectual: If they attempt something practical, "we can be certain that nothing significant will come of it" (1.371/202), as Nietzsche illustrates on Goethe's engagement with the theater.[34] As such, they also failed to overturn the modern pseudo-culture, and so didn't become the founder of a new culture either. Quite the opposite: The philistines are the degenerated form of Goethe's human being, a form in which its major weakness is magnified even further. Thus, both Rousseau and Goethe have ultimately failed in the task to establish a new foundation for culture in the modern times. Rousseau failed because his revolutionary zeal went so far as to fight not just against the corruption of modern culture, but against modern culture as such, and thus also against all in it that is conducive to a genuine culture; and Goethe failed because his zeal wasn't sufficient to fight anything at all. If the third—Schopenhauer's—image of the human being is to succeed where Rousseau and Goethe failed, it will have both to take up human passion and to direct it so that it will be conducive to genuine culture and hostile only to pseudo-culture. And besides this practical task, the Schopenhauerian image of the human being will also show us what Schopenhauer's understanding of life as a whole is, and of the human life that is in accordance with it.[35]

III.3. *SE* 5: The "Schopenhauerian" Affirmation

In *SE* 3, Nietzsche reiterates the idea introduced in *HL* 6 that justice in the sense of legislating the value of all things is one of the chief tasks of the philosopher: "it has always been the peculiar task of great thinkers to

---

34. For Goethe's own account of his failure as a theater director, see the conversation from 27 March 1825 (Eckermann, 2011, p. 553): "I really once had the delusion that it were possible to build a German theater. I even had the delusion that I myself could contribute to it and that I could lay some cornerstones to such an edifice. I wrote my *Iphigenia* and my *Tasso* and thought in a childish hope that thus it would go. But nothing moved, no one was affected, and everything remained as before."

35. I do not think the three modern images of the human being correspond to the three types of the redeeming genius (cf. the following section). But I find it plausible that the former triad correspond to the three useful kinds of history (Church, 2019, p. 164). In my view, Rousseau's human being corresponds to critical history, Goethe's to antiquarian history, and Schopenhauer's to monumental history. Rousseau's kinship with revolutions marks him as critical, whereas the Schopenhauerian heroism of truthfulness at any cost is the most monumental attitude presented in the *UC*.

106 | The Young Nietzsche's Education

be legislators of the measure, mint, and weight of things" (1.360/193). This task demands that the thinker determines not just the worth of all individual things, but of being as a whole. On Nietzsche's account, Schopenhauer succeeded in this task: He set up before him the picture of life as a whole, and answered the question it posed to him (1.363/195): "Do *you* affirm this existence from the bottom of your heart? Are you willing to be its advocate, its savior? For all it takes is one single truthful 'Yes!' from your mouth—and life, now facing such grave accusations, will be set free." The peak of the legislative task of the philosopher is deciding whether life is worth living at all, and the proper measure for making this decision is not any given miserable human life, but the highest kind of life, the life of the philosopher. It is only the highest human life that can redeem the misery of existence that Schopenhauer saw with such clarity, as will be shown in *SE* 5. And his answer to this question was "the answer of Empedocles" (1.363/195), that is, an *affirmative* answer: insofar as life allows for the existence of the philosopher, it is worth living, and this highest possibility redeems all human (and animal) misery.[36] In fact, Nietzsche tells us, this is not just the answer of "Schopenhauer" and Empedocles, but of all the great pre-Platonic thinkers, regardless of all the other differences in their thought (1.361/193–194). The question now is: How did "Schopenhauer"

---

36. It is remarkable, as Lampert (2017, p. 83) emphasizes, that this is the answer of *Empedocles* and not that of the actual Schopenhauer, who famously preached "the vanity [*Nichtigkeit*] of human existence" (cf. *WWR* I, §§ 56–59; *WWR* II, ch. XLVI; *PP* II, ch. XI/*Werke* I.422–47; II.733–54; V.334–60) and declared that "our state is so wretched that complete non-existence would be decidedly preferable to it," as he puts it in his approving comment on Hamlet's "To be, or not to be" soliloquy (*WWR* I, § 59, p. 324/*Werke* I.445). The "answer of Empedocles," as Nietzsche understood it, can be found in his lectures on the pre-Platonic philosophers (KGW II.4, pp. 314–328). Although Empedocles was very sensitive to the many sufferings of existence (which are the consequences of *neikos*, the principle of strife), his fundamental idea was "that *every living being is one*" (ibid., p. 317) thanks to the opposing principle of love or Aphrodite (ibid., 323). Furthermore, he saw it "as the task of his existence" to preach this knowledge and the way of life that follows from it, and thereby "to make good again what *neikos* had spoiled" (ibid., pp. 317–318)—to redeem the entirety of existence. This misdirection from Schopenhauer to Empedocles on Nietzsche's part is an example of the tension between his use of Schopenhauer as the exemplary philosopher and his rejection of the core of Schopenhauer's actual thought. Schopenhauer is connected with Empedocles also in *WB* (1.446/273). Consequently, it is not true that the Schopenhauerian human being prima facie denies the value of existence and therefore needs to be supplemented by Goethe's and Rousseau's human being, as Church (2019, p. 168) thinks; I rather take the Schopenhauerian image of the human being as *the* image of the good life in the *UC*.

arrive at the position from which he was able to affirm and thereby redeem life? What kind of life possesses the ability and the will to make so serious a judgment?

One part of the answer is Schopenhauer's untimeliness, his ability to overcome "the dangers of the age" stemming from the "the worthlessness of the present age" (1.360–361/193). In order to give a just verdict about the worth of existence as such, Schopenhauer's view must not have been skewed by the lowliness of philistine "culture" that surrounded him. More importantly, he struggled against everything within himself that was actually a product of his time and thereby hindered him from attaining his proper greatness, that is, "being free and entirely himself" (1.362/194). It is because being truly oneself requires liberation from the opinions and conventions of one's time—which form, as it were, the dross under which one's true self is smothered and unable to develop—that a great thinker is a "*stepchild*" (1.362/194) of their time rather than its child, as Hegel (1988, 55) would have it.[37]

Here we can reconstruct the full meaning of the term *untimely*. In *DS* it meant "speaking the truth" (1.242/81), which means not just speaking the truth, but in the first place also *wanting* the truth rather than comforting *divertissements*. In *HL* (1.246–247/86–87) it took the form of the critique of the "timely," especially of the historical education that was the pride of contemporary Germany. The purpose of this critique was "to work against the time and thereby have an effect on it, hopefully for the benefit of a future time"—to work toward the overcoming of the timely. In *SE* it means the cultivation of one's soul (1.346/179) and the removal of timely conventions and opinions (1.362/194) that are a major obstacle to be overcome in the process of becoming what we are. Being "untimely" is thus a byword for Nietzsche's overall aspirations in the *UC*: It refers primarily to *wanting* the truth, that is, to truthfulness and the self-cultivation that goes hand in hand with it (and that is necessary to bear the truth); and secondarily to *speaking* the truth, that is, to the critique of the contemporary pseudo-culture and to the public project of cultural renewal that Nietzsche hopes to initiate by these essays.

---

37. "The greatest human beings are always related to their century by a weakness" (Goethe, *Maxims and Reflections*, 97, *Werke* XII.378). Similarly in *CW* Preface: "What does a philosopher demand of [themselves], first and last? To overcome [their] age in [themselves], to become 'timeless'. So what gives [them] [their] greatest challenge? Whatever marks [them] as a child of [their] age."

108 | The Young Nietzsche's Education

In *SE*, the emphasis is on the aspect of liberation from the timely conventions as the path to one's true self—for "once [Schopenhauer] had conquered his age in himself, he could not help but perceive with amazement the genius that dwelled within him" (1.363/195; cf. 1.338/172). This leads us to the question of the philosophic genius themselves and how they fulfill their task. This question is answered by the depiction of the Schopenhauerian human being, which is meant to be an account of how the philosophic genius arrives at the position from which the whole can be judged, affirmed, and redeemed. The basic formula by which Nietzsche summarizes this activity is that the Schopenhauerian human being "*voluntarily takes upon [themselves] the suffering inherent in truthfulness*" (1.371/203) and uses this suffering as a means to mortify their will to life. This denial of the will in turn allows them to attain a higher kind of existence for which the affirmation of life is possible. The lengthy quotation from Schopenhauer at 1.373/204–5 characterizes this as a heroic—or tragic—life, which ends in something akin to the Buddhist *nirvana*. The beginning of this activity is adopting the imperative *be yourself* as one's highest goal and deciding to pursue it regardless of anything else: It is the promise to oneself that "I want to remain my own person!" (1.374/205). Carrying out this decision in one's life has several significant consequences. First, it leads to the intensification of one's passion, and thus also of one's suffering (since all desiring involves suffering from the lack of the desired object, which is not just Schopenhauer's doctrine—cf. *WWR* I, § 56/ *Werke* I.425—but is known already since Plato, at least as far as bodily pleasures are concerned: cf. *Republic* 584e–5b). Second, it leads to the rejection of all the *divertissements* by which ordinary humans keep themselves ignorant both of the voice of their conscience and of the sufferings that are inherent in their existence; and giving up these protective devices further intensifies the Schopenhauerian human being's suffering. However, they don't desire suffering for its own sake—or at all—they desire only to become who they are. Thus they are led to meditate on the two main subjects of their attention, on their individuality and on their suffering, and on the mutual relation of these two: "how did I become what I am, and why do I suffer from being what I am?" (1.374/205).

In this meditation they will understand the manifold kinds of suffering to which they are subjected. Besides those mentions above, they suffer also because this striving alienates their fellow human beings, even those dear to them: One appears unjust to them, a malicious destroyer of what they love and value (1.372–373/204). But their greatest sufferings arise directly from the striving for the truth, from their voluntary shedding of the life-

Schopenhauer as Educator | 109

supporting illusions and exposure to the deadly truth. The Schopenhauerian human being believes that "to be truthful means to believe in an existence that could not possibly be negated" (1.372/203), which means that they seek a permanent, eternal being that would give a stable ground to their existence, and conversely they negate in thought every non-permanent, transitory thing. But insofar as they fail to find a truly permanent, imperishable being, they find themselves ever more without any support for their striving. The effort to *be yourself* and to know the truth begins to appear senseless to them, however noble they may have considered it at the beginning. The more they strive to *be yourself*, the more meaningless their life appears. Thus they come to understand the futility of all desiring: Desiring as such is essentially unsatisfiable striving and therefore senseless suffering. And since desiring is the basic characteristic of all life, life as such bears the essential character of senseless suffering (cf. *WWR* I, § 56, p. 310/*Werke* I.426). This is most evident in the case of animals, especially beasts of prey, who are constantly on the move, looking to kill in order to satisfy their hunger, only to prolong their life and experience the hunger again and again, until they eventually die. The life of the animal is a bad infinity, a perpetual vicious circle of suffering from hunger that can be temporarily satiated only at the cost of exposing one to another bout of hunger, and so on and on and on, until death (1.378/209): "To cling so blindly and madly to life, for no higher reward, far from knowing that one is punished or why one is punished in this way, but instead to thirst with the inanity of a horrible desire for precisely this punishment as though it were happiness—that is what it means to be an animal."

Only humans have the capacity to understand that *this* is the essence of life, to break free from this vicious circle, and thereby to effect the "salvation [of nature] from the curse of animal existence" (1.378/209). However, the vast majority of humans come nowhere near this redemptive understanding. They rather spend their lives in the thrall of their various desires and goals, such as service to the state, military victories, scholarship, or revenge against their enemies; to these goals they assign a value they absolutely do not deserve, being transitory and offering no real satisfaction, only perpetuating the vicious circle of suffering. Moreover, they do not just fail to realize that this is the case, but in a sense actively avoid this realization with the help of the omnipresent *divertissements*: In effect, "the most extensive arrangements of our own lives are made only in order to flee from our true task" (1.379/210). The lives of most humans thus run in the same vicious circle as the life of an animal. Seen from this perspective, we only "desire with

110 | The Young Nietzsche's Education

more awareness what the animal craves out of blind instinct" (1.378/210). And thus, Nietzsche concludes, "we ourselves are those animals who seem to suffer senselessly" (1.378/210).[38]

However, human life does contain the possibility to liberate oneself from this vicious circle, and this possibility arises precisely from the meditation on the suffering of one's existence undertaken by the Schopenhauerian human being. Their meditation on the nature of their existence leads to the realization that life is essentially unsatisfiable striving and hence meaningless suffering. This is the tragic moment, the catastrophe, in the spiritual drama of the Schopenhauerian human being.[39] All their passionate striving and all their suffering led to nothing—to something worse than nothing: to the realization of how futile this striving and all the sacrifices one had undergone for its sake had been all along. The only thing left to do is resignation: to deny one's will and give up all attempts to attain happiness. But at this point, at the point of tragic defeat and resignation of all willing, a momentous transformation occurs: One becomes aware that this insight into the essential nature of life is precisely the kind of permanent, unchanging truth that encompasses the whole of being one had been looking for all along[40]—the truth that reality is essentially the blindly striving Will that can never attain any genuine satisfaction.[41] This insight carries with itself a

---

38. Cf. *Republic* 586a–b. Socrates says this account applies only to those ruled by their *epithymia*, the appetitive part of the soul, but insofar as we all are embodied beings with bodily appetites, we all partake in this kind of suffering. In the note 3 [64] (8.32–33) Nietzsche expands on how such an ordinary existence—what we call today "being a productive member of society"—partakes in the character of the bad infinity: Such people "*all* have *no purpose for their existence in themselves*; and this 'existence for each other' is the most comical of comedies."

39. In contrast, the ordinary humans are thoroughly untragic: a person who rejected the imperative *be yourself* and thereby "has evaded [their] genius" is "all exterior without a kernel, [. . .] a decked-out ghost that can arouse no fear, and certainly no pity" (1.338/172; cf. Aristotle, *On Poetics*, 1452b33–34).

40. Thus I disagree with Church's (2019, p. 167) view that "Nietzsche humanizes being," i.e., that "by 'being' Nietzsche means 'being what [one] is,' being my own unique ideal self." This view effectively turns our "true self"—an entity that "proximally and for the most part" exists only as a projection of our present self—into an eternal and unchanging Platonic Idea.

41. It has to be emphasized that this redeeming insight is not merely discursive; it is transformative of how we understand and conduct ourselves in our life. It has this quality precisely because it was won from the meditation on one's ownmost selfhood and suffering; without this it would be just a metaphysical doctrine among many others.

happiness unlike anything that satisfaction of a desire can provide: While the satisfaction of a desire is always temporary and only spurs one to go further along the vicious circle of desiring, this insight lifts us above the stream of the otherwise sovereign becoming and liberates us from the slavery to the blindly desiring Will. This insight into the whole of life tells us the meaning of our own life (cf. 1.357/189): By comprehending the nature of the whole, we realize that the only genuine happiness and understanding that there is lies in denial of the will, in refusing to follow the vicious circle of desiring any longer. This insight is (1.380/212) "the great *enlightenment* about existence, and the supreme wish that mortals can wish is to participate constantly and with open ears in this enlightenment." One who has attained this "great enlightenment" completes and redeems the entirety of nature, which is "pressing onward toward the human being" for precisely this purpose (1.378/210). In this great enlightenment, nature "feels that for the first time it has arrived at its goal, arrived at that place where it realizes that it must unlearn its goals" (1.380/211): It understands that the only way out of the vicious circle of willing and desiring is to resign at it altogether, to deny the Will and to enjoy the peace resulting from this denial. In this manner the genius, that is, the person who had attained the great enlightenment, redeems not just themselves from the sufferings that are inherent to their life and to the striving to *be yourself* (which, it has to be stressed, is a necessary prerequisite to attaining this insight),[42] but redeems the entirety of nature from the suffering that is inherent to life as such. In the genius—as the peak of all life and nature—a genuine understanding and happiness is attained, and life as a whole thereby ceases to be merely unsatisfiable striving and thus senseless suffering. The existence of the genius thus gives meaning to—*justifies*—the existence of everything else: The whole is made meaningful by the redeeming insight of the genius.

Nietzsche describes the geniuses as "those true *human beings, those no-longer-animals, the philosophers, artists, and saints*" (1.380/211): Through denial of their will and the subsequent "great enlightenment," they have transcended mere animality and attained genuine or full humanity. They exemplify different forms of the highest possible human life. In accordance with Schopenhauer's

---

42. Nietzsche says so explicitly in the note 32 [67], 7.778: "*the same courage that belongs to self-knowledge teaches us also to look at existence without excuses*; and vice versa." Also cf. the note 3 [63], 8.32: "Only in three forms of existence does the human being remain an individual: as philosopher, saint, and artist."

112 | The Young Nietzsche's Education

doctrine,[43] Nietzsche distinguishes three kinds of redemptive genius here: the philosopher, the artist, and the saint. Nature needs each of them for a particular purpose. The purpose of the philosopher and of the artist appears to be the same: "just as nature needs philosophers for a metaphysical purpose, so, too, it also needs artists for the purpose of its own self-enlightenment" (1.382/213). The difference between the philosopher and the artist lies in their way of understanding and communicating the insight underlying the "great enlightenment": While the philosopher *understands* this insight discursively, the artist perceives it as an image, and then *depicts* this image in their works.[44] Both the philosopher and the artist thus serve the purpose of nature's self-knowledge, but each of them in a particular way. The artist creates their works "so that [nature] might finally be presented with a pure and finished *image* of what, in the tumultuousness of its own becoming, it never has the opportunity to see clearly" (1.382/213; emphasis added)—that is, as depictions of life as a whole, of the nature of life. Finally, the saint, "whose ego has entirely melted away and whose life of suffering is no longer—or almost no longer—felt individually, but only as the deepest feeling of equality, communion, and oneness with all living things" (1.382/213–214), *feels* this insight. The saint is, as it were, an embodiment of the "answer of Empedocles": They feel the suffering of all life and affirm it as necessary.

The artist stands in a ministerial relationship to the philosopher. This can be seen not only from *HL*, where art and religion are called "true

---

43. Cf. *WWR* I, § 53, p. 274/*Werke* I.379: "The genuine method of considering the world philosophically, in other words, that consideration which acquaints us with the inner nature of the world and thus takes us beyond the phenomenon, is precisely the method that does not ask about the whence, whither, and why of the world, but always and everywhere about the *what* alone. Thus it is the method that considers things not according to any relation, not as becoming and passing away, in short not according to one of the four forms of the principle of sufficient reason. On the contrary, it is precisely what is still left over after we eliminate the whole of this method of consideration that follows the principle of sufficient reason; thus it is the inner nature of the world, always appearing the same in all relations, but itself never amenable to them, in other words the Ideas of the world, that forms the object of our method of philosophy. From such knowledge we get philosophy as well as art; in fact, we shall find in this book that we can also reach that disposition of mind which alone leads to true holiness and to salvation from the world."

44. Strong's (2000, p. 93) contention that "the philosopher makes becoming available to us" goes directly against Nietzsche's clear statement that the genius's—including the philosopher's—main achievement is precisely rising above the flux of becoming. Indeed, far from needing the philosopher to make becoming available to us, we need them to make something *other* than becoming available to us.

Schopenhauer as Educator | 113

helpers" of philosophy (1.281/118), but also from the note 19 [23] (7.423): "the philosopher should *get to know what is needed*, and the artist should *create* it." The philosopher's knowledge is meant to rule and guide the artist's work. In the note 19 [170] (7.471) we read that "the philosophers are the noblest class of the greats of the spirit," and in the note 19 [195] (7.479) the philosopher is called "the highest type of the great individual."[45] What precisely is the artist to make will be one of the central subjects of *WB*. It is less clear in the case of the saint, who is called "that ultimate and supreme becoming human" in *SE* 5 (1.382/214). However, the saint does not hold this kind of importance in any other work of Nietzsche, and even the *UC* as a whole focus much more on the philosopher and the artist, devoting one essay to each of them (*SE* and *WB*, respectively). Furthermore, in *SE* 1 only the thinker and the artist are mentioned in introducing the imperative *be yourself*. It is much more likely that this declaration of the saint as the highest human type is a piece of rhetoric meant to make *SE* appear more "Schopenhauerian" than it actually is, rather than a serious assertion.[46] The saint's actual role in the project of the *UC* is ministerial, on par with that of the artist. We can see this from notes such as 9 [102] (7.311), where Nietzsche writes that "*art and religion* in the Greek sense [are] identical," or 29 [192] (7.708),[47] where he specifies the educative purpose of these forces: "art and religion are well suited for organizing the chaotic [within us]: The latter gives us love of the human being, the former gives us love of existence."[48]

---

45. Zuckert's (1970, 146–147) view that since Schopenhauer failed in establishing a culture while Wagner has been more successful in this respect, "Wagner represents a higher [degree of freedom], and thus in this respect appears 'more philosophic' than Schopenhauer"—or in other words, that the artist stands higher than the philosopher in the *UC*—thus rests on a misunderstanding of the respective roles of the philosopher and the artist in the project of the *UC*.

46. Breazeale (1998, p. 9) also notes that the three types of genius, especially in their educational modality, are much less Schopenhauerian than they may appear: "despite this Schopenhauerian window-dressing, the actual *function* assigned by Nietzsche to 'geniuses' in general and to philosophers in particular has an explicitly *cultural* and *social* dimension that is utterly lacking in Schopenhauer."

47. The rest of the note makes clear that it comments on *HL* 10, but I do not think there is any substantial difference between Nietzsche's views on art and religion in *HL* and in *SE*.

48. Thus it is not true that "the highest functions of art and philosophy are essentially the same" (Taylor, 1997, p. 87). The suggestion that "in a proper height, everything comes together and into agreement—the thoughts of the philosopher, the works of the artist, and the good deeds" (note 19 [1], 7.417)—should be read as positing the possibility

114 | The Young Nietzsche's Education

The genius, and in particular the philosophic genius, is of supreme importance in the *UC*: It is only their existence that makes life meaningful and worth living, that redeems life from the vicious circle of desiring to which it is otherwise subject. We are now in position to answer Heidegger's (2016, § 97) questions about the principles of the philosopher's originary justice: "in what does the *height* of 'life' consist? [. . .] *Who* determines what height is?" The answer is that the height of life consists in the understanding of the whole, and that the philosopher's legislation of values is derived from their care for the perpetuation and spreading of the kind of life that can attain this highest of heights. It is not an arbitrary legislation, but one that derives from the knowledge of life as a whole and of the specific character of human life. And in regard to his question "who decides which genius is to become the one setting the standard?" (ibid.) we can answer that this "decision" is the result of the philosopher's insight into the whole of life and being.

This view also has important implications for what is to be considered the best way of life, or for the rank order of human values. From the perspective of the genius, the only desire, the only ruling passion that is worth cultivating is the desire to *be yourself*, since it is only through the cultivation of one's self that one may attain the "great enlightenment" and thereby the only genuine happiness there is. Thus, for the genius, as well as for those who believe in the redemptive insight although they do not fully comprehend it themselves, the tasks of culture and education are the only meaningful practical pursuits. Culture understood from the perspective of the genius as its peak means "*to foster the production of philosophers, artists, and saints within us and around us, and thereby to work toward the perfection of nature*" (1.382/213; cf. 1.358/190):[49] the cultivation of the souls of individual humans, and the perpetuation and spreading of the "great enlightenment" that is the peak of self-cultivation. Nietzsche claims that

---

of a single human being who would embody all three types of the genius, rather than as assigning equal value to the three types. In the note 16 [11] from 1883 (10.501), Nietzsche writes: "To become artist (creator), saint (lover), and philosopher (knower) in *one person:—my practical goal.*" However, we should note that the conception of these three types is quite different in this later note, which begins by recounting that "it was necessary *to redeem* myself from the *delusion* that nature must *unlearn* to have goals" (quoting 1.380/211)—i.e., that the conception of the redeeming genius from *SE* is a delusion, that it is fundamentally wrong. Cf. Chapter V.2 below for a detailed discussion.

49. This "fundamental idea of *culture*" is consistent with that of *On the Pathos of Truth* (1.756), where it is attributed to "ethical human beings."

everybody is in principle a genius, although only a few will fully liberate the genius within them and thus attain their true self that is immeasurably high above them.[50] However, even though not everybody will become a genius, everybody can partake in the tasks of culture in a way that will be beneficial both for them and for the culture at large: While the geniuses can benefit from various auxiliary services provided to them by the non-geniuses, the latter can benefit from the educating effect of the genius—as the image of the Schopenhauerian human being "educates us while drawing us upward" (1.376/208). This holds *a fortiori* for the genius in person—especially given their proximity to the genius in the kind of cultural setting imagined here by Nietzsche. What precisely this cultural setting will be, and what kinds of dangers it will have to overcome in the present-day "culture," is the subject of *SE* 6–8.

III.4. *SE* 6–8: The Life of Culture

The ideal of the Schopenhauerian human being, of the genius, is educative also by providing us with a "set of duties" (1.376/207, 1.381/213) that the young souls can fulfill by regular activity and thereby contribute both to their own self-cultivation and to the genuine culture at large. The image of the genius tells the young souls, striving to become themselves and asking themselves "how can your life, the life of the individual, obtain the highest value, the deepest significance?" (1.384/216), that a truly meaningful life can be attained only by unconditional devotion to the cause of genuine culture. The first step in this participation, "the *first sacrament of culture*" (1.385/216), is adopting an educator in recognition of one's current limitedness with regard to whom they themselves desire to be. In the educator they find an image

---

50. Cf. 1.337/171, and the note 34 [8] (7.795): "everyone is a genius in principle, insofar as they are here only *once* and cast a completely new look at things. They *multiply* nature, they create with this new look." Moreover, nobody is exempt from hearing the voice of conscience, even though most people strive hard to ignore it. However, the process of becoming one's true self is exceedingly difficult and painful, as we have seen, and it requires one's full dedication and effort. Hence, only very few individuals come to its end and become a genius in the full sense of the word, a redeeming man—even under the best imaginable external conditions (cf. *HA* 263, even though Nietzsche speaks of a lesser kind of talent there). Many are called, but few are chosen; and this choice is essentially a choice one has to make for oneself and then ceaselessly persevere in it. Cf. Conant, 2001, p. 198.

116 | The Young Nietzsche's Education

of a person they would like to become, and the love they feel toward their educator (and the concomitant contempt for themselves as they are now)[51] provides them with a mighty impetus for self-cultivation in their chosen direction. The second sacrament of culture amounts to an "assessment of external events" (1.386/217) as to whether they contribute to or hinder genuine culture, the production or cultivation of the genius. Finally, they are to work practically with other like-minded young souls to further the cause of true culture, that is, to cultivate the soil from which new geniuses may grow (cf. Parkes, 1994, p. 182). The young souls have already achieved the self-dissatisfaction characteristic of the first consecration, and *SE* now explains them how—and in which direction—to continue this process.

Such an assessment of conditions for true culture shows "*how extraordinarily scant and rare the knowledge of that goal is*" (1.386/217) despite all the ostensible support culture is getting from all sides nowadays. This is a problem for Nietzsche, not only because a conscious effort to produce genius would have a greater effect than leaving its production up to chance, but also and especially because many of the forces that foster culture do this only at the price of perverting it from its proper end to their own ends, which are invariably hostile to the genius. Nietzsche identifies four such culture-perverting forces: the selfishness of the moneymakers, of the state, of those who have an ugly or boring content (i.e., the philistines), and of the sciences. The moneymakers promote culture only insofar as greater education implants more desires to be satisfied and thereby provides more opportunities to make profit. Since their goal is profit, the products of the moneymakers seek to address as many people as possible, and in aiming at the lowest common denominator they are "thoroughly timely" (1.387/218). This "culture industry" does nothing at all for the production of genius; moreover, it operates with a notion that there is a natural connection between one's wealth and level of culture, a notion that elevates the captains of industry to the peak of humanity, and thereby hinders the awareness of the importance of the genius as the redeeming human being.

The state supports culture insofar as it helps to produce loyal citizens and competent bureaucrats—but only insofar. The state is aware that fully cultured individuals consider themselves above the state and thus become

---

51. As well as for others around them, who from this perspective are "like a field strewn with the most precious fragments of sculptures" (1.386/217). Cf. *Za* II On Redemption: "[my eyes] always find the same: fragments and limbs and dreadful accidents—but no human beings!"

Schopenhauer as Educator | 117

dangerous to it, and it tries to manage this danger by supporting only a certain lower level of culture while undermining higher culture, which according to Nietzsche is one of the reasons for the present-day decay of Christianity (which used to be a powerful cultural force—1.389/220). The third perversion of culture is effected by the philistines who completely divorce culture from any effort at self-cultivation and consume it solely as a means of entertainment or *divertissement*—both their own and that of their fellow philistines. They are "the tortured slaves of the three M's, Moment, Majority Opinion, and Modishness" (1.392/222–223) who use culture to hide this fact, to hide their own misery from both themselves and others.

The last of these perversions is the selfishness of the sciences, which supports culture insofar as it is necessary for the production of good scholars. The problems of science and of education based on it were dealt with at length in *HL* 4–9, and Nietzsche only restates them here: First, the sciences strive for partial truths that are useful for the securing of ever more comfortable life, not for *the* meaningful truth about the whole; and second, the education of the scholars damages their souls in ways that make them incapable of self-cultivation and/or unwilling to engage in it at all. Nietzsche then turns to analyzing the all-too-human motivations of the scholar in their research to show how different they are from the motivation of the genius. The three main motivations are a strong curiosity and love of the search itself, the desire to prevail over other scholars, and the desire to validate the ruling opinions and ruling powers, who after all are the hand that feeds them. To these Nietzsche adds twelve[52] other, less frequent motivations, which in one way or another illuminate the smallness of the scholar's spirit, the willingness to limit themselves to a very small and particular field, and/or the willingness to obey and work for the benefit of conventional (political, religious, or scholarly) authorities. These motivations, "a host of very human drives and petty passions" (1.399/230), are then mixed together, and the result is the celebrated modern scholar.[53] This dissection of the scholar's motivations shows why they cannot attain the heights of the redeeming genius. And thus, insofar as the sciences promote culture in order to educate new scholars, they too pervert the true meaning of culture.

---

52. The tentative thirteenth motivation, "the drive for justice" (1.399/229), is added only as a pious wish, for reasons given in the third paragraph of *HL* 6 (1.288–289/124–125).

53. Nietzsche is drawing here on the distinction between the *Brotgelehrte*, "the scholar who works for his bread," and the "philosophic mind" Schiller had made in his lecture *What Is, and to What End Do We Study, Universal History?* (Neymeyr, 2020, 1.182).

118 | The Young Nietzsche's Education

All four perversions of culture represent a giving up of the genuine goal of culture for the sake of lesser goods, chiefly of the comfortable life. So they fail to accomplish what only true culture can accomplish: giving meaning to human life and suffering. The forces that pretend to support culture in the contemporary times are in fact perverting it, and so they worsen the conditions for the production of genius (1.401/231). Nietzsche summarizes here his critiques from *DS* and *HL* after presenting the motivation behind those critiques, the end to which they serve in the overall project of the *UC*: They are critiques of the forces working against genuine culture and its peak, the redeeming genius.

The practical consequence of this assessment of the conditions for culture is that new educational institutions are necessary for the true purpose of culture, for the production of genius.[54] Alternatively, the existing institutions—the universities—could be reformed in accordance with this new "fundamental idea" (1.402/232). However, their original fundamental idea, the education of the medieval scholar (a point confirmed and expanded on by Hadot, 2002, p. 258), is still active in them, and Nietzsche believes the forces of institutional inertia would make such a reform of the universities a much more difficult endeavor than the founding of a new institution. Such an institution would exist in the first place for the sake of the geniuses-in-becoming, who would live there together and strive "to pave the way in themselves and around themselves for the birth of genius and the maturation of his work" (1.403/233), strive to attain their true self in a like-minded community.[55] This institution would provide them with the "the protection of a firm organization" (1.402/233) against the external world, which, as we have seen, is hostile to the genius and to the degree of self-cultivation necessary to bring the genius about. And it would also provide them with various useful services so that they may focus on their task; in this manner, "even those with only second- and third-rate talent" could participate in the work of true culture and thereby attain the "the feeling that they are living for a duty and for a goal, living a life that has

---

54. This is the one crucial exception to Lemm's (2007b, p. 5) otherwise correct view that "Nietzsche's conception of culture in *SE* is inherently anti-institutional." Cf. the remarkable discussions in Drochon (2016, pp. 66, 69n47).

55. Cf. Church (2019, p. 178). It is their true self that is the main object of their striving, and not other, external works of art, as Taylor (1997, p. 133) believes (as a consequence of mechanically applying Schopenhauer's doctrine from *WWR* I, § 36 to *SE*)—these are byproducts of their becoming-oneself, as it were.

significance" (1.403/233)—to the feeling that they participate in the redemption of life as much as is in their powers.[56] For this to happen, however, especially those with lesser capacities must be able to resist the siren call of the sciences that promise to make them great and famous scholars even though they aren't geniuses, whereas in Nietzsche's new institution they would be allegedly "only servants, assistants, tools, overshadowed by higher natures" (1.403/233). The degree to which they will be able to resist this temptation correlates with the degree to which they suffer from existence and feel the need to redeem this suffering (and are aware that only the genius can accomplish this redemption).[57]

In the seventh chapter of *SE*, Nietzsche turns specifically to the philosopher-in-becoming and asks what conditions are necessary for them to attain their genius, and what conditions would increase the effect of their example on his fellow human beings. With regard to the latter question, Nietzsche notes the mismatch between the spiritual greatness of the philosopher (and the artist) and the weak effect their work has on the general public—akin to "the relationship of heavy artillery to a flock of sparrows" (1.405/235). It is as if these highest outgrowths of nature, these redeeming individuals, existed only accidentally, and as if their redeeming work had its proper effects only on very few humans—while for the majority it is only

---

56. The crucial point is that although not everybody can be a genius of the highest kind, everybody can *partake* in the genius and in their work. As Conant (2001, p. 196) puts it, "the person who believes in culture excludes no one else who believes in culture from his concern"; cf. Church (2019, p. 176). This taking part in culture entails not just service to the genius, but also attaining a "higher self"—higher than their *present* self—by communion with the genius (and by making the necessary effort themselves); i.e., it is taking part in genuine culture not just externally, but also *internally* (cf. Taylor, 1997, p. 156). And it is both of these factors that make a life devoted to the fostering of genuine culture meaningful for the non-geniuses. Thus, even though they work for the genius in ministerial positions, they are *not* asked to abandon their self-cultivation and only to "place [them]selves at the beck and call of these 'geniuses,'" as Breazeale (1998, p. 16) thinks. Conant (2001, esp. pp. 209–216) stresses this point repeatedly in his beautiful reading of *SE*. Pearson (2018, p. 17) makes a similar point, but he also claims (ibid., p. 19) that this demands "the sacrifice of our egoistic goals for the sake of elite geniuses," which can be true only if he means the petty egoistic goals of the comfortable life. He is right that, contra Rawls, this is "not conceived as an oppressive social arrangement," but a voluntary one (ibid.).

57. The passage in question is a condensed version of a passage from *FEI* (cf. 1.402–403/232–233 with 1.728, line 10–1.730, line 4). Being ordered "in rank and file" is characteristic of the scholar also in *BGE* 206.

120 | The Young Nietzsche's Education

"a kind of metaphysical pepper" (1.406/236), a welcome distraction from the boredom of their everyday life. It seems as if nature was wise in its ends, but unable to find suitable means toward them, and the consequence is that "something greater and nobler [i.e., the genius and their works] is employed as a means to bring about something lesser and ignoble [i.e., the philistines and their *divertissements*]" (1.405/235). Nature thus needs human aid to accomplish its aims: The effects of the genius, hitherto haphazard and accidental, must be consciously supported so that they reach and transform a much larger number of humans than until now, and so fulfill their proper purpose. Art must complement nature, and by this cultivation nature is to be transformed into a "new and improved *physis*" (cf. 1.334/167). In short, the rule of chance in history must be replaced by conscious purposiveness;[58] human life must be reordered so as to foster both the production of the genius and the redeeming effects of his work.

The way to begin with such a reordering of human life is simply by fostering of true culture. The greatest obstacle to becoming a philosopher in the present day is "the perversity of contemporary human nature" and the "modern ideas"[59] that accompany and justify it (1.407/237)—and this is likewise the greatest obstacle to a more appropriate effect of their work. Thus the fostering of true culture helps both to produce the genius and to spread their effect. Schopenhauer is exemplary here once again, because he was fortunate enough to enjoy in his life precisely those conditions that are necessary for a philosopher to attain their genius. First among these is a certain strength of character, or "unbending and rugged manliness" (1.408/238), which he learned from the example of his father.[60] They also include a manifold freedom of spirit: freedom from parochialisms and local prejudices, which he acquired thanks to traveling with his father as a youth; freedom from the kind of subordination one learns in training to be a scholar or a bureaucrat; freedom from the need to engage in politics; and freedom from having to make a living for oneself, that is, leisure. And finally, he was fortunate enough to make a personal acquaintance with a

---

58. This was first pointed out by Zuckert (1970, p. 141); cf. *Za* II On Redemption on Zarathustra's ambition to be the "redeemer of accidents."

59. This *terminus technicus* is not used here, but it was used in a similar context already in *DS* (1.175/20, 1.190/35). It becomes especially prominent in *BGE* (§§ 10, 44, 58, 202, 203, 212, 222, 239, 242, 251, 253, 260, 263).

60. Cf. Neymeyr (2020, 2.249–251) on Schopenhauer's parents and his relationship with them.

genius, in his case with Goethe.

However, Schopenhauer lived under these favorable conditions—which Nietzsche summarizes as "freedom and nothing but freedom" (1.411/241)—only thanks to an accident, the accident of his good birth. The task of the new institutions will be to provide such conditions to as many worthy contenders as possible, and thereby to promote the production of genius; they will exist, as Zuckert (1976, p. 77) puts it, "as means to the production of the true individual." But they will also promote the effects of the geniuses' work at various levels: Those who work in these institutions in ministerial positions will have the opportunity to be acquainted with the genius and even to adopt them as their educator, and thereby attain higher levels of self-cultivation; and the very existence and working of these institutions will spread the awareness of true culture in Germany and beyond. The institutional framework will allow for the conscious fostering of culture on these three levels (the geniuses, those who aid them, and the population at large), and thus genuine culture will be able to spread wider and grow higher than was hitherto possible. Moreover, the institution doesn't need to be particularly large to begin with: a group of some hundred people, to use the number Nietzsche repeatedly mentioned in *HL* (1.260, 1.295, 1.325/98, 131, 159), would be sufficient to take care of it, and so initiate what would hopefully be a large-scale cultural transformation. This is why founding new institutions of genuine culture is so important to Nietzsche here: It is the first concrete step to promote both the production and the effects of the genius, and so to lead toward a transformation of German and European culture at large.

The last chapter of *SE* deals with the political situation of philosophy in contemporary times. Since its emergence, philosophy has been politically precarious, as is evident from the persecutions of Anaxagoras and Socrates. In response to this danger, the classical philosophers devised a way of presenting themselves as loyal citizens capable of advising statesmen, and so secured a place for philosophy within the state (Strauss, 1988, pp. 27–40). Modernity took this development seemingly even further: The state now doesn't merely tolerate philosophy, but actively fosters it. One of the most interesting developments of modern culture is that the state, traditionally the enemy and censor of philosophy, has now become a major supporter of philosophy by funding chairs of philosophy and promoting the teaching of philosophy at the universities it runs. At first sight, this seems to be the fulfillment of Plato's dream of a state in which "the emergence of the philosopher [would] not be dependent on the unreason of fathers" (1.412/242),

122 | The Young Nietzsche's Education

unreason and anger of the fathers being famously what got Socrates killed. However, just like other purported "Platonic" states and institutions of the past, the modern state's support of philosophy is a sham that falsifies the meaning of philosophy. The support of philosophy that Plato wanted to see in a state must be understood "*Platonically*," that is, so "seriously and sincerely as if it were its supreme task to produce new Platos" (1.413/242).[61] In other words, what Plato wanted was a state of genuine culture whose supreme goal was the education of the philosophic genius, a state in which philosophy would be sovereign not just because it would be ruled by philosophers, but because it understood the self-cultivation of the human soul and philosophy as its highest peak to be *the* good life, the perfection of human existence.[62] However, the modern state—Bismarck's *Kulturstaat*, as Brooks (2018, pp. 1–12) explains—has very different ambitions: It wants to present *itself* as the highest authority on all human things, and it is "afraid of philosophy as such" (1.414/244), which is more than capable of debunking such pretensions. The state's strategy for dealing with philosophy is to ostensibly support it, but in fact to subjugate it precisely by this support. The most important method of this subjugation is changing philosophy into an office [*Amt*]. The state hereby assumes authority over philosophy: It becomes the arbiter of philosophic merit (the "good" philosophers being those who are offered an academic chair), and it even gets to say how many philosophers are necessary. In contrast, the philosophers have to compromise their freedom by teaching regularly at assigned times, and moreover they are forced to teach anyone who signs up for their classes. Especially the latter point means a major curtailing of the philosopher's freedom: As Nietzsche asks, "must [they] not speak before an unknown audience about matters [they] can only safely discuss with [their] closest friends?" (1.416/245). The philosophers can no longer speak freely, because at least as long as they are paid by the state, they (1.415/244) "must recognize something higher than

---

61. Lampert (2017, p. 85) argues that this "Platonic goal can be said to be Nietzsche's most basic political motive from the beginning to the end of his career."

62. Cf. the note 10 [1] (7.348–349) from 1871 (i.e., from the period of *BT*), in which Nietzsche praises Plato for grasping "the authentic goal of the state," which is "the Olympian existence and the ever renewed production of genius, compared to which everyone else is just a preparatory means." His only criticism is that Plato "did not put the genius in its most general concept on the top, but only the genius of wisdom," i.e., unduly privileged the philosophic genius over its siblings, the artist and the saint. According to Drochon (2016, p. 52), this note is an early version of *The Greek State*, originally meant to be included as a chapter in *BT*.

truth—the state. And not merely the state, but at the same time everything the state demands for its own well-being: for example, a particular form of religion, social order, and military organization—upon each of these is written a *noli me tangere*."

The philosopher in the employ of the state is forced to become a sycophant of the state and of the powers that be rather than an independent thinker and critic of the existing conditions. There is a way out of this predicament: transforming "philosophy" into the scholarship of history of philosophy. This however transforms the philosopher into a mere scholar, suffering from all the maladies that befall scholars in other fields; and moreover, philosophical scholarship is, unlike, say, chemistry, utterly impractical. Nietzsche says that, as a result of this subjugation of philosophy, the professors of philosophy he had encountered as a student "always found reasons why it was more philosophical to know nothing than to learn something" (1.419/248), and he adds that "the individual sciences are today more logical, cautious, modest, inventive—in short, more philosophical—than are the so-called philosophers" (1.420/249). The end result of the state's "support" of philosophy is that "university philosophy has fallen into universal disrepute and suspicion" (1.418/247): It is held in contempt by the students, by the scholars from other fields, as well as by the public. The other sciences have no longer any use for philosophy. Being transformed into an academic discipline, philosophy had ceased to be the queen of the sciences, and it has become an object of ridicule instead.[63]

Nietzsche proposes a solution to this problem: to "eliminate from philosophy every form of state and academic recognition" (1.421/250). And, in the most extreme case, even the persecution of philosophy by the state—that is, a return to its pre-Platonic political situation—is preferable to this kind of "support" (1.423/251). He believes that if philosophy ceased to be a way of making an easy and comfortable living, all the pseudo-philosophers currently occupying academic chairs will move on to other, more profitable and less dangerous pursuits (such as becoming a parson, a newspaper editor, or an author of "textbooks for girls' finishing schools"—1.422/250), while

---

63. *SE* 8 is heavily dependent on Schopenhauer's essay *On Philosophy at the Universities* (*PP* I, pp. 137–199/ *Werke* IV.171–242). Schopenhauer made there not just the diagnoses of the character of academic philosophers and of the damage they cause to philosophy itself, but also proposed the solution of separating philosophy from the state as much as possible, and especially ending the state's support of philosophy in the universities (*PP* I, pp. 180, 195–196/ *Werke* IV.222, 240). Neymeyr (2020, 2.20–29) provides a thorough comparison of these two essays.

124 | The Young Nietzsche's Education

those who have a passionate personal investment in philosophy would find a way to continue living in devotion to the truth. The state itself could easily do without philosophy, for it is not concerned with the truth itself, it only wants what is useful to it, such as "legitimation and sanctification of the state" (1.422/251)—and there are always enough sycophants, even educated and authoritative ones, to do that. Nor is education in philosophy necessary to produce loyal citizens (in fact, quite the opposite); and it would also be beneficial for the other sciences to be freed from the union with such "a community of third- and fourth-rate scholars" as academic philosophy (1.424/252). Nietzsche finds it strange that the other scholars do not demand this already, and sees in this one of the signs of the decay of universities in general—the others being the lack of "rigorous education in the skills of writing and oratory," the continuing disregard of ancient Indian thought, and the demotion of Classical Antiquity to "one antiquity among others" (1.424/253) that is no longer held to be exemplary—of the fact that "the spirit of the university is beginning to confuse itself with the spirit of the age [*Zeitgeist*]" (1.425/253). It is precisely because universities are becoming ever more "timely" that it is important that philosophy be separated from universities and cured of the damage wrought by the state's "support" of it. Such a liberated philosophy could function as "a higher tribunal [. . .] with regard to the education [the universities] promote" (1.425/253), as a supporter of genuine culture and a condemner of whatever hinders and opposes it.[64]

However, philosophy itself is more important than the state, universities, and culture at large—and Nietzsche tells us that its current subjection to the state puts its very existence at stake. By becoming ridiculous, philosophy had lost its dignity, and so it is no longer attractive to those who would otherwise be naturally attracted to its uncompromising questioning: to thymotic natures such as the young souls, but also to generals or statesmen (1.426/254). In short, philosophy in the proper sense of the word is dignified and terrible; it is a relentless questioning of everything, as Nietzsche's quotation from Emerson conveys. It should disturb [*betrüben*], and the most damning conviction of current academic philosophy, the most telling indication of its true nature, is that "it never disturbed anyone" (1.427/255). Thus the task of all true friends of philosophy is to "prove by deed that love of truth is something terrible and powerful" (1.427/255). Schopenhauer himself did

---

64. Again reinforcing the superiority of philosophy over art.

Schopenhauer as Educator | 125

this—and the fact that thanks to him philosophy still retains something of its original and proper dignity is the final reason why he is exemplary, and why he is Nietzsche's own educator.[65]

～

In *SE*, the overall project of the *UC* begins to assume a more concrete form. First, *SE* shows us what Nietzsche's "heaven" is: namely the life of the genius, of the individual who alone is able to affirm and thereby redeem the entirety of existence from the meaningless suffering it otherwise is. This affirmation is attained through the striving to *be yourself*, and in it "theoretical" and "practical" knowledge are united: the understanding of one's own life leads to the understanding of life as a whole, and vice versa. The philosopher is the highest and most important kind of the genius for Nietzsche, tasked with establishing originary justice, with determining the value of all things and of the whole anew; the artist and the saint are to help him in this endeavor. A lesser form of this "heaven" is the life of devotion to culture, that is, to the production of genius within and without oneself. In this manner, anyone willing can partake in the work of the genius and thereby make their life truly meaningful.

The tension between truth and life manifests in *SE* in two distinct but related forms. The first concerns the affirmation of life and being presented in *SE* 5, which, although purportedly an affirmation, entails a denial of the will—which seems suspiciously Schopenhauerian and life-*denying*. The second concerns how much the "heaven" of the *UC* consists in becoming one's true self, a genius, and how much it demands devotion to the cause of genuine culture; put differently, we may wonder whether these two facets

---

65. To summarize the other reasons: First, he provided Nietzsche with an aspirational image of the philosopher to guide his own process of becoming-himself. Second, his life showed Nietzsche (some of) the dangers that lie on the path to becoming a philosopher, and the virtues thanks to which he overcame those dangers. Third, his radical, unapologetic untimeliness. Fourth, his image of the human being that can serve as "the visible embodiment of all creative morality" (1.344/178) for the culture at large. And fifth, the favorable conditions of his life that should be consciously replicated in the institutions of genuine culture. Hence it is not true that "the sole direct influence that Schopenhauer's personal example seems to have exercised upon Nietzsche was to confirm him in his belief that a genuine philosopher must live a life that is independent to the point of *solitude*, a belief that is already fully developed in his studies of the ancient pre-Platonic philosophers" (Breazeale, 1998, p. 11).

126 | The Young Nietzsche's Education

are as seamlessly harmonious as Nietzsche makes them out to be. Is the moralistic devotion to cultural renewal really also the way to one's true self? This holds *a fortiori* for the peak figure, the philosophic genius: Is their freedom, their being who they truly are, compatible with an unconditional devotion to a predetermined task? Nietzsche presents these two commitments as if they were unproblematically aligned with each other, but this is not necessarily the case; and when conflict between them comes up, Nietzsche leaves us without a criterion by which to choose the more important one.

Moreover, the idea of becoming one's true self as it is presented in *SE* forces us to raise some serious doubts about its viability. The first of these concerns the primacy of desire or instinct for our self-knowledge and for the way in which we should consequently strive to further cultivate ourselves: It is the sequence of their greatest desiderata that gives the reader "the fundamental law of your authentic self" (1.340/174). These desiderata are not to be examined or questioned, but only recognized as such. This means that the role of reason, of thinking, in the process of becoming ourselves is strictly ministerial; it is to be a "slave of passions," in David Hume's phrase (2007, p. 266). The dubious character of this reliance on instinct was soon to become an urgent issue for Nietzsche: His hopes for Wagner were definitively buried at the inaugural Bayreuth festival, and he entered a profound crisis, which he later characterized as the awareness of "a total aberration of my instinct" (*EH* HA 3). One of the significant outcomes of this crisis was precisely the subordination of instinct to questioning thinking.

The second major doubt here is the peculiar idea that "becoming ourselves" is itself a task, rather than a *result* of accomplishing tasks in which we exert our powers to the fullest, grow, and come into our own. Notably, it is the latter model that Nietzsche employs in *EH* (*EH* Clever 9; Meier, 2019, p. 102), which suggests a significant change in Nietzsche's understanding of the process of becoming-oneself—and given the importance of this subject to his self-understanding, also a change of his conception of what the philosopher is. I address these two doubts, and the way in which the later Nietzsche grappled with them, in more detail in Chapter V.4. To summarize for now, it is precisely at its peak where the project of the *UC* and its image of the genuinely good life appears to be most questionable.

We also see now *how* Nietzsche writes the *UC*: Its rhetoric is crafted to attract to this "heaven" the young souls, the thymotic characters with a powerful conscience, a powerful desire for the yet-unknown genuinely good life, and powerful hopes for the future. Nietzsche strives to channel this power within them both for their own self-cultivation and for the sake

Schopenhauer as Educator | 127

of the project of cultural renewal that can make self-cultivation "easier" and more widespread. Regarding the individuals, *SE* contains magnificent explications of the imperative *be yourself* and of the role of the educator in one's self-cultivation, which build directly on the articulation of the human soul that was developed in *HL*. Here lies one of the main purposes of the *UC*: "*To educate educators! But the first ones have to educate themselves!* And these are who I write for," as Nietzsche wrote in 1875 (note 5 [25], 8.47).

Regarding the cultural renewal, Nietzsche explains at length the importance of a new institution devoted to genuine culture in contemporary society in *SE* 6–8. *WB* will take up this argument by making a concrete proposal for an institution of genuine culture, and so complete the project of the *UC*. This institution, based on Wagner's art, was to appear very soon: In fact, its cornerstone had been laid on 22 May 1872 in Bayreuth, with Nietzsche among those attending this ceremony (1.432/260), and *WB* itself was rushed into print so that it could be sold at the inaugural Bayreuth Festival (Schaberg, 1995, pp. 48–49).[66] By proposing how Bayreuth may be an institution of genuine culture in the modern world, *WB* will answer the last question from *DS* 4, the question about Nietzsche's "courage," or his means to facilitate the attaining of the "heaven," which is an enormously difficult process, as we have seen. *WB* will also thematize the artist in this context—what kind of person they are, and what their works can accomplish.

---

66. Drochon (2016, p. 43) points out that Wagner's Bayreuth project was likely a model also for the very idea of effecting cultural reform by the founding of a new institution.

IV

Richard Wagner in Bayreuth

Wagner, Tragedy, and Free Human Beings of the Future

Music is a torch with which to see where beauty lies.

—Atahualpa Yupanqui

Richard Wagner in Bayreuth, the final completed *UC*, is a complex text. Its complexity is due in a large part to Nietzsche's ambiguous feelings regarding Wagner, which he felt compelled to hide. We have to discuss the history of the text to get a better grasp on this central issue of *WB*. After the publication of *SE* in October 1874, Nietzsche began to work on the next *UC*, which was to be *We Philologists* (15.60). However, the work didn't progress as Nietzsche had hoped—Janz (1978, 1.610) reports that despite having made extensive notes for it (which can be found in 8.11–96), by late May 1875 he hadn't written a single line of the actual text and abandoned it. Around August 1875 Nietzsche started writing *WB* instead (15.64), but this work didn't go as planned either, and eventually it too was abandoned. A major reason for the difficulties Nietzsche had in writing *WB* was his private misgivings about Wagner and his project, which, as Prange (2013, ch. 1) documents, started as early as February 1870.

Nietzsche developed his honest assessment of Wagner at some length in his notebooks in early 1874 (7.756–775; he also reports about it in the letter to Erwin Rohde from 15 Feb. 1874—cf. KGB II.3, p. 202). One point that keeps recurring in these notes is Nietzsche's explanation of Wagner's artistic peculiarities and shortcomings through his having a nature of

130 | The Young Nietzsche's Education

"a transposed actor" (note 32 [8], 7.756; cf. 7.759, 761, 762, 766, 770, 773). This judgment also appears once in *WB* (1.467/292) but is stated there simply as a matter of fact, not as a criticism. In the note 32 [10] (7.756), he views Wagner's art in a sober and unflattering light: Considering the individual components of Wagner's *Gesamtkunstwerk*, Nietzsche judges that "the music isn't worth much, the poetry also ⟨not⟩, the drama also not, the acting is often just rhetoric—but everything is on a grand scale one and on a high level."[1] Even more damningly, Nietzsche finishes this note by saying that "Wagner the thinker is on the same level as Wagner the musician and poet" (7.757), that is, not particularly high. Consistently with this assessment, in the note 32 [41] (7.766) Nietzsche comments that "as a writer, [Wagner] is a rhetorician without the power to persuade"—that Wagner's theoretical writings are useless for their intended purpose of winning over new supporters to his artistic project (cf. 1.478/302). Nietzsche's critique doesn't spare even the greatest of Wagner's works: The note 32 [43] (7.767) finds "excesses of the most alarming kind in the *Tristan*"—in Wagner's *Tristan and Isolde*, which Nietzsche went on to call "the true *opus metaphysicum* of all art" (1.479/303) in public.

A second critical strand in these notes considers Wagner's lack of success so far and his own contributions to this failure. First of all, Wagner *is* unsuccessful so far in his chief goal, in reforming the theater (cf. 1.448/274): "for until now, everything remains as it used to be" (note 32 [28], 7.763). Nietzsche goes on to consider two causes of Wagner's failure. First, "there is something comical about it: Wagner cannot persuade the Germans to take the theater seriously," because "in Germany everyone takes their own matters seriously, and so they laugh about those who pretend to be the only serious person" (ibid.). In other words, Wagner doesn't really understand the Germans, and that is why he wasn't able to devise a rhetoric that would persuade them. He would first have to understand that his project "does not fit into our social and economic relations" (ibid.)—and then work (rhetorically and otherwise) to provide access to his project to those whom it strikes as bizarre for these overarching external reasons. The second cause of Wagner's failure is his lack of prudence in political matters. This is detailed in the note 32 [39] (7.766), which examines Wagner's dealings with the powers that be. The first of these is Ludwig II of Bavaria, who "half betrayed [Wagner's work]

---

1. However, a slightly later note, 33 [5] (7.789), applies this judgment only to Wagner's "earliest works."

Richard Wagner in Bayreuth | 131

by premature performances"[2] and who, thanks to his more than generous financial support of Wagner, gave the latter "a highly unpopular reputation": Wagner came to be seen as the cause of Ludwig's excesses.[3] Second was his engagement in the revolution of 1848, which lost him the support of rich patrons and gained him nothing in return from the socialists. And third, he alienated the Jews, "who now own the most money and the press in Germany," by his unprovoked outbursts of anti-Semitism ("when he first did it, he had no reason for it: later it was revenge").[4] In short, Wagner's lack of prudence in his abortive political engagements had cost him the support of almost all potential allies and powerful factions and made him dependent on Ludwig II, which dependence made him even less popular.

A final strand of interest in these notes is concerned with the general outlines of Wagner's project, to which Nietzsche is broadly sympathetic. Wagner's art is "a tremendous attempt to assert himself and to dominate—in a time hostile to art" (note 32 [56], 7.774). To this end, he "gathers all the *effective* elements" in his works, all the artistic means that still have the power to affect modern humans (note 32 [57], 7.774). And the goal for which he seeks to attain this power is a highly laudable one: namely "the renewal of art from the only foundation that still remains, from the theater" (note 32 [61], 7.775), a renewal of the true significance of art for human life.[5] But even here, at the very core of Wagner's striving, Nietzsche has a reason to seriously doubt whether Wagner understands what the true significance of art for life is. In the note 32 [44] (7.767–768), he finds in

---

2. Referring to the performances of the first two parts of the *Ring* cycle before its completion that Ludwig II demanded from—and was granted by—Wagner (Gutman, 1968, pp. 304, 308).

3. Large (1978, p. 164) reports that "Wagner's scandalous affair with Cosima von Bülow, his luxurious living at public expense, and his repeated interference in local politics soon alienated the people of Munich" and adds that Wagner's stay at Tribschen was also financed "at Ludwig's personal expense" (ibid.).

4. The most infamous, but by far not the only, instance of Wagner's antisemitism is the pamphlet *Judaism in Music*, first published anonymously in 1850, then reissued in an expanded version under his own name in 1869. Rose (1992, p. 1 et passim) argues at length that "Wagner did not suddenly change from being a revolutionary to being a racist—for him, the German idea of revolution contained always a racial and antisemitic core."

5. In the same note, Nietzsche comments that "there is no doubt that, were he Italian, Wagner would have attained his goal"—but, to reiterate, as a German he wasn't able to find the right means to address his fellow Germans.

132 | The Young Nietzsche's Education

Wagner's art "something like an escape from this world, it negates the world, it doesn't transfigure this world"—a tendency that is the very opposite of what tragedy should do according to Nietzsche. Lampert (2017, p. 106) judges this note to be "an early installment in Nietzsche's condemnation of romantic pessimism" (cf. *GS* 370). He goes on to say that "Wagnerism, to the degree that it had a core, harbored an antilife, romantic tendency, part of the reason it so naturally tended toward Christianity" (ibid., p. 107)—and Nietzsche was aware of this *fundamental* problem of Wagnerism to a large degree already in 1874.

Thus, because of his grave doubts about Wagner's artistry, the means he uses, and even his ends—all of which stand in a sharp contrast to the text of *WB*—Nietzsche considered the manuscript of *WB* unpublishable. However, he allowed his admirer Peter Gast to read it, and his enthusiastic reaction persuaded him to finish the work. *WB* was thus completed at Gast's insistence and rushed into print so that it could be sold at the inaugural Bayreuth festival in June 1876 (Schaberg, 1995, pp. 48–49; Lampert, 2017, pp. 104–105). Naturally, this meant that Nietzsche's misgivings about Wagner were not resolved, and some of them are expressed in a veiled manner in the text. One class of the shortcomings Nietzsche perceived in Wagner was presented as "elements of his character that he had overcome on his way to becoming a great artist and human being" (Parkes, 1994, p. 108): the "grotesque indignity" of entire periods of his life (1.441/269), his pandering to the modern audiences in the first period of his career (1.474/298), the utter failure of the project of his second period (1.477/301–302; cf. Chapter IV.1), or the clumsiness of his writings (1.501–502/323–324). Other of his shortcomings are only briefly touched upon in *WB* and assume a much larger significance only in Nietzsche's later thinking about Wagner. Here belong his subservience to the powers that be (1.504/326; cf. *GM* III.5; also cf. Drochon, 2016, p. 134), and especially the diagnosis of Wagner's "natural theatrical gift" (1.467/292), discussed at length in the notes cited above, which later became Nietzsche's central critique of Wagner (*EH* UC 3, *CW* 8–12).

What this rhetorical strategy amounts to is that "Wagner" as he is presented in *WB* is far removed from Wagner as Nietzsche actually understood him at this point. The general thrust of the rhetoric of *WB* is to present "Wagner" as the exemplary artist and as an exemplary individual, as a man who had managed to complete his life's task, who has become what he is. *WB* doesn't speak about Wagner as he actually was, but about what he *could* and *should* have been, and what he *could* and *should* have

Richard Wagner in Bayreuth | 133

accomplished for the cause of genuine culture: The Wagner of *WB* is a "monumental ideal" (Lampert, 2017, p. 124).[6] As Nietzsche wrote later, "the entire picture of the *dithyrambic* artist is a picture of the *pre-existent* poet of *Zarathustra*, sketched with abysmal profundity and without touching even for a moment the Wagnerian reality" (*EH* BT 4).[7] Insofar as Nietzsche still had any hopes for the fruitfulness of Wagner's project at this point, I agree with Montinari (1982, p. 46) that *WB* should be read as "a challenge to Wagner, whom Nietzsche proposes a certain interpretation of his life and work. [. . .] will Wagner remain faithful to himself?"[8] It was one last attempt to guide Wagner toward the genuine heights his project could potentially attain, were it oriented in the right direction.

Because of the huge difference Nietzsche perceived between the actual Wagner and the "Wagner" of *WB*, in the remainder of this chapter the name "Wagner" refers to the monumental fiction of Wagner rather than to the actual Wagner (unless specified otherwise).

The rhetorical intention of monumentalizing Wagner is clearly present in the opening chapter of *WB*, which tells us that the founding of Bayreuth is a genuinely great event in which "art itself [. . .] was discovered" (1.433/261)—an event in which art in its highest form and in its utility for internal and external culture (re)appeared in the world. But a great event requires also that it be understood by its audience; otherwise its effect will be only temporary, a momentary flash (1.431/259). This in turn means that a great event must be a necessary event, and Nietzsche intends to explain the necessity behind Bayreuth to his readers. He will make the necessity of Bayreuth evident to us. *WB* thus aims in the first place to help the audiences of the Bayreuth festival to understand what they are about to experience, so that this event may have its proper effect on them,

---

6. I submit the preceding as a fairer assessment of the rhetorical style of *WB* than its usual condemnation. Gray (1995, p. 405) characterizes it as "uninhibited idolatry" and says that, as a consequence, *WB* "is often merely read as a curiosity" (ibid., p. 408); Large (2012, p. 100) writes that "the text strikes us now as positively cringeworthy on account of the depth of its hero-worship"; and Brooks (2018, p. 188; cf. p. 212) speaks of its "cringingly reverential tone."

7. Drochon (2016, p. 134) sees this disconnect between the "Wagner" of *WB* and the actual Wagner, but thinks this occurred unconsciously rather than being a deliberate strategy on Nietzsche's part.

8. We can find a similar evaluation also in Janz (1978, 1.706). Wagner himself wrote to Nietzsche on 21 September 1873: "I swear to you by God that I hold you to be the only one who knows what I want!" (KGB II.4, p. 295).

134 | The Young Nietzsche's Education

and thus accomplish its *"great future"* (1.434/262). *WB* is an "exhortation" to the audience of Bayreuth to make it the great event it promises to be (Lampert, 2017, p. 108).

The final paragraph of *WB* 1 tells us about a peculiar look Wagner had after the laying of the cornerstone of the theater at Bayreuth, which was to become the permanent home of his art in the form he had always envisioned: "he was silent and for a long time turned his gaze inward with a look that would be impossible to describe in words" (1.434/262). Not one word, not even a few words suffice to explain this look [*Blick*] or moment [*Augenblick*, as it is called a few lines later]: In fact, the remainder of *WB* is an interpretation of this singular moment.[9] In this *Augenblick*, the whole of his life in its unity—his past, present, and future, or "how he had become what he is, and what he will be" (1.434/262)—became manifest to Wagner.[10] That this *Augenblick* of Wagner is not just a throwaway rhetorical device for Nietzsche, but a crucial phenomenon, is made clear by Nietzsche's comment on this passage in *EH* BT 4: "the *look* spoken of on the seventh page [i.e., at 1.434/262] is Zarathustra's distinctive look; Wagner, Bayreuth, the whole wretched German pettiness are a cloud in which an infinite *fata morgana* of the future is reflected." To summarize, this *Augenblick*, this insight into the unity and direction of one's life, is something that can be experienced only by a genuinely great individual, by one who has become what they are. And it is not just Wagner's life that becomes comprehensible from this *Augenblick*, but "only from this Wagnerian look will we ourselves be able to understand the greatness of his deed" (1.434/262). Nietzsche tells us that Wagner's art must be understood from the artist (cf. Heidegger 1991, vol. I, ch. 12).

---

9. We can see this structure of *WB* also in the note 11 [47], 8.239–240.

10. This *Augenblick* is very similar to that described by Heidegger in *Being and Time* as the authentic present (translated as *"moment of vision"*: § 68a, p. 387; § 68c, p. 398). And insofar as *WB* is an interpretation of a single, particular *Augenblick*, Nietzsche goes beyond Heidegger's account of this phenomenon by not just indicating its formal structure, but also showing us the content that fleshed it out in this unique instance. This leads one to suspect that Heidegger was inspired by the *UC* in more than just the three useful kinds of history from *HL* that he discusses in § 76—on which occasion he remarks that Nietzsche "understood more than he has made known to us" (p. 448). Also cf. Chapter III, fn. 6 above.

Richard Wagner in Bayreuth | 135

IV.1. Becoming Richard Wagner

The next two chapters of *WB* turn to Wagner's past, to the path he had to go to become who he is today: Here he is depicted as an exemplary case of becoming oneself, or of attaining one's genius. Nietzsche first tells us about Wagner's pre-dramatic period, his merely biographical youth. His soul appears chaotic in this period; his various passions and talents manifest themselves more or less accidentally and struggle against each other. His passions weren't ordered by any kind of strict education, and it seemed as if "he was born to be a dilettante" (1.436/263). Then Wagner's "ruling passion" (1.435/263) manifested itself—the passion for theater, which, as he understood, can be the most effective of all arts: he understood that "theater had the potential to exert an incomparable influence, an influence greater than that exerted by any other art form" (1.472/297). Here, with the appearance of Wagner's ruling passion or ruling thought (1.472/296),[11] commences his *spiritual* youth and the drama of his life (1.436–437/264). The conflict of this drama revolves around the question of what kind of effect he should strive for in his musical-theatrical productions.

In attempting to answer this question, the chaos of passions in his soul "seems to be simplified in a terrible way" (1.437/264): His passions order themselves into two powerful conglomerations. The first of these is characterized by Nietzsche as a strong and tyrannical will that yearns for the manifold pleasures and satisfactions that the world can offer to a popular composer—things like wealth, fame, prestige, or honors (1.439–440/267). This tyrannical will demanded of Wagner that his art pander to the audiences in order to achieve the greatest possible effect of *this* kind, that he should provide the modern masses with the most entertaining *divertissements* he possibly can, and reap the bountiful rewards that await such a provider. The other major player in Wagner's soul is "an entirely pure and free force" (1.437/264) that can best be characterized as his love of art itself and of the joy his artistic creating gives him.[12] This force told Wagner that he should

---

11. The second of these formulations—ruling thought—seems more accurate in the light of the argument that follows, according to which Wagner's spiritual drama revolves around the struggle of his two principal passions to interpret the "ruling thought" and use it for their respective ends.

12. The note 11 [42] (8.235) glosses on the subject as follows: "*Faithfulness to the spirit of music* became his religion."

136 | The Young Nietzsche's Education

strive for the greatest genuinely artistic effect, that his works ought to be *"collective deeds of his many-voiced being"* (1.445–446/273), and that his creative activity ought to pay no heed to the demands of petty selfishness (the various forms of which have united themselves into the "tyrannical will").[13]

The further unfolding of Wagner's spiritual development, or of his spiritual *drama*, lies in the relation of these two principal forces of his soul to each other. The principle of this development is not the suppression of the tyrannical will in favor of the purely artistic force within him, but rather an *integration* of the former into the latter, a process of unifying his soul under the rule of the highest within it (cf. 1.474/298–299). The power of his lower passions wasn't suppressed—it was channeled and made useful for the purposes of the higher, ruling force.[14] Wagner understood this process under the slogan of *"faithfulness, selfless faithfulness"* (1.438–439/266): as these two forces keeping faith to each other, the lower (ever more) willing to accept the guidance of the higher, and the higher in turn not abandoning the lower in disgust over its excesses.[15] This is how Wagner fulfilled the imperative *be yourself*: by persuading the two principal forces of his soul to keep faith to each other, and consequently by his soul as a whole keeping faith to his ruling passion for genuine art, practicing it in an ever-higher sense. The more he succeeded at the former, the more he succeeded also at the latter. This is why the motif of faithfulness is so central to all of Wagner's works (1.438, 1.484, 1.507–509/266, 308, 328–330): It is an expression of the solution he found to the central internal conflict of his life.

However, the preceding account makes this drama look much simpler and easier to resolve than it actually was. During the long period in which this drama played itself out, Wagner could never be sure that this great

---

13. This "tyrannical will" is not analogous to the "plastic force" of *HL*, as Church (2019, p. 204) thinks: While the former is a set of particular desires, the latter is a general structure at work within every soul. Cf. Chapter II.1.

14. Parkes (1994, p. 114) explains one of the utilities of the tyrannical will for the overall unification of Wagner's soul by pointing out that "there is a strong suggestion that the chaos can be ordered only by a will that derives its *initial* strength from intensely tyrannical desire" (emphasis added)—that the tyrannical will did the essential preparatory work of reining in the many lesser desires under its auspices.

15. Nietzsche also stresses *love* as characteristic of Wagner along with his faithfulness (1.439, 1.456, 1.464, 1.471, 1.500/266, 282, 289, 295, 322). I understand this love as continuous with his philanthropy—whether it works within his soul or on others, it is a selfless and self-sacrificing love of the higher for the lower, for the sake of raising the lower up. We can consider it as Wagner's way of practicing his "tragic sensibility" (cf. Chapter IV.2 below).

Richard Wagner in Bayreuth | 137

necessity of his life, this faith, will actually be kept; it was "it was the only thing that was not within his own power" (1.439/267). This uncertainty was a major source of his suffering, which is an instance of the more general class of "sufferings of someone who is developing [*des Werdenden*]" (1.439/267): Such sufferings await all who strive to become their true self, their genius. The suffering of uncertainty was moreover compounded by the temptations the world offered to his lower part, to the "world within him" (1.440, 1.472/267, 296), and from the disgust of his higher part over this "world" and its desire to abandon it altogether. "His dangers lie in this temptation [to the 'world'], as well as in the rejection of this temptation" (1.440/267); the principal dangers for Wagner's becoming lay in each of his two principal forces refusing to keep faith to the other. The danger was that either the tyrannical will may refuse to obey the artistic force any longer, or that the artistic force would abandon Wagner[16] and leave him only with the tyrannical will and its desiderata.

This internal struggle and the uncertainty of its outcome left Wagner in a peculiar state of mind: "although he did not despair, neither did he believe" (1.441/268). This state of *hopelessness*—neither hoping nor despairing—that was characteristic of Wagner for a long time is, it seems to me, a specifically modern affliction. At this point, Wagner has an inkling of what he wants to be and do, but he cannot accomplish it yet, nor can he be sure he will ever get to that point. This hopelessness that Wagner felt is a feeling of the pointlessness of life, a feeling that one lacks the direction toward doing anything meaningful, that a way toward living meaningfully is out of sight, out of reach; and given the uncertainty of one's spiritual development at this point, there is a distinct possibility that it will never get better than this. The symptoms of this hopelessness are described at length at 1.441/268–269: the grasping at momentary delights as if there were nothing more to life—for there may not be anything more to it; the incapacity to attain any genuine satisfaction by accomplishing what one strives for; the sense that one's work has only ephemeral significance and that one need not bother oneself with it too much. It is in this context that Nietzsche speaks of the "grotesque indignity" of "entire stretches of his life" (of which Wagner was moreover painfully aware), and he says that for a person in such a state of mind, death or even suicide may appear as

---

16. By "abandoning" I mean here that the force would cease to strive for its original goal. The result would be a Wagner making popular art with a defeatist attitude such as "it is not good art at all, but in *this* world it is impossible to make good art." It would be a state of despair in the sense of the following paragraph.

138 | The Young Nietzsche's Education

desirable, as a sweet release from an endless chain of sufferings. In short, what Wagner experienced—and overcame—at this stage was the misery of the precarious modern, post-death-of-God existence, in which there is no pre-given meaning and no guarantee of success for our projects (or, indeed, of the meaningfulness of our projects at all).[17] This suffering too belongs to becoming what we are, and Wagner is exemplary in overcoming it.

Wagner also overcame the dangers of the present age oversaturated with learning, which Nietzsche analyzed in *HL* 4–9. He possessed a great plastic force (cf. 1.251/89), stemming from the combination of the great force of his desires and of his clear plan for life, which is to say of his well-ordered soul. (The latter is most prominent in the last stage of his life, but already in the earlier stages Wagner possessed a psychic order sufficient to guide his learning for the purposes of his artistic production.) In this way, Wagner was capable of directing his studies of all the arts, history (which he used as an artist rather than as a modern "objective" historian—1.443/270, cf. 1.290/126),[18] and philosophy always so that new knowledge would be incorporated into the existing order of his soul and used for its overarching goals: "the larger and heavier the edifice becomes, the greater becomes the tension on the arch of his ordering and ruling thought" (1.442/269). His new knowledge would expand his world and his capacity to act without breaking apart the structures of meaningfulness that order his world. Consequently, he used knowledge as a stimulant for action rather than as an opiate to satisfy him even with inaction or incapacity for action, as is so often the case with modern humans (cf. Chapter II.3). In Wagner's case, knowledge serves life rather than vice versa. It is in this rather peculiar respect—in his capacity for action, in his philanthropic striving to reform modern society and the souls of modern humans, and *not* in the power of his thinking—that Wagner is "most like a philosopher" (1.445/272).

Parallel to this spiritual drama runs the drama of Wagner's outward activity: His spiritual drama is reflected not just in his works and in the prominence of the motif of faithfulness in them, but also "in the entire constitution [*Gestaltung*] of his life" (1.435/262; cf. 1.163, 1.264, 1.340/9, 102, 174). This drama unfolded itself in three distinct stages, which Nietzsche recounts in *WB* 8. The first was that of the "grand opera," in

---

17. Goethe has a similar account of the attractiveness of suicide in the modern times—and admits to have struggled with it himself—in Book 13 of *Poetry and Truth* (*Werke* IX.583–585).

18. This may be referring to Aristotle's thesis that poetry is more philosophic than history (*On Poetics*, 1451b6–7).

which he strived simply to become a popular and successful composer in the style of Giacomo Meyerbeer, the period up to and including *Rienzi*. This stage led to his understanding, and disgusted rejection, of "the whole mendacious nature of modern art," and it is only after the rejection of the modern art-as-*divertissement* that he actually becomes a composer and an artist (1.474/298).

In the second stage his concerns changed diametrically. He recognized "*the poeticizing common people* [*Volk*]" as "the only hitherto existing artist" (1.475/299), and he realized that the modern culture industry—including his own previous works—is derivative of the *Volk*'s creativity, and perverts the fruits of this original creativity "for the gratification of *illusory needs*" (1.475/299). Wagner thus became a social revolutionary, and strived to liberate and re-create the German people through his art. He wanted to accomplish this by gathering a multitude that would feel the same basic need that he did, the need for "selfless faithfulness." And insofar as Wagner created his works to satisfy his innermost need, to produce mythical and musical expressions of such faithfulness, his works would provide the same kind of satisfaction to this multitude, which would then find "the same type of happiness [as Wagner] in this gratification" (1.476/300). The principle of this re-creation of the people, namely uniting them around the satisfaction of the same supreme needs he himself has, is the same as in *HL* 4 (1.278/114–115).[19] Thus Wagner's works of his second period, most prominently *Tannhäuser* and *Lohengrin*, in effect ask their audience, "Where are those who have the same suffering and the same need as I?" (1.477/301) and invite them to become members of a re-created genuine people. However, this ambitious enterprise failed miserably: "no one gave an answer, no one had understood his question" (1.477/302), and insofar as his works were discussed, they were utterly misunderstood. This failure rested on Wagner's insufficient understanding of what his supreme need is—for his supreme need was not the need to establish a national faithfulness; indeed, faithfulness itself was just a symbol of his true need—namely creating art that expresses the full capacities of his unified soul. He had to improve his understanding of himself and of human life in general before he would be able to succeed.[20]

---

19. At the same time this draws on Wagner's own words: cf. Neymeyr (2020, 2.500).

20. Drochon (2016, p. 134) overlooks the failure of Wagner's social-revolutionary phase and also imputes the same wish for social revolution to Nietzsche himself. On my reading, the significance of Wagner's art for Nietzsche, as well as the focal point of Nietzsche's project, lies not in the social-political sphere, but rather in the domain of the human soul.

140 | The Young Nietzsche's Education

Wagner's career thus entered into its third stage, from *The Rhinegold* onward. Here he lost all hope at worldly success—but this moment of resignation is, as with the Schopenhauerian human being, actually the moment of his great triumph. His lower, tyrannical will, having lost all prospects of satisfaction, now fully integrated itself into his artistic will, his soul attained full unity, and Wagner became the "dithyrambic dramatist" that he *is*. He now sees "suffering in the nature of things" (1.478/302), and his works become mythical expressions of the world as a whole. He now creates as if only for himself, "he speaks only through his art and only with himself" (1.478/302–303) and makes no concessions to any prospective viewers. The exemplary result of this approach is *Tristan and Isolde*, "the true *opus metaphysicum* of all art" (1.479/303). And now also genuine friends appear, people who understood his art and want to help him in its creation and preservation for posterity. Finally, the Franco-Prussian war of 1870 showed him the virtues that Germans still possess and that his art can cultivate in them, their bravery and presence of mind (1.481/305; cf. 1.160–161/6–7).

The preservation of his work in its undistorted intended form now becomes Wagner's chief concern. He wants to publicly show and teach how his works are to be performed and thus to found a "*stylistic tradition*" that is inscribed "in effects upon the human soul" (1.481/305). It is in this context and for this purpose that he came up with "the *idea of Bayreuth*" (1.483/307): Bayreuth is to be an institution where his art would be preserved, where its proper performance would be carried on, and through which it could have a lasting influence. So he began to seek allies for the project of Bayreuth, founding Wagner societies, and his friends—including Nietzsche[21]—contributed what they could. This is Wagner's final act of faithfulness to his art, and the expression of his friends' faithfulness to him.

IV.2. Wagner's Tragic Art

After this outline of Wagner's past, we turn to his present with the question of what his art is and what kind of influence it could and should

---

21. Nietzsche became an official patron of the festival, for which title he had to contribute 900 *Reichsmark*, a huge sum of money. The sale of these expensive Certificates of Patronage was one of Wagner's main means of amassing funds for the completion of the Bayreuth Festival Theater (Large, 1978, p. 167). Nietzsche in fact received his Certificate from his sister, which delighted Wagner so much that he sent her another one for free (Janz, 1978, 1.531).

exert. Nietzsche ascribes no small significance to Wagner and his art: He is to be a *"counter-Alexander"* (1.447/274), a re-Hellenizator of the world. That he can assume this world-historical task at all depends in part on the opportune historical moment in which we find ourselves. Nietzsche tells us that throughout its history, Western civilization has oscillated between two poles: the Hellenic and the Oriental. And now, after the death of God—Christianity being "a bit of Oriental antiquity" (1.446/273)—that stands in the background of Nietzsche's thought already in *DS* (cf. Chapter I.3), the pendulum of history begins to swing back toward the Hellenic pole, "the Earth [. . .] now yearns once more for Hellenization" (1.447/274). Given the current exhaustion of the Oriental, the only other option available is the absence of any culture proper, that is, descent into barbarism. Wagner thus finds himself in a time of great danger and great opportunity; the question is how he will make use of the situation in which he finds himself.

Wagner's means toward this reform of culture as a whole is a reform of the theater. Nietzsche's model of cultural reform stands on the questionable premise that the various domains of modern life are interconnected with such necessity and reciprocity that a genuine change in one domain will lead to change in all others. Thus, theater is not a privileged site for such a reform—"the same can be said of any [other] true reform" (1.448/275)—but it is one of many possible starting points, and the one Wagner has chosen. This reform is to consist in changing "the position of our arts with regard to life" (1.448/275): Whereas nowadays they are a *divertissement* from the genuine tasks of our life and an opiate, they are to play an essential role in our self-understanding and to become a stimulant for action. That is to say, theater and the other arts are to become for us what they were for the Greeks.[22] In thus restoring the proper relation of art to life, Wagner will re-Hellenize our culture—and in this he resembles Aeschylus, the inaugurator of the greatest period of Attic tragedy (1.446, 1.467, 1.490/273, 292, 313), and may even surpass him (note 11 [25], 8.212).[23] If this Wagnerian reform of the theater succeeds, if tragedy is indeed reborn in modern Germany, the reform will spread to other domains of life, where a discerning eye can detect a lot of hidden rot underneath the pompous facades. In a word, "the greatest empires stand waiting" (1.450/277), are ripe for the taking, and

---

22. Nietzsche follows here Wagner's own ideas from *Art and Revolution* (cf. Neymeyr 2020, 2.421–423).

23. Besides Aeschylus, Wagner is prominently analogized also to Alexander the Great (1.434, 1.447/262, 275).

142 | The Young Nietzsche's Education

Nietzsche voices high hopes for the domain of education in particular and for the downfall of the entire philistine system of pseudo-culture in general.

THE TRAGIC SENSIBILITY

The means to this reform of theater and consequently of the entire culture is Wagner's art, his *tragedy* in the form of musical drama (or *Gesamtkunstwerk*). These tragedies present to us mythic images of the world—for myth, as Wagner and Nietzsche understand it, is not a primitive, obsolete way of explaining natural phenomena, but "myth itself is a kind of thought; it communicates an idea of the world, [not in concepts] but in a succession of events, actions, and sufferings" (1.485/309). This is "a truly depth-psychological conception of myth" (Parkes, 1994, p. 83): Myth thus understood conveys to us universal features of the world and of the human condition through the depiction of the struggles of individual characters, which then assume a paradigmatic significance. Being tragedies, Wagner's works always depict the "struggle of these individuals against everything" (1.451/278), the struggle of the heroes against the "world" and its alleged "necessities" that conspire against their strivings—and their eventual defeat. Wagner shows us individuals attempting great deeds against overwhelming odds, and their perseverance in their endeavor at any cost, including at the cost of their own life. And this is genuinely noble (*kalon*), Nietzsche tells us (1.451/278; cf. 1.319/153): "The individuals can live in no more beautiful way than by preparing themselves to die and sacrificing themselves in the struggle for justice and love." In presenting such images of heroic struggle against the "world" to us, Wagner gives us "the *semblance* of a more simple world" (1.452/279, cf. 1.447/274): They show in an oversimplified form what is right and wrong, what is noble and base, what kind of life is worth living.[24] They provide us with a way of ordering our desires and giving us a compass for the complex world of actual experience, teaching us that a life on unconditional devotion to our highest values—a moral life—is to be preferred to everything else. These mythic images are, however, *not* history, not even in Nietzsche's expansive sense of the word: "art is no teacher or educator for immediate action," and the desiderata of the tragic heroes "are not things worth striving for in themselves" (1.452/279; contrast with 1.258/96, where Nietzsche paraphrases Polybius on history as

---

24. This, and more broadly the entire account of the tragic sensibility, is the "didactic role" of art that Church (2019, p. 213) doesn't see.

Richard Wagner in Bayreuth | 143

"the proper preparation for governing a state and the best teacher," that is, a teacher for immediate action; and with 1.262/100, where monumental history ceases to be history when its monumentalization goes so far as to create a "mythical fiction").[25] But if Wagner's mythic images of the world are useless for practice, as Nietzsche admits here, we have to ask what are they good for at all.

Art has no *practical* use, Nietzsche tells us, because it is "the activity of the human being in repose" (1.452/279). It is a means of relaxing ourselves in between the episodes of our own struggles with the "world," it is a safe haven in the midst of a stormy and perilous world, and thereby it strengthens us "for further and higher willing" (1.449/276; cf. 1.324/158): It is a stimulant for further action. And even more than that: Art, and in particular Wagner's art, provides us with solace [*Tröstung*] in the face of "the greatest suffering that exists for the individual" (1.451–452/278):

> the lack of a knowledge shared by all human beings, the lack of certainty in ultimate insights, and the disparity in abilities [. . .] We cannot be happy as long as everything around us is suffering and inflicts suffering on itself; we cannot be moral as long as the course of human events is determined by violence, deceit, and injustice; we cannot even be wise as long as all of humanity has not entered the competition for wisdom and led the individual to life and knowledge in the wisest possible manner.

These are, as Lampert (2017, p. 112) notes, *spiritual* sufferings—and this is the more remarkable, the more one knows of the extent of Nietzsche's physical sufferings.[26] To understand what exactly these sufferings are, it is helpful to

---

25. I thus disagree with Brooks's (2018, p. 204) claim that the Wagner of *WB* is "the monumental historiographer described in *HL*": he is a *mythopoet* rather than a historian of any sort. Church (2019, p. 209) also takes Wagner to be a historian, namely the "true historian" of *HL* 6. Contrary to Zuckert (1970, p. 165), it is *facts* rather than values that are distorted in Wagner's art; although the desiderata of the tragic hero are not desiderata in themselves, his art nevertheless accurately depicts the tragic sensibility, and in this central sense it doesn't distort "values."

26. "No philosopher ever suffered as Nietzsche suffered" (Huenemann, 2013, p. 67). His sickness consisted of three sets of symptoms: an eye affliction that made "reading and writing extremely difficult and painful" (ibid.); severe migraines that would render him incapacitated for days; and various kinds of digestive issues, such as "vomiting for hours without having eaten anything beforehand" (letter to Carl von Gersdorff, around

144 | The Young Nietzsche's Education

consider what they are privations of. What we lack is the commonality of knowledge to all human beings, the certainty of our knowledge, and the equal capacities to act on the part of all humans. The reason why these insights into the essential limitedness and inequality of human capacities constitute the greatest human suffering is that they create a tremendous tension within the soul of the knower, namely "the tension between the universal knowledge of things and the intellectual-moral capacity of the individual" (1.453/279). In other words, they produce a tension between, on the one hand, the genius' love of humanity, their *philanthropy*, which desires—demands, even—that the redeeming insight into the being of life, of the world as a whole, and its concomitant happiness become universal, that every human being be given the means to be as happy as is humanly possible in this world; and on the other hand, the *knowledge* that the gap between the few and the many is unbridgeable, that most human beings will never attain the genuine human good of having become who they are, that the goal of the philanthrope in us is unattainable. *This* tension between philanthropy and knowledge is, for Nietzsche of the *UC*, the greatest suffering one can suffer: to know that however much one may strive to bring about genuine and universal human goods, the majority of human beings are nevertheless condemned to a life that amounts to senseless suffering. This is also the highest level of the insoluble conflict between truth and life.

Wagner's art provides its audience, and especially the highest kind of its audience, those who have attained the insight of the genius, with a temporary illusion—for a mythic fiction is factually untrue by definition—that allows them to forget this knowledge, this "deadly truth," and thus to relax the immense tension they normally have to bear: "art exists *so that the bow does not break*" (1.453/279). Wagner's art thereby allows us to keep on working on our tasks, which ultimately means on the task of becoming what we are—which is, not accidentally, also the task from which Wagner's own sufferings arose and which he depicts in various guises in his tragedies.

But Wagner's art relaxes this spiritual tension also in a second way. Being art, it is in principle accessible to everyone, unlike philosophy—and so any

---

26 June 1875; KGB II.5, p. 64). Nietzsche's sickness manifested itself as early as 1871 (15.27) and continued to plague him throughout his active life. It was apparently at its worst in 1879, at the end of which year he reported to his sister that "last year I had 118 days of *heavy* bouts of sickness" (15.112), but it was severe already in the period of the *UC* (Janz, 1978, 1.609, informs us that since the middle of 1875 the condition had become serious and permanent), and it was the main outward cause for Nietzsche's early retirement from his professorship in Basel.

Richard Wagner in Bayreuth | 145

human being as such can draw inner strength from its joyful illusions. Thanks to this it is possible that it becomes the basis of a universal community, a community that anyone—and so potentially *everyone*—can belong to and take part in. It is in this sense that Wagner's art points to a future in which "the stigma that until now was attached to the word 'common' will then be stripped away" (1.504/325): a future in which all human beings, high and low, can equally enjoy Wagner's art, and learn from its mythical images of the world the meaning of their own life. It promises the possibility of a genuine human brotherhood, even though this brotherhood would rest on the shared enjoyment of illusions. This universal accessibility of Wagner's art is also the reason why it is not merely German, but *"supra-German"* and belongs to all *"human beings of the future"* (1.505/326; cf. Chapter IV.4).[27]

The argument of *WB* 4 culminates in the final paragraph of this chapter, where Nietzsche names the attitude that Wagner's heroes exhibit and that his art instills in its audience: It is *the tragic sensibility*. This tragic sensibility is the attitude that "the individual should be consecrated to something supra-personal" (1.453/279); that the struggle for noble goals is worthwhile in itself, regardless of the eventual result, may one fight for them against the entire world and its "necessities"; that striving for our highest goals is worth infinitely more than the comfortable life of petty selfishness; or, to use a Platonic phrase, that "the most important thing is not life, but the good life" (*Crito* 48b). But it is not just individuals who can profit from incorporating this sensibility, by far not: The survival and

---

27. By this pronouncement Nietzsche interprets away Wagner's own *völkisch*-nationalist tendencies (cf., e.g., Wagner, 1983, 9.106/2014, p. 187) as irrelevant to the true, universal importance of his art; cf. also the note 11 [4], 8.190. Hereby he incidentally provided an invaluable benefaction to Wagner and his legacy: "without Nietzsche, [the reception of Wagner's work] would have been completely dominated by the anti-Semitic nationalist ideology in which Wagner's oeuvre was enveloped at the most official and authoritative source, the Bayreuth of the composer's widow and of Houston Stewart Chamberlain" (Berger, 2017, p. 375). Nietzsche describes Wagner's art as supra-German also in *BGE* 256. His idea of the "good European," which appears from *HA* onward (Prange, 2013, p. 170), is prefigured here for the first time. Contrary to Taylor (1997, p. 10), who thinks that the early Nietzsche is concerned with "the regeneration of *German* culture and society" in particular and even believes that Nietzsche frequently invokes "the "German Spirit" as a source of the highest value and significance" (ibid.), I believe Nietzsche's thought always had universalist ambitions, and its concern with German matters is simply a function of Nietzsche (and Wagner) being German: Germany and the Germans were the closest objects of his attention, the environment in which he was raised and with which he was most familiar. Cf. the note 29 [47] (7.645).

146 | The Young Nietzsche's Education

spreading of the tragic sensibility is the sole hope and guarantee for "the future of what is human" (1.453/280). If and only if we adopt the tragic sensibility can humanity become united by the realization that we share the same supreme need and that Wagner's art provides a satisfaction of our shared need. Humanity could thus become *one* and transcend the barriers set up by conventions of all sorts, and face its future, up to and including its inevitable doom, "*as a whole*" (1.453/279).

Only in this way can the rule of chance and conventions over the human affairs, which was hitherto the case, be overcome—not just by a few extremely fortunate individuals as it was until now, but in an important sense by humanity as a whole. The only real alternative to this is, again, descent into barbarism, accelerated if not effected by our newfound awareness of the deadly truths (including the truth of the eventual demise of our entire species, as we have just seen). "This supreme task," the spreading of the tragic sensibility, "comprises all the ennoblement of the human being" (1.453/279); and herein thereby lies the possibility of the only genuine "Fortgang der Menschheit"—of the *progress of humanity* (1.453/280). What a word for *Nietzsche* to use in all seriousness! And he confirms his seriousness by emphatically stating, "This is how I feel!" (1.453/280). In a word, *this* is the true promise of Bayreuth, *this* is the mission of Wagner's art in human history: the unification and ennoblement of humanity in the only genuine way, by teaching people to value living well more than merely living. A "world-historical accent" (*EH* BT 4) indeed, if there ever were one: Nietzsche imagines here a global cultural reform on the utmost limits of the humanly possible, and quite likely beyond them.

THE EXPERIENCE OF WAGNER'S ART

Wagner's art is supposed to have these immense effects on its audience thanks to the immense artistic powers Wagner disposes with. It is his incomparable artistry that gives his nature its "demonic ability to communicate" (1.485/308; cf. 1.466/291), its capacity to convey feelings and states of mind with such power. Nietzsche describes several notable features of Wagner's artistry in *WB* 9. One of them is his work with the German language, which he "forced [. . .] back into a primal state" (1.486/309), into a state resembling that before its modern corruption (which was amply exemplified in *DS* 11–12; Wagner's analysis of this corruption is related at 1.455–456/281–282, and it will be discussed in Chapter IV.3). Another one is Wagner's chief innovation in music: According to Nietzsche, he is

Richard Wagner in Bayreuth | 147

the first to develop a musical language "of pathos, of passionate willing" (1.491/314). In this he went beyond Beethoven, who expressed pathos not directly, but through a sequence of individual states, from which the listener had to "*intuit*" the entire line of the passion (1.492/315). But Wagner went further than expressing just a single passion in his compositions: Indeed, "everything that speaks through [his music], human being or nature, has a strictly individualized passion" (1.493/316). His music thus depicts the world as a dynamic interplay of various passions, each struggling for its own goal and many struggling against each other, but the ultimate effect of this apparent chaos and discord is a harmony of a higher kind, a *harmonie aphanes* (Heraclitus B 54). Thus, Nietzsche tells us, Wagner's music as a whole is (1.494/316) "a likeness of the world in the sense in which it was conceived by the great Ephesian philosopher, as a harmony that discord produces out of itself, as the union of justice and strife."

The combination of the poetic and musical elements of Wagner's artistry allowed him to present his heroes to us with a hitherto unprecedented clarity and intensity. In a Wagnerian work, we see the passion of the hero, and indeed every dramatic process, "on three mutually clarifying levels: verbal expression, gesture, and music" (1.488/311–312). Thanks to this, the passion of a Wagnerian hero is transmitted "immediately to the souls of the audience" (1.488/312), unlike in a spoken drama, where the audience needs to process the speeches to grasp the underlying passion. And finally, although Wagner is well aware of his manifold artistic mastery, he doesn't show it off, "he has nothing epideictic about him" (1.495/318): On the contrary, his sole concern is to effect the greatest possible absorption into his work on the audience's part, and thus to ensure the greatest possible effect of his work on them. Therefore he composes so that "one only feels what is *necessary*" (1.495–496/318).

On this basis Nietzsche describes the experience of absorption in the Wagnerian tragedy in the fourth paragraph of *WB* 6, and in the rhapsodic single-paragraph *WB* 7 (1.468/293), as a descent into a cave in which our notions of life, nature, and reality itself will be shaken. In the former passage, Wagner's art itself is said so speak to its audience as follows (1.464/289):

> You *must* pass through my mysteries, [. . .] you need to experience their purifying and disruptive power. Dare to do it for the sake of your own salvation, and leave behind you for once that dimly illuminated bit of nature and life that is all you seem to know. I will lead you into a realm that is just as real; after you

148 | The Young Nietzsche's Education

> have returned from my cave to your daylight, you yourselves shall decide which life is more real, which, in fact, is daylight and which is cave. Inner nature is far richer, far more powerful, blissful, and terrible; you do not know it, given the way you usually live. Learn how to become nature again yourselves, and then let yourselves be transformed with and in nature by the magic of my love and fire.

Brooks (2018, p. 213) takes these passages to constitute a reversal of the famous Platonic image of the cave, which culminates in the ascent out of the cave. For Brooks this means that in the *UC*, all knowledge is considered to be a human fabrication ("knowledge of nature exists inside the cave because knowledge of nature is created in the cave"—ibid.), and an ascent out of the cave into the light of the sun is impossible: "for the early Nietzsche, there are only caves because life flourishes within the closed horizon of a cave" (ibid., p. 214).

Such a reading of these passages rests on a misunderstanding of the image of the cave. Eugen Fink (1970, p. 54 ff.) points out that Plato didn't invent this image: He took it over and adapted it from the Eleusinian mysteries. The initiates into these mysteries "die" and are "reborn," and in this process they attain " 'insights' through which they themselves are fundamentally transformed" (ibid., p. 55). These insights have to do with the unity and eternity of all life, which is found "not beyond becoming, but precisely *in* becoming" (ibid.): They are insights that, as far as I can tell, are quite similar to Nietzsche's "answer of Empedocles" (cf. Chapter III.3). And, crucially, the initiation into these mysteries took place "in caves and underground chasms at night, illuminated by torchlight" (ibid., p. 56)—in the same conditions into which Plato placed the *prisoners* of his cave. Knowing all this, it becomes clear that Plato's allegory of the cave presents philosophy as "*reversed Eleusis*" (ibid.), as a new and higher form of life-changing insight that (among other things) replaces the Eleusinian principle of the Earth by the principle of Light.

It also becomes clear that what Nietzsche points to in using the language of the mysteries to describe the effect of Wagner's art is not a rejection of Plato's image of the cave and its concomitant rationalism—it is rather a restoration of Eleusis.[28] Just as the initiates of the ancient mysteries, the

---

28. We can see this idea of a unity between art and religion, particularly of Attic tragedy and Greek mystery religions, already in *BT* (1.66, 1.68, 1.73/*BT* 47, 49, 52), and also in notes such as 3 [77] (7.81); 9 [102] (7.311): "*Art and religion* in the Greek sense

Richard Wagner in Bayreuth | 149

audience of Wagner's art will descend into the depths of a "cave," of the Bayreuth Festival Theater, in order to be shaken and purified, and consequently to attain an insight that will transform their entire being. They will encounter "a sudden vision," as the initiates in Eleusis did (Hadot, 2002, p. 70). In this vision, everything visible wants "to deepen itself and intensify its inwardness by becoming audible," and conversely, everything audible wants "to emerge and rise up into light as a phenomenon for the eye"; Wagner thus manages "to retranslate visible motion into soul and primal life and, on the other hand, to see the hidden fabric of the inner world as a visual phenomenon and to give it the semblance of a body" (1.467/292). In other words, Wagner makes the motions, desirings, and strivings of his heroes into visible and audible representations of the fundamental drama of human life or soul, of the drama of becoming what we are. It is this capacity of Wagner to make the essence of human life manifest that makes him the "dithyrambic dramatist" (1.467, 1.471, 1.472/292, 295, 296).

Seeing this vision, the audience will be overwhelmed by the power of Wagner's art that "suspends the resistance of reason" (1.468/293): not of reason as such, but rather of the "common sense" of the ordinary everyday experience. Here the question will arise: "Why do *you* actually exist?" (1.466/291)—and the realization may come that they have no good answer to it, that their everyday life is a pointless bad infinity. They will realize that they don't know what nature is "given the way you usually live" (1.464/289), when possessed by the petty concerns of the philistine " 'seriousness of life,' that is, profession and business, together with wife and child" (1.170/16). It is this realization, this shaking of our self-assured "reason," that Wagner's art effects by depicting the fundamental drama of the human soul. This shaking can provide the starting point for the effort "to become nature again" (1.464/289), for the effort of living in accordance with the nature of the erotic-historic soul, to those who weren't able to come to this perspective by their own unaided striving.[29] In this sense, Wagner's

---

[are] identical"; 19 [36] (7.429); or 19 [38] (7.431), which describes religion as a work of art that "corresponds to an extraordinary need" (cf. 1.278/115). Without delving too deeply into this issue, I would like to point out that the fact that our principal sources on the Greek gods are poets—above all, Homer and Hesiod—was salient to Nietzsche's reflections on the close relation between Greek religion and art. Cf. Herodotus II.53 and Hegel (1970, pp. 299–306). Patočka (1996, pp. 142–143) offers an interesting account of the shared roots of myth, religion, and poetry in ecstatic experiences.

29. I.e., to people less "heroic" than the likes of Nietzsche, Goethe, Wagner, or Schopenhauer.

150 | The Young Nietzsche's Education

art is return to *nature* ("this music is the return to nature, while at the same time it is purification and transformation of nature"—1.456/282): It re-naturalizes the *natura denaturata* of modern humans. Wagner creates his works in order to make his audience equal to himself (in the sense of them all desiring the same good, of having the same ruling passion)—"in order finally to find love and not just devotion" (1.471/295). He wants equals rather than followers, he wants people who share his understanding of human life—that is his philanthropy.

The phrase "you yourselves shall decide which life is more real, which, in fact, is daylight and which is cave" (1.464/289) refers to the above-mentioned shaking of the petty, ordinary "common sense": The light of this "common sense" is in fact much dimmer, much more of an illusion than the illusions on show in Wagner's "cave." Wagner's art thus leads us into the cave not from the bright light of the sun, as Brooks (2018, p. 213) thinks, but rather from another, even deeper cave of the philistine pseudo-culture. The ascent from the cave of Wagner's art is a further task that each individual must accomplish for themselves and for which that art can serve only as a stimulant in hours of relaxation.

But isn't there nevertheless an implied critique of Plato in this appeal to the liberating power of *art*? After all, Plato had the poets cast out from the city in the *Republic* (398a), as Nietzsche reminds us at 1.468/293, and relied on philosophy alone.[30] Doesn't this indicate for Nietzsche a short-coming on Plato's part, consisting in an undue devaluation of art? There is a comment of this kind in the fragment 10 [1] (7.349), where Nietzsche judges that Plato "in his perfect state did not put the genius in its most general concept on the top, but only the genius of wisdom." However, this fragment is from early 1871, and the discussion of Plato in *WB* 7, written some four to five years later, takes a different direction. Nietzsche is silent here on the various kinds of genius, and instead he points out that we need a poet like Wagner precisely because we *don't* live in a state like a Greek *polis*—let alone in the city of the *Republic*—but rather in denatured modern society (cf. Lampert, 2017, p. 116). His art can lift us up only from the artificial second cave into the natural first cave: That is the chief purpose and the utility of the illusions his works present to us moderns.

---

30. This is of course leaving aside the artistry of Plato himself: the dramatic form and content of his dialogues, the vivid characters he presents us, his imagery, and the myths he invents. I also take the issue of the musical education of the guardians in the *Republic* (and in the *Laws*) to be separate from this; it will be discussed in Chapter IV.3.

Richard Wagner in Bayreuth | 151

From there on, the striving toward our true nature that is "immeasurably high above [us]" (1.340–341/174) is up to us, and the poet can only help us by relaxing the spiritual tension that this striving builds up in us. This relaxing—which is not to be mistaken for *divertissement*—is, on my reading of the *UC*, also what the tragic poets accomplished for the inhabitants of the natural cave of the Greek *polis*.

~

This account of tragedy bears strong continuities with that of *BT*. As in *WB*, tragedy in *BT* provides metaphysical solace against the "deadly truth" that kills all action: "knowledge kills action; action requires one to be shrouded in a veil of illusion" (1.57/*BT* 40). However, the "deadly truth" in *BT* is quite different from its counterparts in the *UC* (cf. 1.319, 1.452/153, 278): In *BT* it consists of the awareness of the undifferentiated mass of human sufferings that is expressed in the wisdom of Silenus, according to which the best thing for us is "not to have been born, not to *be*, to be *nothing*. However, the second best thing for you is: to die soon" (1.35/*BT* 23). Human existence thus understood is in need of an aesthetic justification, and this is what tragedy provided for the Greeks, and what Wagner's art can provide for us moderns according to *BT* (1.47, 1.69, 1.152, 1.154/*BT* 33, 50, 114, 115). The accounts of the Dionysian experience of the spectators of a tragedy are quite similar as well (compare, e.g., 1.109/*BT* 80–81 with 1.465/290 or 1.468/293; cf. Parkes, 1994, p. 112), even though Nietzsche doesn't use the term "Dionysian" in *WB*. But there is a crucial difference in the *purpose* of tragedy. In *BT*, this justification of existence seems to be a goal for itself, unconnected with any other, higher goals: Tragedy was *the* way to make life livable before the ascent of Socratic rationalism and will become this again after the imminent collapse of Socratic rationalism (cf. *BT* ch. 18). On the other hand, in *WB*, the justification of human sufferings effected by tragedy serves higher goals: namely the (self-)education of genuine human beings and the creation a genuine community. The imperative *be yourself*, the idea of becoming the genius that is dormant within us, which is so central to the project of the *UC*, is entirely absent from *BT*.

Nietzsche's claim is that all this can have an immense effect on the culture and the world at large once the transformed audience starts changing their own lives. Wagner's art is exceptional because of the clarity and intensity with which it presents the fundamental drama of the human soul to its audience. This makes it powerful enough to effect a change in the

152 | The Young Nietzsche's Education

audience's lives, to alienate them from their regular comfortable existence and to make them desire to undergo this drama themselves, inasmuch as they are capable of it—and in this sense it re-naturalizes them. It also instills in them the tragic sensibility, the sense that to undergo this drama is good for them regardless of the suffering involved and of the eventual outcome: It gives them the *courage* to live more nobly, and it provides the solace against the greatest human suffering, the suffering from the awareness of fundamental inequality of human beings. On a larger scale, it can create a *people*, a group of individuals who are united by the same supreme need they feel and by the satisfaction of this need with which Wagner's art provides them (cf. Lampert, 2017, pp. 120–121).[31] And, at the highest possible level, this universal character of Wagner's music may even effect, or at least contribute to, the unification and ennoblement of humanity as a whole.

Two caveats must be added to this account. First, we must carefully distinguish two groups within Wagner's audience: those who actually strive to attain their higher selves, the would-be geniuses, and those who don't. For the former group—for Nietzsche of necessity a small minority—the main use of Wagner's art is the solace they can derive from it, the relaxing of their spiritual tension that prevents them from breaking down. For the latter group, Wagner's art is in effect an illusion which they admire, not a reality which they enact; but insofar as they enjoy this illusion and admire its core teaching—the tragic sensibility—they can take part in (or at least not hinder) the projects of those who carry out the imperative *be yourself* in their own lives. The actual community Wagner's art can create is hierarchical. The allegedly universal, egalitarian community in which the word "common" is no longer an insult (cf. 1.504/325) is based on an illusion, on the noble lie that the highest human good is universally accessible, and that the audience of Wagner's works is actually accessing it in the act of enjoying these works. Insofar as there is equality in this community, it would be limited to the act of spectating Wagner's works. Wagner's art is thus a provider of salutary illusions, a "true helper" (1.281/118) of philosophy.

---

31. While Church (2019, p. 149) is correct that philosophers are legislators of values for Nietzsche, this does not make them the founders of a people (ibid.)—that is a separate task that belongs to the artist. He is more accurate in saying that Nietzsche thought Wagner to be the best hope for a transformation of culture at large, but this does not make him a "distinctively modern exemplar" (ibid., pp. 227–228), as is shown also by the multiple comparisons of Wagner to Aeschylus (1.446, 1.467, 1.490/273, 292, 313).

Second, it is highly questionable how far Wagner's work could change humanity as a whole, even if one admits that it has the capacity to (re)create a people. For there are many peoples and many artists, and it is difficult to imagine that, as powerful as Wagner's art may be, it would work equally powerfully on everyone regardless of their mother language and other differences, and that Wagner would achieve an unquestioned preeminence over all other artists. But perhaps a weaker version of this argument would be defensible: If Wagner succeeded in (re)creating a people—be it the German people, a "people" of Wagnerians of various nations, or anything else—and if the ennobling effects of his art among this "people" were visible enough, perhaps other artists would follow Wagner's suit, create works with similar potential, and (re)create other noble(r) peoples. The Earth would then not be united, but it would at least be divided into multiple noble cultures that would compete with each other in human excellence, as the Greek cities did in Nietzsche's view.[32] A multitude of noble cultures in an *agon* with each other for eternal glory among the mortals would for Nietzsche surely be a great breeding ground for genius of all kinds, and definitely a major improvement over the contemporary situation.

IV.3. Wagnerian Musical Education

Looking forward into Wagner's future, Nietzsche sees another way in which his music would be particularly beneficial for the denatured modern people: It could serve as a basis of a *musical education*. That is to say, it could serve as a means by which one could "found the state on music" and thereby follow the example of the ancient Greeks (1.458/284). To see what precisely is entailed by this proposal, we need carefully to follow the argument of *WB* 5–6.

Wagner understands the crisis of modernity through one of its most visible symptoms—the alienation of language. In the modern world, "language

---

32. Cf. *Homer's Contest*, and Nietzsche's account of the Seven Sages in his lectures on the Pre-Platonic philosophers (KGW II.4, pp. 226–230). Here he points out that only four names are always present among the Seven (Thales, Solon, Bias, and Pittacus), whereas the holders of the other three "places of honor" were *sought*, and cities strove to add their particular wise man to this exclusive group. There were in total 22 men who were (at various times and places) counted among the Seven; Nietzsche characterizes this situation as "a great contest of *sophia*" (ibid., p. 228).

154 | The Young Nietzsche's Education

always had to climb up to the very last rungs it could reach" (1.455/281) so as to provide an adequate conceptual apparatus for the rapidly expanding edifice of science. It thus becomes ever more adapted to the needs of modern science, and its registers become oriented ever more on thought rather than on feeling (1.455/281). But there is a major unforeseen consequence to this "theoreticization" of language: Through this process it also becomes ever less capable of fulfilling its primary task, namely "to enable suffering human beings to communicate with one another about their most basic necessities of life" (1.455/281)—these needs being *felt* and thus requiring language likewise oriented on feeling. Thus, thanks to this alienation of language from its original purpose, modern humans have become alienated from their true needs. They are unable to communicate them and even to express them for themselves. Simply said, they no longer have the words for them—this is what Nietzsche means when he says that we moderns have to suffer also "under *convention*" (1.455/281) in addition to our other, more universal sufferings. And, Nietzsche tells us, this is a major problem, as feeling is more primary for humans than thinking and concepts, and we can hardly be "a being who thinks and reasons correctly" if we are not first "someone who feels correctly" (1.456/282).

Nietzsche's expression in *WB* for this self-alienation of the modern humans is "incorrect feeling"—a term loosely based on an argument from Wagner's *Opera and Drama* (cf. Wagner 1983, 7.225/1966, II.231). He then proceeds to analyze the influence of the incorrect feeling on modern life in terms consistent with the critique of the philistine pseudo-culture in *DS* 1–3. The two principal instances of incorrect feeling in the modern world, discussed at 1.462/287, are the valuation of moneymaking over higher human pursuits, and the valuation of the timely affairs over "concern for the matters of eternity." Incorrect feeling means the instinctive attitudes of the sick modern soul (cf. Chapter II.3) that doesn't know its genuine good and seeks its good instead in pursuing the satisfaction of various insatiable—in fact, unsatisfiable—desires that are mere extensions of our animality (cf. 1.378/209–210). Nietzsche emphasizes the latter feature of "incorrect feeling" with phrases like "here there is no hunger and no satiety" (1.460/286) or "the omnipresence of a filthy, insatiable greed" (1.462/287). In short, the incorrectly feeling moderns "call their unhappiness 'happiness' and willfully collaborate in their own misfortune" (1.461/287).

This alienation can go so far as to make them into "will-less slaves of incorrect feeling" (1.461/287),[33] into automata whose lives are completely

---

33. This phrase harks back to "the tortured slaves of the three M's, Moment, Majority

Richard Wagner in Bayreuth | 155

governed by external structures such as work, journalism, and public opinion, and whose decisions and plans are mere choices from pre-given options provided by these conventional structures (cf. Chapter I.2); as Hutter (2006, p. 31) puts it, "in such conditions, human beings do not live, they are being lived." The only power within them that objects to the barbaric life they lead is their conscience, and therefore they strive hard to silence it. Their learning has a *"preparatory apologetic* character" (1.463/288) against the accusations of their conscience, against the voice that tells them—if only ever so quietly—to "be yourself! You are none of those things that you now do, think, and desire" (1.338/172). Art for them becomes "either a nothing or an evil something" (1.461/286), its task is "to stupefy or intoxicate" them (1.463/288): It is *divertissement*, a way of temporarily silencing the incorruptible critic within their souls. This is why under these circumstances "we must even consider the *avowed enemy of art* to be a true and useful ally" (1.460/285): Their hostility to art is hostility to its contemporary debased form, to art as *divertissement*. In short, the alienated modern humans have no way of facing their conscience squarely and of carrying out what it asks of them—that much is said by the word "incorrect feeling"—and thus "they prefer to be hunted, wounded, and torn to pieces rather than to have to live with themselves in solitude" (1.461/286).

Such is Wagner's diagnosis of the alienation of modern humanity. Moreover, he sees music as a necessary corrective against this alienation. He sees evidence of the *necessity* of this relationship in the fact that it is precisely now, in the modern times, that music achieved an unheard-of preeminence above the other forms of art, and in the emergence of "a series of great artists" from Bach through Beethoven to Wagner himself in the recent past (1.454/280–281). But how can music help us overcome the affliction of incorrect feeling, insofar as we are an "existence that fights for *conscious freedom* and *independence of thought*" (1.454/280)? How is music, in Wagner's—and Nietzsche's—view, capable of teaching us *"correct feeling"* (1.456/282)? What is the relation between music and life—genuinely *human* life—that they saw?

I believe the answer has to do with the "content" of Wagner's music, with what it "represents." If we take our bearing from the argument of Chapter IV.2, what "actually resounds" (1.456/282) in Wagner's music is a very intense articulation of the need to live nobly rather than comfortably, an articulation that is unique to the medium of music. We need not believe with Schopenhauer that music is "a *copy of the Will itself*" (*WWR* I, § 52, p.

Opinion, and Modishness" from *SE* 6 (1.392/222–223).

156 | The Young Nietzsche's Education

257/*Werke* I.366) to know from personal experience that it has an extraordinary power of appealing to our passions, whether by rousing or soothing them, whether by putting them into a tension or by harmonizing them. In a word, music has a unique way of speaking to our feelings. If we keep this in mind, it is no longer that surprising to claim that music may be able to play an important role in their cultivation, in the sentimental education of modern humans. And it becomes even less surprising when we remember that there is another thinker, central not just to Nietzsche's thought, but to all of Western philosophy, who stressed the power of music to affect the irrational parts of our soul—in common language, our "feelings"—and the educative uses of music: namely the divine Plato, who gave a prominent place to musical education ("musical" in the wide sense of everything that is "of the Muses," i.e., what we could call cultural education) both in the *Republic* (376e–403e) and in the *Laws* (Books II and VII).

For Plato, the purpose of education in general is properly to order the irrational passions of the human soul even before reason becomes capable of doing such ordering, so that reason faces less resistance from the irrational parts of the soul when the time comes for it to assert itself as the soul's proper ruling faculty. As the Athenian Stranger explains in the *Laws* (653b), education effects that "Pleasure and liking, pain and hatred, become correctly arranged in the souls of those who are not yet able to reason, and then, when the souls do become capable of reasoning, these passions can in consonance [*symphonia*] with reason affirm that they have been correctly habituated in the appropriate habits." Education, then, aims at the young (in the biological sense), whose reason is not yet fully developed. Their passions nevertheless need to be ordered in a way that is in accord with the future order in which reason is the rightful ruler of one's soul. However, since reason cannot do this work yet, we need non-rational means for this ordering. And these means are the various musical arts, as the Stranger goes on to explain: He says that (*Laws* 653d) "the gods have ordained the change of holidays as times of rest from labor. They have given as fellow celebrants the Muses, with their leader Apollo, and Dionysus—in order that these divinities may set humans right again." He then adds that the gods have also given us "the pleasant perception of rhythm and harmony" (*Laws* 654a), perceptions that allow us to enjoy songs and dances, and finally suggests that choruses—a chorus being "the combination of dance and song taken together as a whole" (*Laws* 654b)—divided by age and sex groups, with a content suited for each particular group, would be the best way of habituating the souls of the citizens of Magnesia to virtue.[34]

Musical education for Plato entails not just dancing, but also gymnastics in a wider sense: Gymnastics arises from, and cultivates, the natural human tendency to move and jump around that we exhibit as soon as we can. Music, its counterpart, cultivates our natural tendency to make noises of all sorts: "these motions and cries were the source of music and gymnastic" (*Laws* 672c). Nietzsche was familiar with this Platonic conception, as can be seen from the note 5 [14] (7.95–96), in which he made notes on some of the same passages I discussed in the preceding paragraph. We may, then, safely assume that he was also aware of the basic principle underlying the Platonic musical education: As the Athenian Stranger puts it (*Laws* 659d), "education is the drawing and pulling of children toward the argument that is said to be correct by the law and is also believed, on account of experience, to be really correct by those who are most decent and oldest."[35] It follows that "the things we call songs" are in fact "incantations for souls" that lead them toward feeling correctly about each and every matter relevant to virtue, but "since the souls of the young cannot sustain seriousness, these incantations are called 'games' and 'songs,'" and are treated as such" (*Laws* 659e). In short, the purpose of Platonic musical education, both in the *Laws* and in the *Republic*, is to "make the irrational realm [of the soul]

---

34. Valiquette Moreau (2017) offers a valuable account of why the *musical* part of "musical education" is essential to its efficacy, which served as an inspiration for the argument of this section. She shows that in the *Republic*, Socrates argues that "the soul has a musical structure" and that it "requires tuning in order to achieve harmony" (ibid., p. 203)—i.e., tuning by the means of suitable music. That is why in the *Republic*, "music is the means by which [the guardians] are to preserve the system of education upon which the harmony of the city depends" (ibid., p. 201).

35. Cf. also the forceful formulation of the same principle in the *Republic* (401d–2a), where Socrates tells Glaucon that "the rearing in music is most sovereign" because "rhythm and harmony most of all insinuate themselves into the inmost part of the soul and most vigorously lay hold of it in bringing grace with them; and they make a man graceful if he is correctly reared, if not, the opposite. [. . .] And, due to his having the right kind of dislikes, he would praise the fine things; and, taking pleasure in them and receiving them into his soul, he would be reared on them and become a gentleman. He would blame and hate the ugly in the right way while he's still young, before he's able to grasp reasonable speech [*logos*]. And when reasonable speech [*logos*] comes, the man who's reared in this way would take most delight in it, recognizing it on account of its being akin."

158 | The Young Nietzsche's Education

that which it is capable of being without knowing it, namely *a realm of unconscious rationality*," in Jan Patočka's (2022, p. 84) words.[36]

Such a conception of musical education is, roughly, what Nietzsche has in mind when he says that the Greeks demanded of themselves to found the state on music. This is also why he considers music to be a great "educational force" (1.458/284) that has (re)appeared in modern times.[37] If we look at Wagner's music from this perspective, we'll see that it produces in its audience a sensitivity to their genuine needs (cf. 1.333/166)—to what is necessary for their spiritual growth and/or for the cultivation of their tragic sensibility. In other words, it *attunes* them to these needs, and conversely, it tunes them out of caring for the pseudo-needs that are propagated by the empty modern conventions and by the alienated modern language.

Furthermore, by instilling this correct feeling in the souls of its listeners, Wagner's music also "expresses the longing for its natural sister, *gymnastics*" (1.458/283): It demands that appropriate outward motions accompany the inner motions—the feelings—it has awakened within the soul.[38] That is to say, it fosters within us "the true concept of form as a necessary formation" (1.457/283), as opposed to the modern conception of form as an arbitrary convention that bears no relation to the "content" it presents (cf. 1.275/112). Thus it promotes not just the unity of style that is a sign of genuine culture, but also the unity of one's thinking and actions, and it

---

36. Gabriel Richardson Lear argues along similar lines that "Plato believes that, with sufficient repetition, the practice of mimesis will train us to take some sort of non-rational pleasure in the outward manifestation—in the appearance—of the character-type imitated" (2011, p. 197). If she is correct that for Plato, the real danger of dramatic poetry is "the *multifariousness* of mimesis"—i.e., the variety of characters being imitated (and especially bad characters) rather than *mimesis* as such (ibid., p. 198), this would make Nietzsche's Wagnerian-Platonic musical education especially conducive not just to the cultivation of one's soul, but to an external culture defined as unity of artistic style (1.163/9) as well.

37. The idea of music and tragedy as means of education appears very early on in Nietzsche's thinking: cf. notes such as 5 [9] (7.94); 7 [139] (7.195); or 19 [274] (7.505).

38. Wagner offers a somewhat similar conception of the relation of music and gymnastics in his essay *On Musical Criticism* (Wagner, 1983, 6.385, 389/1966, III.68, 71), a conception that also harks back to the ancient Greeks (in particular to the Athenians). Nietzsche takes up Wagner's words and uses them in his much more ambitious conception. Nietzsche thus makes his conception of musical education appear much closer to Wagner's conception than it actually is: He uses the same *words* as Wagner, and thereby masks the difference of *concepts* underlying those words. More generally, *WB* contains a wealth of borrowings from and allusions to various writings of Wagner, which are documented by Mazzino Montinari in KGW IV.4, 119–160.

Richard Wagner in Bayreuth | 159

works contrary to the modern tendency toward the "weak" or "split" personality that consists precisely in the lack of connection between thinking and action (cf. Chapter II.3). It also works against the related phenomena of philistine pseudo-culture, which is "the chaotic hodgepodge of all styles" as opposed to the unity of style (1.163/9), and of the use of culture as a "'*beautiful form*,'" a mere decoration, by those who "are conscious of an *ugly or boring content*" (1.389/220).

Such a "spiritual" understanding of gymnastics again has its precedent in Plato, who has Socrates argue in the *Republic* that although gymnastics is apparently done for the sake of the body, its ultimate importance is for maintaining the proper harmony within the soul: Souls that lack gymnastic training become cowardly and easily excitable, while souls that lack musical education become savage and misologistic (*Republic* 410c–11e). Nietzsche's reasoning here is analogical: While the term "gymnastics" refers primarily to exercise of the body, its true importance lies in its promoting of the plastic force of one's soul, that is, of the robustness of the order within one's soul.

The practical form a gymnastics thus understood would assume would be various kinds of "dancing"—rhythmic motions with emphasis on breathing and on becoming aware of the organic rhythms of one's living body [*Leib*]: We can consider yoga and martial arts (Hutter, 2006, p. 195), or the dancing of Xenophon's Socrates (Hutter, 2006, p. 71; cf. Xenophon, *Symposium* II.15–19), as kindred practices. This "gymnastics in the Greek and Wagnerian sense" (1.459/284) is, then, in an important sense a spiritual exercise, a "gymnastics of willing"[39] that teaches us to take control of our outward lives and to shape them according to our innermost needs. This is another way in which Wagner's music is capable of re-naturalizing its audiences and their spiritual development.[40]

The structure and purpose of this Wagnerian musical education are, then, fully analogous to its Platonic forerunner. Music in concert with gymnastics is to train or harmonize the various feelings or passions that

---

39. On this term and its potential practical applications, cf. Hutter (2013).

40. Alternatively, Hutter (2006, p. 187) suggests that Plato's (and hence also Nietzsche's) conception of musical education "would seem to follow a social practice known from many traditional cultures in which communal orgiastic abandonment to chaotic forces of the soul periodically interrupt the normal performances of social labor." On this account, this "gymnastics" would also be a way of discharging various normally repressed passions in a controlled manner, thus preventing their festering in the subconscious part of the soul and occasional uncontrolled, chaotic outbreaks of such passions. This would be yet another way in which gymnastics contributes to a healthy balance of forces within the soul.

160 | The Young Nietzsche's Education

coexist within our soul in the correct way before we are able to do this consciously.[41] It is a pre-rational or pre-conscious preparation of the order the soul requires for its proper work, which can be performed only at a later stage of spiritual maturity (and which would be significantly more difficult if the lower elements of the soul were striving in a direction that is contrary to this work). The main difference between the Platonic and the Wagnerian musical education lies in the particular order that it is supposed to prepare in the soul: For Plato this means a soul that is harmonized under the rule of the *logistikon*, the "rational part" of the soul, while for Nietzsche the goal is a soul that knows itself in the sense of knowing "the fundamental law of [its] authentic self" (1.340/174), and which is willing and able to follow this innermost tendency wherever it leads. For Nietzsche, the "correct feeling" that Wagner's music should instill in the young is feeling that is consistent with the imperative *be yourself*—it is this imperative itself in the form of affective preference rather than of conscious understanding. It is a subconscious preparation for the later conscious choice of the life of culture.

However, it has to be emphasized that the musical education sketched in this section is just Nietzsche's vision or speculation. If it is at all possible that Wagner's music could accomplish these effects, it would be a matter of quite distant future. This education would first have to be elaborated in detail, institutionalized, and given a solid place in the structures of German culture. And even then, its efficacy in shaping the souls of the young would depend on how early in their life it begins and with what precision and regularity it is practiced. As Plato's Socrates says (*Republic* 377a–b), "Don't you know that the beginning is the most important part of every work and that this is especially so with anything young and tender? For at that stage it's most plastic, and each thing assimilates itself to the model whose stamp anyone wishes to give to it." The earlier the age at which the education starts, the better the eventual results (cf. *Republic* 429d–30b). And, being based on the same principles, the same holds for the possible Wagnerian musical education of the future. Its influence on the present-day people should be sought rather in the effect of alienation from the alleged

---

41. In accordance with the twofold audience of Wagner's art we can distinguish a twofold emphasis in the process of harmonizing one's passions: the emphasis on one's genuine needs for the would-be geniuses, and the emphasis on the tragic sensibility, or unconditional devotion to a higher cause, for the lower type of audience. The difference between these two groups is fundamentally a matter of self-selection; cf. Chapter III, fn. 50.

Richard Wagner in Bayreuth | 161

certainties and necessities of one's unreflective existence so far, which was described in Chapter IV.2.

IV.4. Finale: The Free Human Beings of the Future

We have seen the importance that Wagner's art holds according to Nietzsche: It is capable of strengthening those who strive for their higher selves to persevere in their difficult endeavor; it can induce a feeling of alienation from everyday life in its audience, a feeling that is conducive to their turning toward this striving; by articulating this fundamental human need, it can create a community of those who feel it and who find a satisfaction in watching Wagner's heroes pursue the same goal; and finally, it may become a basis of a new system of musical education based on the Platonic model. In sum, it provides us with the means to pursue the genius within us. Wagner's art thus provides us with the answer to the last of the questions posed at 1.177/23: It is Nietzsche's "courage." The questions Nietzsche posed to D. F. Strauss—and implicitly to himself as well—are now all answered, and the project of the *UC* is almost fully laid out. The last remaining task is gather all its strands together, and so to show what future is this project meant to lead toward: What kind of human beings will it educate, and what kind of world will they create and live in?

Nietzsche describes the character of these human beings of the future in the first two paragraphs of *WB* 11. He first insists that Wagner—and by extension also Nietzsche himself—is no utopian: His goal isn't remaking human beings according to some fanciful notion that has no foundation in experience, such as that all people should be brothers and sisters and live in perfect harmony. Nietzsche and Wagner rather strive to change the changeable in us in accord with the unchangeable necessity (cf. 1.445/272), with human nature and its true height as they came to know it from their own experience, from their own struggle to become what they are. Their legislation of human greatness is originary justice based on their knowledge of that which is. Their teaching is meant to help others cultivate themselves in a similar manner, to help them become spiritually as free and healthy as Nietzsche and Wagner are.

These men of the future may not look very appealing to us on the first sight: Nietzsche says they might "seem on the whole even more evil" than the people of today, and it is possible that the sight of them "would shake up and terrify our soul" (1.506/327). This is because these people

162 | The Young Nietzsche's Education

will be characterized above all by *openness*, for good as well as for evil. However, this doesn't mean they will not have any standards; they won't be spiritual anarchists for whom "anything goes." It is rather that the current (post-)Christian moral conventions of good and evil (*böse*) will hold little importance to them. *Their* standard will be human nature and the process of growth inherent in it; and in terms of this standard, they will be good rather than bad (*schlecht*) human beings.[42] Nietzsche sums up the attitudes of these free human beings as follows (1.506–507/327–328):

> Or how do these statements sound to our ears: that passion is better than stoicism and hypocrisy; that being honest, even where evil is concerned, is better than losing oneself in traditional morality; that the free human being can be both good and evil, but that the unfree human being is a disgrace to nature and shares neither in any heavenly nor in any earthly consolation; finally, that any person who wants to become free must accomplish this through himself, and that freedom does not fall like a surprise gift into anyone's lap.

They will know that following the imperative *be yourself* is the path to the only humanly attainable freedom and happiness, to the genius within them; that this is a task only they themselves can accomplish; and that their passions, rather than conventions, are what they should take their guidance from. Moreover, they will also *feel* these attitudes, attitudes that are "*precisely* what I earlier called correct feeling" (1.507/328; emphasis added): They will incorporate them so deeply that they will become a second nature to them, a "new and improved *physis*" (1.334/167).

The key distinction in their ethical thinking will be between the naturalness of themselves and their striving to further growth, and the unnaturalness of the spiritually crippled modern society. Their naturalness will be the source of their freedom: the freedom from the degrading influence of modern society, the freedom to pursue their own genuine self that is immeasurably high above them and to genuinely act as a consequence of this pursuit. They will know that the modern unfree humans don't live, but are "being lived" (Hutter, 2006, p. 31); that they are not capable of

---

42. Nietzsche's argument here recalls the ancient conception of *arete* ("virtue") as the excellence that is proper to a particular kind of being, and prefigures the "good–bad" vs. "good–evil" distinction of *GM* I.

any greatness whatsoever (cf. *Republic* 495b); and that they are "a disgrace to nature and shares neither in any heavenly nor in any earthly consolation" (1.506–507/328).[43] Ultimately, they will see *the* fundamental choice we as human beings have to make as between genuinely *leading* one's life, that is, a life that seeks to grow and that finds meaning in the further unfolding of itself, and "leading" a comfortable life that can find no such meaning, that amounts to senseless suffering—and knows this if it doesn't anesthetize itself with *divertissements*. Nietzsche concludes with the sharpest possible formulation of this distinction, which marks the free humans beings of the future as life-affirming and their unfree counterparts as life-denying because they lack any genuine way of coming to terms with the suffering life inevitably entails: "the [unnatural] does *not* want to be; the [natural] wants to be *different*"[44] (1.507/328).[45]

These free humans will use Wagner's art as it is meant to be used—as art *as such* ought to be used: It will provide them with salutary mythic images of their own life and striving, and it will strengthen them for the trials and sufferings they have to undergo. They will furthermore strive to make a "people" of their kind, a free people, a genuine community based on a shared highest need and a shared satisfaction thereof, that is, on a shared highest goal (1.506/327; cf. 1.278/115, and Lampert, 2017, p. 121). We can see what their shared highest need or ruling passion is from the satisfaction they derive from Wagner's art, from the myths it provides them with: It is the need to become their true selves, wherever it may lead them and whatever it may cost them. Wagner will thus be for them "the interpreter and transfigurer of the past" (1.510/331), but this will be a mythical-symbolic account of their own past strivings, not an actual interpretation of the historical past, as has been argued above (cf. 1.262/100; contra Brooks, 2018, p. 204).

Bayreuth is to be the central institution of this program: a meeting place for the community or "people" of those devoted to the new, genuine culture, and a place of their spiritual renewal. Here they will be able to relax their spiritual tension and draw strength "for further and higher willing" (1.449/276); and here they will meet and discuss their various projects to

---

43. Nietzsche will quote and affirm this passage at the end of *GS* 99.

44. "Different" in the sense of being ever higher and higher than it currently is.

45. Cf. *CW* Epilogue: "The Christian wants to *escape* from [themselves]. [. . .]—On the other hand, noble morality, master morality, is rooted in a triumphant *self*-directed Yes,—it is self-affirmation, self-glorification of life."

164 | The Young Nietzsche's Education

spread and enhance their new, genuine culture. Plans for new educational institutions seem to be of particular importance for Nietzsche—institutions of Wagnerian musical education on the one hand, and on the other hand the "philosophical monasteries" that Nietzsche hoped he would soon found.[46] These "monasteries" would be institutions focused on the more talented of the young souls, who could find a refuge from the external world in them and work on cultivating their souls, which is to say, strive to "complete their work" (1.403/233). The conditions of these "monasteries" would be conducive to the practice of various kinds of "gymnastics of willing" or spiritual exercises: The members of these communities would be learning to live philosophically in a sense similar to the understanding of the ancient philosophical schools.[47] Thereby they would become ever more "themselves" and produce new geniuses—all thanks to the work of Nietzsche and Wagner that provided· the foundations for this process.[48] The Bayreuth festival

---

46. As discussed in *SE* 6 and Chapter III.4. This idea appears as early as in the letter to Rohde from 15 December 1870, where Nietzsche plans "a new *Greek* academy"—the word *Greek* pointing to the Platonic Academy, of course—and explicitly connects this idea with "*Wagner's* plan for Bayreuth" (KGB II.1, p. 165). In the same letter Nietzsche speculates on how to get funds for this plan, including trying their luck in lotteries, and generally using "any not forbidden means" (ibid., p. 166). Also cf. the notes 16 [45] (8.294) and 17 [50] (8.305)—both from 1876—which call for the establishment of modern "monasteries" for "free spirits." In the letter to Reinhart von Seydlitz from 24 September 1876 he describes his upcoming stay in Sorrento as "a kind of monastery for free spirits," and expresses the hope of founding "my monastery, I mean "the school of educators" (where these educate *themselves*) in a *higher style*" (KGB II.5, pp. 188–189). The usage of the word "monastery" probably denotes that these new institutions are to be places of contemplation sequestered from the outside world (cf. *GS* 280). It is one of several similar approximations: Elsewhere Nietzsche says it could be "also called a modern monastery, an ideal colony, [or] université libre" (15.71). Hutter (2006, pp. 32–33) notes that Nietzsche strived to establish such an institution not just in his early years, but throughout his active life. For evidence we can turn, e.g., to the postcard to Peter Gast from 26 March 1879, where he asks, "*Where* do we want to renew the garden of Epicurus?" (KGB II.5, p. 399); or to the letter to his mother and sister from 28 November 1884, where he says he wants to stay in Nizza [today's Nice] "for the purpose of *my* future 'colony,'" which now seems more possible to me (I mean: nice people whom I can teach my philosophy)" (KGB III.1, p. 563).

47. Cf. Hutter (2006, pp. 32–33) on the exercises practiced in these schools, including the importance of "gymnastics" in the general sense of cultivation of the body for one's spiritual growth. For a more thorough account of the ancient spiritual exercises, but without reference to Nietzsche, cf. Hadot 1995, ch. 3.

48. Again, there are multiple statements of Nietzsche on this subject in his notebooks. Cf. the notes 5 [11] (8.43): "There lie my hopes: the breeding of significant people";

Richard Wagner in Bayreuth | 165

would in effect be the annual council of the chief representatives of this new culture and its flagship event.

At the center of this entire project lies the conception of the human soul and its natural growth, articulated principally in *HL* 1 and *SE* 1, but operative throughout the *UC*. Everything in these essays is written with reference to this conception of the soul and the structures that constitute it: the ways in which the soul should be cultivated, the goal of becoming the genius within oneself, the choice of Nietzsche's audience (the "young souls"), the rhetoric he uses to appeal to them, the project of the educational institutions of the future, as well as the image of the free human beings these institutions will educate. From the critique of the contemporary pseudo-culture in *DS*, through the diagnosis of the psychic pathologies underlying this pseudo-culture in *HL*, the appeal to the young souls' conscience and exposition of how one learns what one's authentic self is in *SE*, up to the powers ascribed and the tasks assigned to Wagner's art in *WB*: All this emerges as a single, coherent project when seen in the light of the erotic-historic conception of the human soul, and of the growth of such a soul as guided by the fundamental law of its unfolding (cf. 1.340/174). Already in the *UC*, psychology is "the queen of the sciences" and "the way to the fundamental problems" (*BGE* 23).

The project of the *UC* is one of reshaping, or rather re-naturalizing the world by teaching individual souls how to counter their current denaturalization, how to (re)shape themselves, and thus how to attain the genuine human good (as Nietzsche understands it at this point), with the hope that these methods and attitudes of self-shaping will soon become an influential force in German, and eventually European, culture. It is a project of establishing a new originary justice, a new legislation for life, a new way of life that is founded on insight into that which is, into "the unalterable character and bone structure of human nature" (1.506/327; cf. 1.445/272). This project is open to anyone willing to devote themselves to it, and it offers to each person the satisfaction of their innermost need—of the need to spend their life in a truly meaningful way—according to one's capacity of understanding this need. There will be ways of contributing to it for the smallest as well as for the highest of human capacities, and satisfactions that any of them may require. And there will be a community of all who find their satisfaction in this striving—a community in which, at least for the

---

5 [22] (8.46): "My religion, if I still may call something that, lies in the work for the production of genius; and 5 [25] (8.47): "*To educate educators! But the first ones have to educate themselves!* And these are who I write for."

166 | The Young Nietzsche's Education

duration of Wagner's artistic illusions, "the only supreme blessings and joys that exist are those common to the hearts of all people" (1.503–504/325).

This is the future as it was projected by the twin geniuses of Nietzsche and Wagner,[49] of the latter-day Plato and Homer working together for their shared goal, as Wagner wrote to Nietzsche in 1870: *This* is "the great "renaissance" in which Plato embraces Homer, and Homer, filled with Plato's Ideas, now really becomes the greatest Homer of all" (KGB II.2, 146). Indeed, "[*WB*] is full of world-historical accents" (*EH* BT 4), as Nietzsche tells us twelve years later, in 1888: And the meaning of its immense hopes and projects can be properly understood only on the foundation that the previous three *UC* provide. The world-historical hopes of *WB* are the hopes of the project of the *UC* as a whole. The only thing to be done now is to execute the project, and that will happen soon enough: The future shall begin on 13 August 1876.

---

49. At 1.498/320 Nietzsche describes Wagner with a quotation from Schopenhauer's essay *Ideas concerning the Intellect generally and in all respects* (*PP* II, p. 87/*Werke* V.105). This quotation characterizes the genius as such and forms the finale of the entire essay.

V

The Failures—and the Successes— of the *Untimely Considerations*

What I, in my "younger years," once wrote about Schopenhauer and Richard Wagner—or rather, what I *painted* about them, perhaps in an all-too-audacious, overly confident, and overly youthful *al fresco*—is something I certainly have no desire to examine in detail today as "true" or "false." But provided I have erred back then: At least my error dishonored neither them nor me! It *is* something to err *in such a way*; it *is* also something to seduce *me* of all people to error in such a way. [. . .] And whoever reads those writings with a young and fiery soul may be able to guess the serious vows by which I have bound myself for life back then—by which I have decided for *my* life: May this reader be one of those few who *can* decide for the same kind of life and for the same vows![1]

However, the prophesied future did not come to pass. The inaugural Bayreuth festival did begin on 13 August 1876, and it was Wagner's great triumph after decades of hardship and struggle, as Nietzsche himself admits—"Bayreuth signifies the greatest victory an artist has ever achieved" (*HA* II Preface 1)—but its reality was far removed from the grand hopes Nietzsche had expressed for it in *WB*. Bayreuth turned out nothing like the triumph of the new, genuine culture Nietzsche had hoped it would be. With attendees like the German Kaiser Wilhelm I or the Brazilian emperor Pedro II, whose presence signaled the admission of Wagner into the officially recognized

---

1. *Nachlass* from 1885, note 41 [2], 11.670–671.

168 | The Young Nietzsche's Education

canon of German greatness and into high society, the festival was pandering to the old philistine pseudo-culture and to the German *Reich*. The Wagners themselves mostly ignored Nietzsche, as they were too busy entertaining the various rich and powerful elites in attendance (Janz, 1978, 1.716). Wagner in effect chose popular success over any of the ambitions and aspirations to a cultural revolution he had professed in the past.[2] As Nietzsche put it twelve years later, "Wagner had been translated into German! The Wagnerian had become master over Wagner.—*German* art! The *German* master! *German* beer!" (*EH* HA 2). In a word, the reality of Bayreuth was a fiasco from Nietzsche's perspective. It shattered all the hopes he might have had left for Wagner at this point—his break with Wagner was more or less immediate[3]—and he found the festival so difficult to bear that he had to take a break from it and go to a spa in Klingenbrunn to recover from this shock (which included also various physiological difficulties, mostly with his eyes; cf. 15.68, and Janz, 1978, 1.715–716). The letter to Elisabeth Nietzsche from 6 August 1876 (KGB II.5, pp. 182–183) is very telling in this respect: "I know certainly that I *cannot* endure it [in Bayreuth], actually we should have known it beforehand! [. . .] I feel so tired and exhausted from the short stay there that I cannot recover at all."[4]

This event opened the question of how Nietzsche could so mislead himself that, despite all he privately knew about Wagner, he didn't realize Wagner would choose popular success over the cause of genuine culture.

---

2. On this subject consider Nietzsche's later critique of Wagner as essentially an actor for whom avowing principles of any kind was just a means to enhance his stature and to increase his popular success: "Wagner could not care less about principles, even his own!" (*CW* Postscript; cf. *CW* passim).

3. The last personal meeting of the two men took place in late 1876 (cf. 15.70–71 and the letter to Elisabeth Nietzsche from 28 Oct. 1876, KGB II.5, 197). They ceased to have any contact thereafter, expect for the last letter Wagner sent to Nietzsche: a copy of the text of *Parsifal* accompanied by a short greeting, signed "Richard Wagner, Chief Church Councilor" (letter from 1 Jan. 1878, KGB II.6.2, 788), upon which Nietzsche comments in *EH* HA 5. Critical references to Wagner started to appear in Nietzsche's works, at first in a veiled manner (e.g., *HA* 215), but later on (especially after Wagner's death) also openly. Wagner too hadn't refrained from a veiled critique of Nietzsche in his essay *Audience and Popularity*, published after *HA* showed Nietzsche's break from him to be definitive.

4. The letter speaks apparently only of Nietzsche's physical state, but it is fully plausible to read it as simultaneously commenting on his spiritual state after the great disappointment of Bayreuth—a disappointment he did not expect, although he seems to think he should have known better, given his private critiques of Wagner discussed at the beginning of Chapter IV.

The Failures—and the Successes—of the *Untimely Considerations* | 169

All of Nietzsche's earlier hopes, however conditional they may have been, have come to nothing. And if he was as wrong about Wagner as has now become apparent, what *else* was he wrong about? Did he have an adequate understanding of what genuine culture is? And how about the basis of culture, that is, about the nature of the human soul? The shock caused by the reality of Bayreuth had triggered a deep crisis in Nietzsche: a crisis that consisted in a sudden loss of all ground, in a realization that what were up to now his central beliefs are nowhere near as evident as he had thought, and that he has to rethink the very premises of his intellectual activity and of his way of life. He described this crisis in retrospect as "a total aberration of my instinct" (*EH* HA 3). This strong phrase points to the core problem behind the immediate disappointment of Bayreuth: If Nietzsche's instinct had led him into such a dead end, how can he trust it again? How does he know that the instinct will not lead him into a similar disappointment in his next engagement? Can the instinct be trusted *at all*? In sum, Nietzsche realized that he needed a thorough examination of his thinking and of his actions as a public writer so far, which he tells us he had undertaken in the years of writing *Human, All Too Human* and its two sequels.[5]

The retrospective note 9 [42] (12.354–355) from 1887 is very instructive in this respect. Nietzsche comments here, first, "*around 1876*, when I understood what Wagner is driving at now, I was terrified I would see my entire striving hitherto *compromised*," and second, "around the same time I felt to be inextricably *incarcerated* in my philology and teaching." Third, and most importantly, he had realized that "my instinct drives at the opposite of Schopenhauer's instinct: at a justification of life, even at its most terrible, most ambiguous, and most mendacious:—for that I had the formula "Dionysian" in my hands." In short, he became aware of his bad choice of allies, bad choice of occupation, and that his instinct failed to hit the target it aimed at, that his conceptualization of the goal of life-affirmation was completely inadequate. A reflection was overdue on all these fronts.[6]

---

5. "*Human, All Too Human* is the monument of a crisis" (*EH* HA 1). For a thorough account of this self-examination, cf. Meier, 2019, ch. IV, esp. pp. 104–106.

6. We find contemporary evidence for the third point, for his realization of the inadequacy of his earlier Schopenhauer-influenced presentation of philosophy and "life-affirmation," in the letter to Cosima Wagner from 19 December 1876. Nietzsche confesses here "a disagreement with Schopenhauer's teaching which came about gradually, but which I realized almost in an instant," and goes on to say that "On virtually all general propositions I am not on his side; already when I was writing about Schopenhauer [in *SE*], I noticed that I'm beyond everything dogmatic; all that mattered to me was the *human being*" [i.e., Schopenhauer as his educator; cf. Chapter III, fn. 26 and 65] (KGB II.5, p. 210).

170 | The Young Nietzsche's Education

Here we come the second meaning of "the young Nietzsche's education": It is Nietzsche's own self-critique and self-education in the light of the failure of the project of the *UC*. The would-be educator of the young souls disgusted by the poverty of contemporary pseudo-culture came to see how much he was entangled in that very pseudo-culture he strived to fight against. He had to radically reflect on and examine the premises of his own thought and rethink the principles of his activity as a public writer.

Now that the project of the *UC* and the thinking behind it have been fully laid out, I reconstruct this reflection and rethinking with reference to the *UC* themselves. I take a synoptic and critical look at the *UC*—both at their weaknesses and failures that had set up the situation in which Nietzsche's crisis fully manifested itself, and at their successes that withstood the crisis and were further developed in his later thinking. I assess these failures and successes from the perspective of the mature philosopher Nietzsche. I begin with a couple of critical points about the *project* of the *UC*, addressing in particular its unrealistically grandiose scale. Thereafter I critique the *thought* behind the *UC* with the aim of diagnosing the core from which the many other problems of Nietzsche's early thinking issue. After this critique I take a twofold look at the successes of the *UC*: first, at those aspects of his early thought that had proved their worth in the examination of the crisis; and second, at those attitudes that, although they ultimately were not fully adequate to Nietzsche's mature thought, were instrumental in helping him carry out the necessary self-examination—attitudes that, as it were, formed a ladder on which the young Nietzsche climbed up to what he is, to the philosopher Nietzsche.

V.1. The Failure of the Project of the *UC*

Beyond the effect the *UC* may have on individual readers, their project relies heavily on Wagner's planned transformation of the entire German culture: Nietzsche conceived Wagner's project as a vehicle for his own project, or as the first stage thereof. However, it remains very unclear how exactly their transformation of German and European culture is supposed to have looked. Let us imagine for a moment that Bayreuth had in fact fulfilled Nietzsche's expectation, that it had been a triumphant presentation of the new, genuine culture: What would the next step be? Nietzsche tells us simply that with the reformation of the theater "the modern human being would thereby be changed and reformed: in our modern world one thing is so intimately connected with another" (1.448/275). But he doesn't

The Failures—and the Successes—of the *Untimely Considerations* | 171

discuss or even suggest any concrete mechanisms or processes by which this transformation of the entire German culture, in the extensive sense of "all the vital self-expressions of a people" (1.163/9), would proceed. Even if we imagined that Bayreuth were a complete and resounding success in the narrower cultural-artistic sphere, and consequently the entire musical-theatrical establishment converted to Wagnerianism in a meaningful sense, it by far does not follow that this success would do anything to challenge (let alone transform) powers like the state or capital, which Nietzsche had singled out as great dangers to the cause of genuine culture (1.387–389/218–220). However influential Wagner's cultural productions may become, they would still be in no position to challenge the logic of the profit motive or the state's monopoly on violence. Art may at best hope to influence these powers to treat it favorably for some time, but this hardly amounts to a reform of the entire culture in the extensive sense.

The idea that Wagner's reform of theater will re-create "the onetime reality of the Greek theater" (1.449/276), that theater can have the same effect for us as it did for the Greeks, is questionable as well. It is true that theater can be deeply meaningful for individuals, and in this sense it may well be the opposite of the modern art-as-*divertissement*.[7] But it can hardly have the same effect on the community of citizens. Modern theatrical performances are always played for a relatively small audience, as opposed to the performances of tragedies at the Athenian Dionysia, which were observed by a large part of the citizen body. This is a question of scale: Given how much larger modern political communities are, theatrical performances cannot serve the same purpose in them. In the modern world, theater is a medium for small, elite groups, and not the communal (in the sense of relating to the entire community) affair it was in the ancient city.[8]

Nietzsche's hopes for the transformative effect Wagner's art could have had on the culture at large were out of proportion to what it could

---

7. Incidentally, the technical level of the 1876 props and special effects was so low that it *detracted from* rather than contributed to the audience's absorption into Wagner's mythic stories (Janz, 1978, 1.717–718, 722–723).

8. It is an interesting but tangential question whether modern mass media—especially television and cinema, these heirs of the Wagnerian *Gesamtkunstwerk* in their artistic means—could produce a similar effect in modern societies. They have long overcome the technical limitations of Wagner's time. And the problem of scale no longer exists in them: Thousands and even millions of human beings can be the audience of a single event or artwork simultaneously.

172 | The Young Nietzsche's Education

realistically accomplish. But his hopes went even further than that in seeing Wagner as a potential founder of a new people and, in a certain sense, even a potential unifier of humanity under the banner of the tragic sensibility (cf. Chapter IV.2). This is not to say that great art doesn't have the capacity to create a people by shaping its self-understanding: The Homeric epics, the Torah, the Aeneid, and the Chronicle of Kosmas clearly exemplify this foundational capacity of great art (cf. *Za* I On the Thousand and One Goal; Gmirkin, 2016 passim; Patočka, 2006, pp. 264–266). But this is not a free-standing, absolute capacity: It has certain preconditions that allow it to occur, such as political independence of the community and a long period of uncontested influence of the artwork in question. It would take centuries until Wagner would have changed the self-understanding of the German people and become "the interpreter and transfigurer of the past" (the last words of *WB*: 1.510/331) for them—centuries in which his art, moreover, would have to maintain its preeminence against all past, present, and future competitors. It certainly would be far beyond the lifespan of anyone living at the time of the publication of *WB*. The second possibility, the creation of a supra-national Wagnerian "people," is even more difficult to imagine. Barring a political revolution to this effect (which we have no reason to expect, as no such suggestions were made by either Wagner or Nietzsche), such a "people" would in effect consist of fragments of other peoples who have no political power, organization, or independence of their own, with no power to defend themselves against an external enemy or to compel unity and obedience internally. A "people" of this sort, if it were somehow to arise in the first place, if it were to constitute itself on the basis of a shared fundamental need that they find expressed and satisfied in Wagner's works (cf. 1.278, 1.477, 1. 506, 1.509/115, 301, 327, 330), would be a rather short-lived experiment.

If this is the case regarding Wagner's prospects for the creation of a people, it holds *a fortiori* for the global cultural renaissance and transformation of human life, for the spread of the tragic sensibility among the peoples of the Earth, that this people is supposed to spearhead. Simply put, these are utterly excessive hopes, out of proportion to anything art had *ever* accomplished; and despite his many qualities, Wagner was not in a position to make such a groundbreaking event happen. Even if Wagner actually were committed to the ideals and principles that he publicly professed, and that Nietzsche promotes tirelessly in *WB*, reality would remain far behind their expectations, and Wagner would remain just an artist.

The Failures—and the Successes—of the *Untimely Considerations* | 173

Setting these grander hopes aside, we also have to wonder whether Nietzsche's proposal of new educational institutions would be viable. As described in Chapter IV, fn. 46, Nietzsche dreamed of establishing a philosophic school throughout his productive life. But the description of this institution we get in *SE* (1.402–403/232–233) seems to have a particular twist: the suggestion that *all* members of this institution, the difference in their natural capacities notwithstanding, would be able to live meaningfully and thus become their true self. The suggestion is that *be yourself* is not just the imperative for the future geniuses whose purpose in the institution is "to complete their work," but also for those "with only second- and third-rate talent" (1.403/233). All members of these institutions would contribute to the production of the genius according to their capacities and would in turn be able to cultivate their own genius according to their capacities. This is a surprisingly harmonious—even utopian—picture of the social body, one that is without parallel in Nietzsche's oeuvre before or after the *UC*. Nietzsche would deny that there can be a society in which everyone has become what they are as early as in *The Greek State* with the principle that "*slavery belongs to the essence of a culture*" (1.767). It would be strange if this new, genuine culture should not require some kind of "slavery"—that is, ministerial subordination on part of its less talented members. Nietzsche emphatically returns to the principle from *The Greek State* in his post-*UC* works: cf. *WS* 275; *GS* 4, 21, 23, 116, 296, 356; or *BGE* 262. While the details vary to a certain extent, the principle remains constant: that one can either be a good individual (i.e., attain their true self), or a good (i.e., useful) member of society—but not both, and that not every member of a society can be a good individual. Moreover, this is a well-established principle of Western political thought: In the terms of *Republic* IV, the person who is like the just city is not identical with the citizens of the just city (with the possible exception of the rulers); and Aristotle expresses it as the difference between a good human being and a good citizen (*Politics* III.4). Nietzsche's abandonment of this principle in *SE* is most likely a piece of deceptive rhetoric to match the rhetoric of the culture-perverting forces that likewise (falsely) promise freedom and countless other goods to their followers (1.403/233).

The preceding points are only tangential to the central problem of the project of the *UC*: namely its inseparable connection to Wagner's Bayreuth project. This connection has its roots in the young Nietzsche's misunderstanding of who Wagner was and what he stood for. On one level, Nietzsche

174 | The Young Nietzsche's Education

was deceived by Wagner—deceived into taking Wagner and his professed ideals and plans for a cultural reform "seriously," as he tells us in *CW* 3. The deep friendship Nietzsche shared with Wagner in the latter's Tribschen period certainly contributed to this. But Wagner's great actorly capacity, his ability to project a persona designed to seduce the observer, was also a highly significant factor. Already in this early period Nietzsche ascribed "a natural theatrical gift" to Wagner (1.467/292), and already here he sees it as a problem (albeit he says so only in his private notes—7.756–775—that were discussed at the beginning of Chapter IV). But he thinks Wagner is an actor only in relation to his artistic productions, not to his life as a whole: In fact, in the note 32 [41] (7.766) he writes, "[Wagner's] talent as an actor shows itself in that he is *never* actor in his personal life." Nietzsche had to completely rethink Wagner's relation to his alleged principles, and the deconstruction of Wagner's theoretical writings at the beginning of *CW* 10 is very instructive in this regard. Put simply, Wagner's "principles" were a pose, a mask meant to attract a particular kind of audience and turn them into devotees of Wagner. The audience in question were thymotic or idealistic young men[9] who saw very well the corruption and pettiness of contemporary German culture and yearned for something new and better, for a genuine culture. In other words, they were very much like Nietzsche's principal audience in the *UC*—the young souls—and like the young Nietzsche himself. In his later years, Nietzsche would describe this group as "German younglings."[10] As Nietzsche's principle is not to attack persons, but rather to make use of them "as of a strong magnifying glass" to demonstrate a more general phenomenon on their example (*EH* Wise 7), Wagner isn't special or particularly corrupt with regard to his masks and deceptions. Artists are rather inherently in a position of dependence on some powers that be: "in all ages they have been valets of a morality or philosophy or religion" (*GM* III.5), and so it is imprudent to expect of them any serious intellectual leadership.

The final, and intellectually most interesting, factor that led Nietzsche into Wagner's trap was the latter's Schopenhauerian pessimism—Schopenhauer being also the subject of their very first conversation and thus the beginning of their friendship (cf. Chapter I.1). In *GS* 370, Nietzsche admits

---

9. Nietzsche attributes quite different motives to the typical female Wagnerian (cf. *CW* Postscript), although in principle it is possible that a woman could belong among the "German younglings."

10. Cf. the note 37 [5] (11.579), discussed at the end of Chapter III.1, with the usage of this phrase in *CW* 10 and *CW* Postscript.

The Failures—and the Successes—of the *Untimely Considerations* | 175

that in his younger days he misunderstood the pessimism of Schopenhauer and Wagner "as if it were a symptom of a superior force of thought, of more audacious courage, and of more triumphant *fullness* of life." However, rather than being the expression of a fullness of life that affirms itself and the entire world, the *Romantic* pessimism of Wagner and Schopenhauer is rather a symptom of their suffering from life, and an attempt to revenge oneself on the world by pronouncing the suffering *they* feel to be the essence of all things. In Nietzsche's own words, it is an expression of a "tyrannical will of one who suffers deeply," who "would like to turn what is most personal, singular, and narrow, the real idiosyncrasy of [one's] suffering, into a binding law and compulsion—one who, as it were, revenges himself on all things by forcing *his* own image, the image of *his* torture, on them, branding them with it." Nietzsche says he mistook this life-denying pessimism for a pessimism of strength. But if we make the "*backward inference* [. . .] from the ideal to those who *need* it," as Nietzsche invites us to do in *GS* 370, we see that this was not just an accidental cognitive error. If Nietzsche put himself into the company of these life-deniers and put his hopes in them, if he subscribed to a life-denying ideal, he apparently had suffered from life himself at this point. And he admits this much in *Ecce Homo*. In *EH* HA 3 he explains us that the "total aberration of my instinct" of which he became aware at Bayreuth included also his professorial way of life, which was bad not just for his philosophic development, but even for his health in the usual sense of the word: "Crawling scrupulously with bad eyes through ancient metrists—that's what I had come to!"

Living in bad health, lacking the kind of company he needed, spending his time in a profession he did not care much for and that made his health even worse—no wonder that Nietzsche suffered and that he would consequently find the Schopenhauerian life-denying ideal attractive (even if he never fully subscribed to it). Wagner's music was of eminent use to him in this situation: First, it is "the antitoxin against everything German par excellence—a toxin, a poison, that I don't deny . . . ," a counterpoison or a *pharmakon* against the Germans to which he found himself "*condemned*" (*EH* Clever 6). And given that Nietzsche didn't suffer just from the Germans, but also from other aspects of his situation at the time and was in need of an escape from himself, Wagner's "narcotic art" (*EH* HA 3) was very welcome to him. To state this as a principle, "one anti-nature formally *compels* another one" (*EH* HA 3); it was because he lived against the needs of his nature that he suffered, and it was because he suffered that he needed an art like Wagner's that provided him with a temporary escape from his suffering.

176 | The Young Nietzsche's Education

We have seen the substance of two critical points from the note 9 [42] (12.354–355)—Nietzsche's bad choice of allies and of occupation. The third one, the inadequate character of his early thought, comes to light in the admission that he used to admire a life-denying ideal. But what exactly, beyond the misunderstanding of Wagner and what he stood for, is wrong with the thought of the *UC*? How is it itself aberrated? How is the denial of life expressed in it? Is it only a tangential tendency in these four essays, or is the thought behind the *UC* life-denying at its core?

V.2. The Sickness of the Thought of the *UC*

Nietzsche's thought in the *UC* contains, of course, many elements that appear inadequate when compared with how the same subjects are treated in Nietzsche's later works. For example, the young Nietzsche's critique of modern culture and of the "modern ideas" (1.175, 1.190, 1.407/20, 35, 237) is quite rudimentary, but it already grasps the main symptoms of these phenomena that he will keep on emphasizing in his later years, such as human dignity, social equality, or the allegedly necessary moral progress (cf. *GS* 377). One important exception to this trend is pity [*Mitleid*] and morality of pity, which is held in high regard in the *UC* (1.195, 1.382/40, 214), apparently because of the influence of Schopenhauer—whereas Nietzsche subjects pity to a thorough critique in his later works as one of the most important reactive "feelings of vengefulness and rancor" (*EH* Wise 6) and as "the *practice* of nihilism" that multiplies misery and makes life palpably more miserable for everyone involved (*AC* 7).[11] Pity is in Nietzsche's later thought one of the key features of Christian morality and one of its most powerful means for winning over the allegiance of the multitudes of weak, decadent human beings. The critique of pity thus points to the core of the later Nietzsche's critique of morality: to the distinction between master morality and slave morality as the two basic *types* of morality (*BGE* 260, *GM* I, *CW* Epilogue, *EH* Destiny 4–5), with corresponding characteristic

---

11. I consider the fact that Schopenhauer's doctrine of pity made its way into the *UC* as another symptom of the young Nietzsche's suffering from life. Pity undergoes a thematic critique in *D* 133–138. Nietzsche considers it to be especially dangerous to the philosopher: cf. *GS* 271, and *EH* Wise 4, where Nietzsche describes the entire fourth part of *Zarathustra* as dramatizing the danger of pity to Zarathustra, the overcoming of which is "his real *proof* of strength." Other relevant passages include *HA* 50, 103, 321, 499; *AOM* 68, 377; *WS* 45; *GS* 13, 118; *BGE* 202, 222.

The Failures—and the Successes—of the *Untimely Considerations* | 177

sets of evaluations (good–bad vs. good–evil) and pathoses (affirmation of life and oneself vs. denial thereof). The oblique presence of these distinctions at 1.507/328 is merely foreshadowing this.

At the same time, the identification of Christianity and Christian morality as a case of slave morality par excellence leads to the late Nietzsche's understanding of history as the struggle between these two basic types of morality and the human types they value and produce (*GM* I.16, *AC* 3–5). But although Nietzsche has a clear preference among the contenders in this struggle, he does not understate the power and appeal of Christianity. His mature critique of Christianity is so forceful precisely because he sees both the power of Christianity (*AC* 23 and Meier 2019, 207–209) and the life-denying end toward which it leads (*AC* 62). In the *UC* we find the appreciation of the power of Christianity at quite an advanced stage (1.389/220), but the critique of it is present only vaguely and its consequences are not being drawn out (1.305, 1.345/140, 178).[12]

However, as important as the shift between the early Nietzsche's and the late Nietzsche's critiques of "modern ideas," morality, and Christianity is, his earlier position cannot be described as a symptom of an underlying sickness of thought. The early critique describes the surface-level phenomena faithfully enough, without any significant distortions, and the later critique is a deepening and a consequence of the early critique. The fact that the early critique lacks what would come to be the core of the late critique is due to its rudimentary form and not to any corruption of Nietzsche's thinking.

Let us now return to the question of life-affirmation and life-denial in the *UC*. At first sight it appears simple enough to conclude that the thought of the *UC* is life-affirming. The purpose of working on the production of the genius within and without oneself—which is "the fundamental idea of *culture*" (1.382/213)—is precisely to bring about the exemplary human beings who by their insights and works redeem existence and thereby justify the nonsensical bad infinity that is the existence of the animals and of the vast majority of human beings. And although Schopenhauer is held up as an exemplary philosopher in *SE* (and in the *UC* as a whole), Nietzsche refuses to accept his negative judgment of the value of existence and refers us instead to the affirmative "answer of Empedocles" (1.363/195; cf. Chapter III, fn. 36). But things start to appear in a different light once we follow the logic

---

12. However, this critique is developing in private already in 1875: cf. the notes 5 [148] (8.79–80), 5 [166] (8.87–88), and especially 5 [146] (8.77–79), which articulates many of the points of *AOM* 220, published in 1879.

178 | The Young Nietzsche's Education

of the idea that there is a *fundamental and insoluble conflict between truth and the needs of life*. This is one of the central thoughts of the *UC*: It appears obliquely already on the first page of *DS* with the claim that "errors can be of the most salutary and blessed nature" (1.159/5); it is famously prominent in *HL* in the statement about "doctrines I hold to be true, but also deadly" (1.319/153), but also in the description of the genuinely just individual, of the philosophic legislator, who "in every moment must do penance for [their] own humanity and tragically consume [themselves] in pursuit of an impossible virtue" (1.286/122); in *SE* it is manifest in the notion of "*the suffering inherent in truthfulness*" (1.371/203) that leads to the knowledge that life as such is unsatisfiable striving and hence senseless suffering, that "we ourselves are the animals who seem to suffer senselessly" (1.378/210); and it culminates in *WB* with the account of "the greatest sufferings that exist for the individual"—of the insoluble conflict between the genius' philanthropy and their knowledge of the reality of human life—and with the awareness of the inevitable eventual extinction of humanity (1.451–453/278–280).

What this means in practice is that happiness—understood not as some kind of exceptional, exalted state of mind, but more widely, including even a basic level of satisfaction with one's life that is necessary for continuing to live it as one did until now—is essentially incompatible with the truth: Happiness is of necessity a product of either ignorance or illusion. By saying that this is *essentially* so, I mean that it is the case for all kinds of human beings, even for those at the highest levels of knowledge that the philosophic conception of the *UC* knows of. The philosophic legislator of *HL* 6 (1.286/122) and the genius of *SE* 5 and *WB* 4 (1.378, 1.451–453/211, 278–280) suffer from the truth, and indeed, the more they know, the more they suffer: It is at these highest levels of human understanding that one encounters "the *greatest* sufferings that exist for the individual" (1.451–452/278; emphasis added). The life of this genius is thus *not self-sufficient*, not sustainable by itself: Living in the tension between one's philanthropy and one's knowledge of human nature is a huge drain on one's psychic powers, and it would ultimately be unbearable if one didn't occasionally indulge in illusions such as those depicted in Wagner's art. "Art exists *so that the bow does not break*" (1.453/279) is how the young Nietzsche expresses this crucial *limitation* of his conception of the life of the thinker in the *UC*.[13]

---

13. Church (2019, p. 54) takes Nietzsche's project in the *UC* to be one "not of embracing but of dispelling illusion and self-deception." However, given the unbearable nature of the truth in the *UC*, this can be the case only to a limited extent and at the personal cost of the individuals who choose to expose themselves to the truth. It certainly cannot be the

The Failures—and the Successes—of the *Untimely Considerations* | 179

The path traversed by Nietzsche in the ten years after *WB* becomes apparent when we look at *BGE* Preface, where the centuries-long struggle against Christianity had created "a *magnificent* tension of the spirit" (emphasis added) that allows us to "shoot for the most distant goals." *This* spiritual tension is productive rather than self-destructive: Whereas the tension in *WB* is one whose resolution is structurally impossible and living with it passively drains one's forces just so one can go on with living, the tension in *BGE* is an agonistic tension in which we strive to mobilize and exert our forces to overcome the opponent, in the process increasing our forces and—metaphorically speaking—aiming and shooting further than we were able before. And while it is true that in *BGE* 39 Nietzsche says that the strength of a spirit can be measured by "how much of the 'truth' one could still barely endure," in *BGE* 30 we get a suggestion that it is possible to be so strong so as to bear all of the truth, that is, so as *not to suffer from the truth at all*: "there are heights of the soul from which even tragedy ceases to look tragic." Similarly, in *EH* Destiny 5 Nietzsche says of Zarathustra's *Übermensch* that this type of the human being "conceives reality *as it* is, being strong enough to do so" (and analogously in *GS* 347 regarding certainty). Such claims have no parallel in the thinking of the *UC*. That is to say: Nietzsche of the *UC* is not yet aware of such heights of the soul.

Closely connected to the insoluble conflict between truth and life is the idea that the world is meaningless by itself and needs to be redeemed [*erlöst*] (1.363, 1.377–384, 1.404, 1.469/195, 209–215, 234, 294)—the idea of *nihilism*. We saw that the life of animals amounts only to senseless suffering, and so does the life of the majority of humans (1.378/210). Moreover, human history has so far been ruled by chance and is therefore nonsensical; and, as we have seen above, not even those individuals who are aware of all this are an exception to the rule that life is suffering—for they suffer from that very knowledge, and apparently they suffer even more than the lesser, more ignorant people (1.451–452/278). As a consequence, life—life of all living beings, life as such—doesn't amount to much: To the best understanding of the *UC*, life so far appears to be "a tale told by an

---

case for a culture at large, as Church claims: "Nietzsche does not simply enjoin cultures to embrace illusion [. . .] all such illusions are unjust, and [. . .] we must provide a new [and truthful] justification for modern culture" (ibid., p. 73). The necessity of illusions ultimately comes to the fore in Church's reading as well, e.g., when he discusses (what he understands as) the natural teleology in *SE* 5 as an ideal with a "regulative status" (ibid., p. 174) or as a "rhetorical means" (ibid., p. 180) that Nietzsche substantially "cannot defend" (ibid., p. 182)—i.e., as a *falsehood*, strictly speaking.

180 | The Young Nietzsche's Education

idiot, full of sound and fury, signifying nothing." Life has to be redeemed, and this redemption is the work of heroic individuals, of geniuses such as Schopenhauer, Nietzsche, or Wagner, who willingly take the suffering of truthfulness upon themselves in order to make life livable for others. They sacrifice themselves and their own happiness so that the lesser people can live happily, that is, live in a culture that provides them with the best possible conditions of life and growth, with the most salutary illusions. This redemption is in principle the establishing of a cultural-political order of life, or originary justice, that fosters human greatness—an establishing that has to take place through the production of salutary illusions, such as those of Wagner's art. This new order of life will redeem all previous existence (human and animal) by becoming the *ex post* meaning of all the suffering that had hitherto been meaningless, and by making all future that will happen under its sign meaningful as well. The project of the *UC*, in conjunction with the project of Bayreuth—the project of a cultural renewal centered on Wagner's tragedies and the new educational institutions planned by Nietzsche—was intended to be such a redemption. It was to be the founding of a new culture based on the insight into the true nature of human existence; this new culture was then to prevail over the old pseudo-culture and spread its constitutive tragic sensibility all over the world, thus in a nontrivial sense unifying humanity; it was to be a world-historical redemptive event not just in its meaning, but also in its intended scope.[14]

---

14. Church takes the problem of nihilism to mean simply the value-less character of our natural existence, "natural" understood in terms of the Kantian distinction between nature as the realm of necessity and culture as the realm of freedom. He interprets the "wisdom of Silenus" (1.35/*BT* 23) as expressing this valueless character of natural existence (2015, pp. 18, 30) that is compounded by the self-contradictory character of human nature (2015, pp. 30, 58). Church, 2019, refrains from talking about nihilism in these terms but doesn't offer an alternative reading of it. This valueless and contradictory human nature is then to be "redeemed" simply by creation of autonomous meaning, of which Church recognizes a multitude: redemption by the just individual (2019, p. 103), by one who adopts the suprahistorical perspective (2019, p. 107), by the lives of exemplary individuals (2019, p. 126), by education (2019, p. 143), or by Schopenhauer's reform of culture (2019, p. 155); in short, by just about any act of self-determining freedom (2019, p. 140). I think this account misses the core of the problem of human existence as Nietzsche sees it in the *UC*: namely, that our lives are essentially unsatisfiable striving and hence senseless suffering, a bad infinity (a view that Church, 2015, pp. 101–102 ascribes only to Schopenhauer); and a redemption of life thus understood consists not in *any* given act of freedom, but rather in the insight into this fundamental character of

The Failures—and the Successes—of the *Untimely Considerations* | 181

Nietzsche has dramatized a thoroughgoing critique of this kind of project in his *Zarathustra*. In *Zarathustra's Prologue*, Zarathustra presents his initial, *futuristic* teaching to the people: the teaching of the future coming of the *Übermensch* who is to be "the meaning of the Earth" (*Za* I Prologue 3), and for whose coming Zarathustra's disciples are to prepare the way. This teaching is analogous to the project of the *UC* in that it aims toward a redemptive event in the near future that is supposed to provide meaning for the entire world that would remain meaningless without it. Meier (2017, pp. 92–103) shows how this futuristic teaching comes into a crisis in *Za* II On Redemption and how Zarathustra abandons it on substantial philosophic grounds. Already a brief consideration of the presuppositions behind the idea of such a redemptive event shows how untenable this idea is. Would all life remain forever meaningless if the redemptive event fails to occur, as it happened with the project of the *UC*? If the event succeeded in establishing the redeeming order of life, but this order was to break down at a later point in time, would this make life meaningless again? Would it all have been in vain? And even if the redemptive event fully succeeded, how would it change the fact that life is essentially senseless suffering, a bad infinity? Wouldn't it rather merely cover it up?

Zarathustra does in fact conclude that the futuristic doctrine is untenable because of these and related reasons and turns from the failure of the doctrine to the failure of the thinking that produced it: He uses the crisis as an occasion for self-critique. Zarathustra tells us that that as long as he held fast to the futuristic doctrine, he saw everyone as "fragments and limbs and dreadful accidents—but no human beings!,"[15] and that as long as this was the case, he was "also, as it were, a cripple" (*Za* II On Redemption), that is, was not complete and self-sufficient because of projecting all his hopes onto an uncertain future.[16] He comes to see that "the

---

life and in the consequent denial of one's will to live, in the cessation of participation in this bad infinity. Acts of self-determining freedom may (and in most cases do) participate in this bad infinity, and thus by themselves cannot be considered "redemptive" in the sense developed above.

15. The young souls are to see spiritual cripples in everyone who has not yet been transformed by the redemptive event, including themselves—just like Zarathustra. Cf. 1.385–386/216–217 and Chapter III, fn. 51.

16. Church (2015, pp. 235–236) sees nothing problematic with this futuristic teaching and reads *Za* II On Redemption as an affirmation thereof rather than as a profound critique.

182 | The Young Nietzsche's Education

futuristic doctrine is rooted in outrage at reality" (Meier, 2017, p. 95), that this doctrine is ultimately a projection of its author's own dissatisfaction with life. Doctrines and projects such as Zarathustra's futuristic doctrine and the project of the *UC* come from the "spirit of revenge." which is "the greatest danger for the philosopher" (Meier, 2017, p. 97; cf. Heidegger, *Who Is Nietzsche's Zarathustra?*, in Heidegger, 1991, vol. II, pp. 209–233), from the will's anger at everything that refuses to bend to its demands, in particular everything past. As an act of revenge against these immovable rocks, the thinker's will devaluates them—thereby exercising some form of power against that which in fact shows the will's impotence or at least the limits of its power—and then comes to see these now-worthless things, this now-worthless world, as in need of being given meaning and worth. Now the thinker's will can fully assert itself and take revenge on everything that had previously resisted it: It bestows its own meaning and laws on everything, including the previously immovable past, and thereby the will subjects everything to itself.[17] But as glorious as this "triumph of the will" (cf. Hutter, 2006, p. 64) may appear, reflection shows the untenable nature of such futuristic projects that aim to make the world meaningful by bringing about some world-historical redemptive event—including the project of the *UC*. Zarathustra concludes that what needs redemption is not the world or life as such, but the thinker's will: It needs to be "redeemed" from its need to redeem things, from its need to bring everything under its control at least in its mental constructs. The will needs to learn to accept the world and the things *as they are in themselves.*[18]

Underlying this desire for redemption of the whole of life is a basic attitude of dissatisfaction with life, a creeping sense that life by itself is *not good.* If life, including its highest forms, is unbearable, if the truth about

---

Brooks (2018, p. 130) also reads the late Nietzsche as "the redeeming philosopher-artist depicted in the combined teaching of *SE* and *WB*" and believes that "the redeeming task of such philosophers [as Nietzsche or Zarathustra] is bound up with the fact that they are the creators of values, truths, and even of 'nature' itself."

17. Meier (2017, p. 99) points out that the logic of the spirit of revenge ultimately leads to making (the "unredeemed") life itself into suffering and punishment so that it can ascribe the greatest possible significance to its "redeeming" act.

18. Cf. *AC* 14, which directly contradicts the notion that animal life (including human life) is somehow imperfect and in need of redemption. This of course does not imply a practical attitude of complacent quietism—cf. *EH* Za 6, and fn. 55 below. Golomb (1999, p. 5) also argues that "the salvation from [our need for] salvation was to become a central motif on Nietzsche's mature philosophy."

The Failures—and the Successes—of the *Untimely Considerations* | 183

life is that life is livable only under the spell of some illusion, why bother with the truth? Why is the life of the redemptive genius who is a "true *human being*" and a "*no-longer-animal*" (1.380/211)[19] desirable at all, given that it consists of suffering more intensely than the lesser kinds of life? And if this highest kind of human life is not desirable, can we consider life desirable at all? Such an understanding of life is *not* life-affirming. This becomes clearer when we take a closer look at the "Schopenhauerian affirmation" of *SE*. This "affirmation" presupposes the insight that all willing as unsatisfiable striving and hence senseless suffering, and that one ceases to play this game. In other words, it presupposes a denial of the will, a cessation of striving and desiring.[20] But denial of the will in the strict sense in which it is used here—not merely a self-disciplining of some unruly impulse or another, but a complete cessation of striving (Schopenhauer, *PP* II, p. 322/*Werke* V.380; quoted at 1.373/204–205)—is incompatible with Nietzsche's psychological theory already at this point. Life that is essentially willing or desiring, life as "that dark, driving, insatiable power that lusts after itself" (1.269/106), cannot cease willing or desiring without ceasing to be what it is. As long as a living being is living, it is willing or desiring; as soon as it ceases to desire, it ceases to live; the only *natural* cessation of willing or desiring is death. This "affirmation" is a vision of transcending the limits of the human condition, but it runs against the conditions of its own existence. It is self-contradictory, and, as Nietzsche will understand in a few years, sickly (cf. *AOM* 349). It is unclear whether Nietzsche actually believed something like it was possible when he was writing *SE*—given its psychological impossibility, and given that *SE* rejects Schopenhauer's doctrines in most cases, I am inclined to think he didn't—but in any case, he apparently didn't have anything better to offer to his audience as an image

---

19. Regardless of how seriously Nietzsche meant this metaphysical notion of the genius, he soon came to critique it explicitly: cf. *HA* 162–164, *AOM* 378.

20. At 1.374/206 we read about ceasing to be a toy of eternal becoming; at 1.375/207 we read that the power of the Schopenhauerian individual "lies in their self-oblivion"; the redeeming insight at 1.380/211 is that "[nature] realizes that it must unlearn its goals"; at 1.472/296, the tragic wisdom is described as ending in "an ecstatic demise and end to willing"—all these phrases say, more or less directly, that genuine wisdom and happiness lie in the denial of one's will. The same is true of the description of the redemptive geniuses as "true *human beings*" and "*no-longer-animals*" (1.380/211)—they are such in contrast to the regular humans who have not denied their will and who thus are not fully human, but rather "the animals who seem to suffer senselessly" (1.378/210).

184 | The Young Nietzsche's Education

of the insight into the being of the whole at this point.[21] Thus the image of the highest knowledge and happiness the *UC* offer to us is a sham, and there is no genuine affirmation of life in the *UC*. This "affirmation" tells us that life can be affirmed only by ceasing to be life. The thought of the *UC* is, despite its best efforts, *life-denying*.

The best life that the *UC* knows of is a tragic or heroic life: a life that is in an inescapable conflict both internally (truth vs. the needs of one's life) and externally (opposition of the individual against the "world" that is in the wrong and needs to be redeemed), in which the task of the tragic-heroic individual is to sacrifice themselves and their own good for the sake of a greater, common good, which they will not be able to enjoy (and, as discussed above, it is questionable how far that alleged greater good is genuine). This kind of life consequently does not admit the possibility of inner peace or happiness other than in the cessation of itself, be it in death or in the fabled "Schopenhauerian affirmation" of the three types of the redeeming genius.[22] There is a hope that this may be different for the free human beings of the future after the redeeming event takes place, but there is no such hope for Nietzsche himself and for the present-day young souls, who "also have to suffer from these antidotes [to the historical sickness]" (1.331/164) and can only hope that they will one day manage to overcome this sickness (1.332/166). Such a life, a life ruled by the ethos of the tragic sensibility, by the belief that a self-sacrificing tragic struggle

---

21. We can see Nietzsche's difficulties with this subject in the letter to Franz Overbeck from 30 July 1874. Nietzsche reports here that *SE* is almost finished, apart from what would become *SE* 5, i.e., precisely the account of the affirmation of life: "Admittedly I dread what is still missing, a little chapter in the middle about the most difficult—and difficult to say—thing!" (KGB II.3, 252). As for the intention behind using the trinity of redeeming geniuses as images of the good life, I think they were to be a conception that honors the eminent role of philosophy in human life, but one that is not limited to philosophy and that can take into account the great diversity of human types without simply condemning all non-philosophers as worthless. The multiple audiences recognized by the later Nietzsche can be seen as resulting from a similar, but more carefully considered intention (cf. fn. 35 below).

22. While strictly speaking it is true that "these exemplary individuals make many appearances in Nietzsche's work early and late" (Church, 2015, p. 64), the artist and the saint are radically devalued compared with the role they have in the *UC* (cf., e.g., *GM* III.5 for the artist and *BGE* 47 for the saint), and the philosopher is understood in a completely different way, as I momentarily show. They certainly no longer appear as types of the redeeming genius.

The Failures—and the Successes—of the *Untimely Considerations* | 185

with ourselves and with the world is the best life available to us, is fundamentally a *moral* life.[23]

The moral character of this way of life is reflected also in the way Nietzsche conceives of his primary audience, of the young souls. In accord with the larger theme of the tragic-heroic life, they are thematized as believers willing to sacrifice themselves for a task assigned to them from outside (e.g., at 1.403/233), as "camels" in Zarathustra's sense (cf. *Za* I On the Three Metamorphoses). In contrast, the free spirits, one of the later Nietzsche's primary audiences, are characterized by two qualities that mark them as the opposite of the young souls: their intellectual independence or skepticism (as a character trait), and their having freed themselves from harmful ideals they had hitherto believed (as an experience they have undergone). It is in this sense that Nietzsche speaks of himself as a "*spirit that has become free*" in *EH* HA 1, and of his desired readers in *AC* 36. Although both the young souls and the free spirits can be fruitfully characterized as thymotic natures, the free spirits have attained a higher level of maturity, both in an experiential and in a spiritual sense. Their experiential maturity shows itself in having overcome the kind of rash and passionate devotion to causes one finds admirable, the taste for the unconditional, which Nietzsche criticizes as characteristic of "youth" in passages like *HA* I Preface 3, *HA* 599, *BGE* 31 or *EH* HA 4. The spiritual maturity of the free spirits is their actual spiritual independence, their having attained the stage of Zarathustra's "lion" (cf. Hutter, 2009, p. 214). Seen from this perspective, *nobody* in the *UC* is actually free—even the philosopher is bound by their moral, redemptive purpose (as well as by the task of producing genuine culture), to which they are to contribute without regard for their own good.

A moral life is fundamentally different from the philosophic life as the mature Nietzsche understands it. First of all, whereas the philosophic life strives to attain one's own good, understood as the increase of one's power and knowledge, as the increase of one's virtue or *virtù* in the sense of *AC* 6 or *EH* Clever 1, the good of the moral life is determined by a heterogeneous moral purpose that is in principle unconnected to one's own good in the

---

23. Thus, although Fink (2003, p. 33) is incorrect that in the *UC* Nietzsche merely "constructs his metaphysics of art on the basis of Schopenhauer's philosophy," he is right that "the concept of culture [in the *UC*] is firmly based on the tragic world-view" (ibid., p. 28).

186 | The Young Nietzsche's Education

above sense.[24] The life of the *UC*'s redeeming genius is ruled by such a moral purpose that requires them to suffer for its sake, to suffer from truthfulness more than any other human being suffers (1.371, 1.451–452/203, 278), and to do so even though it doesn't contribute to their good: "[their] strength lies in [their] self-oblivion" (1.375/207). Second, it is a life based in *belief* rather than knowledge. On the one hand, the actions and projects of such a life are based on the belief that the moral purpose is the unconditional good: They are not actions and projects that correspond to the knowledge of what one's good is and how this good is grounded in the being of the human being and of the whole. The thinker's philanthropy is such a moral belief to which one is to devote oneself, even at the cost of one's own good. On the other hand, it is a life that believes in the future redemptive event and derives its own meaning (and, as we saw, the meaning of everything else as well) from bringing that event about. But, this being a *future* event, it is of necessity uncertain, and as such it is a matter of belief rather than of knowledge. Here it should be emphasized that because the thought of the *UC* in general holds truth to be deadly and deadening, it places a great premium on belief of whatever kind—on belief that is known to be an illusion at least to the thinker—as the motivating force of life and action. Thus Nietzsche tells us, "only in love, only in the shadow of the *illusion* of love, does the human being create—that is, only in the *unconditional belief* in perfection and justness" (1.296/131; emphases added); or that "the foundation for all [human] security and tranquility [is] [our] *belief* in what is lasting and eternal" (1.330/164; emphasis added); that the motivation of the young souls is "*the belief in the metaphysical significance of culture*" (1.401/231); and even that truthfulness means "to *believe* in an existence that could not possibly be negated" (1.372/203; emphasis added)—that

---

24. This includes philosophy as a way of life in the ancient sense, as it was described in Chapter II.3 above, at least insofar as the standards according to which one lives and orders one's soul are not the product of original insight into one's own good, but just doctrines one believes in, i.e., products of another thinker meant as a public teaching. The philosophic life in the mature Nietzsche's understanding means precisely *not* following any master, being a "skeptic" (*AC* 54)—one who takes nothing for granted and examines (gr. *skeptomai*) everything. On a related note, the philosophic life no longer has to be externally visible: It is rather the internal devotion to the truth, or the passion for knowledge, understood as one's genuine good; all its external manifestations (or lack thereof) depend on the thinker's circumstances and judgment. In this regard, consider also the prominence of the concept of the *mask* in the mature Nietzsche's thinking (e.g., *BGE* Preface, 25, 40, 270, 278, 289, or *GM* III.9–10; cf. Kaufmann 1982).

The Failures—and the Successes—of the *Untimely Considerations* | 187

truthfulness itself is a matter of *belief*. In a word, knowledge is not its own goal and its own reward in the *UC*: It is just a means to bring about the redemptive event on which one's hope and belief are oriented.[25]

This emphasis on belief has in turn important consequences for how the *UC* conceive of the philosopher. These four essays contain no thematic reflection on what it means to be a philosopher, to be engaged in a life of thinking, what the good of such a life is and what kind of happiness it entails.[26] They consider the philosopher only from the outside (and consequently also "from below"—*BGE* 30), from the perspective of what the philosopher is supposed to accomplish for the sake of genuine culture and for the redemptive event.[27] It is this instrumental conception of the philosopher that makes it possible to speak of Wagner as a "philosopher" at all (1.445/272). We have already seen that in the *UC* it is impossible to speak of the happiness that a life devoted to the truth entails, a subject of eminent importance to the mature Nietzsche. Insofar as happiness is possible for the thinker in the *UC* at all, it would be tightly bound up with the success of the redemptive project; their life would be "tragic" in the sense of it being a struggle against overwhelming odds, and the possibility of success (and of the consequent happiness) is minuscule. Furthermore, given that the conflict between truth and life is a background of this entire conception, it is questionable how genuine even the happiness of bringing about the redemptive event would be.[28] In any case, this life would be unbearable for the most part, and it would have to be complemented by artistic illusions (cf. 1.453/279). The philosopher, as they are conceived in the *UC*, is an

---

25. In retrospect, Nietzsche names *Glaube* (belief or faith) as one of the principal prejudices of which he freed himself during his crisis (*EH* HA 1).

26. Two years later, in the letter to Mathilde Maier from 15 July 1878, Nietzsche points out very clearly that "now I *myself live* striving for wisdom, up to the smallest detail, while earlier I just admired and raved about *the wise*," and comments that his pre-crisis "philosophizing," combined with his devotion to Wagner's art, was what "eventually made me sick and sicker, and almost alienated me from my good temperament and my talent" (KGB II.5, p. 338).

27. Cf. Meier (2019, p. 108n32 and p. 117) for an instructive discussion.

28. A consequence of this is the image of the "theoretical person who thirsts for life" (1.503/325) in which truth and life are once again pictured in irreconcilable conflict. In *D* 41, the theoretic or contemplative life appears already in a much more positive light, as something that possesses its determinate worth despite how most of the world misunderstands it and despite the fact that it is suitable only for a small number of people.

188 | The Young Nietzsche's Education

unhappy and not-self-sufficient existence, guided by a moral purpose—in sum, not much to be envied.

Nietzsche would later admit that in his early works, including the *UC*, he was practicing "Jesuitism," defined as "the conscious holding on to illusion and forcibly incorporating that illusion as the *foundation of culture*" (note 16 [23], 10.507). We have seen ample evidence of how the illusions of Wagner's artworks were supposed to fulfill this cultural role.[29] But the crucial problem here is that Nietzsche, an aspiring philosopher, is here prescribing a moral view of life not just for others, but for himself as well. He has no sight of a life higher than that, a life that would be "for himself," in which he would be nobody's servant. The core to which the moral life should point and for which it should be a preparation—the philosophic life in the proper sense of the term—is missing in his thinking here. And insofar as Nietzsche is a *philosopher* above all else, this way of thinking leads him in a totally wrong direction; it constitutes a "total aberration of my instinct," as he later called it (*EH* HA 3). That his thought, guided by the idea of the insoluble conflict between truth and life, leads him to a moral life instead of the philosophic life, is *the* sickness of his thought. This sickness is, ironically, the same as what he diagnosed in the philistines: running away from himself and using *divertissements* to hide this fact from himself (Wagner's art and Wagner's project being his *divertissements* of choice—*EH* HA 3). And the ultimate result of this sickness is that the thinking he presents in the *UC* is *life-denying* or *nihilistic*: the very opposite of Nietzsche's innermost aspiration.

～

To summarize this line of critique, when Nietzsche diagnosed the crisis of his time in *HL*, he articulated a profound insight: namely that truth is not necessarily compatible with the needs of human life, that the life of societies and of the vast majority of individuals depends on some kind of illusion for its health and flourishing. But he overestimated the validity of his insight and went on to claim that truth is *essentially* in conflict with the needs of life. His further development put the lie to this, as he discovered that the life devoted to the truth, the philosophic life, the life in which the

---

29. This directly contradicts Church's (2019, p. 57) claim that the *UC* embrace the modern culture's "unconditional valuing of truth and knowledge" and merely seek to slightly correct this culture of truthfulness. Cf. Chapter II, fn. 18.

The Failures—and the Successes—of the *Untimely Considerations* | 189

soul is ruled by the *passion for knowledge*, is not just possible, but is in fact the best life available to human beings. Whereas truth can be, and indeed often is, deadly, it need not be so. What the young Nietzsche believed to be impossible turned out to be merely something of which he was not yet capable; his insight was genuine, but he unduly absolutized it. And this incapacity gave rise to the most serious intellectual error of the *UC*. The incapacity to live well turned him—temporarily—into a life-denier. This new insight found its correlative in a new, more structured rhetoric that distinguishes between different kinds of audience and hides the dangerous truth while pointing to it in oblique ways (cf. *BGE* 30). Nietzsche thereby entered into a tradition of a philosophic art of writing that goes back at least to Plato's *Phaedrus* and its apparent paradox of criticizing writing in the medium of writing itself.

Nietzsche explicitly rejects the thesis of the necessary conflict between truth and life in *D* 550, where he tells us that "knowledge of even the ugliest reality is itself beautiful," that is, that even though the world may be terrible, the knowledge thereof is *not* terrible—that knowledge makes one happy and thus leads to the genuine affirmation of even what would otherwise be a "terrible" world. If knowledge has the capacity to make one happy, then there is no *necessary* conflict between truth and life.[30] The path then stands open to a conception of a life devoted to the truth, or to put this in terms of Nietzsche's desire-based psychology, of a soul that is ruled by and ordered according to the needs of the "passion for knowledge." This passion—another innovation of *Daybreak* (cf. *D* 429, 482)—is, unlike other passions, capable of giving an account of itself and self-correction in a way that other passions with their determinate desiderata are not. Thereby it provides a solution to the core problem of the crisis: The passion for knowledge may be the guiding force of one's soul precisely because it does not have to *believe* that its present goal is unconditionally good; it is rather capable of questioning and correcting its own direction, and thereby the direction of one's entire life. Not instinct, but a passion for questioning and examination of each of the beings—and especially of oneself—is now to guide Nietzsche's life: That is the core of his mature conception of the philosophic life, and the solution to the crisis into which he was plunged by the failure of the project of the *UC*. Such a life is emphatically *not* a life of suffering or renunciation (*D* 440). From then on, the connection

---

30. Cf. *AC* 11: "an action demanded by the instinct of life is proved to be *right* by the pleasure that accompanies it."

190 | The Young Nietzsche's Education

between knowledge and happiness, happiness and love of the whole, and love of the whole and the affirmation of the whole[31] will become a regularly (if somewhat obliquely) discussed subject in Nietzsche's books, in passages such as *Za* IV At Noon; *BGE* 30, 152; or *AC* 1.[32]

It is fundamentally because of the thought of the essential and insoluble conflict between truth and life that Nietzsche in the *UC* aims at the same time too low and too far. *Too low* because he did not yet see the height of the genuinely philosophic perspective from which the world is good and justified as it is—or rather, in no need of a justification at all. Consequently, he wasn't able to see the life of knowledge, a life ruled by the passion for knowledge, as the good life. And *too far* because the tragic perspective conditioned by the thought of the insoluble conflict between truth and life led him to believe that happiness is impossible, that the world is not good, and consequently that it needs to be redeemed. He then conceived of the task of the philosopher as the striving to bring about a redemptive transformation of this worthless world, which is far beyond what any philosophy can hope to accomplish. Life-denial, conditioned by the young Nietzsche's incapacity to live well, stands at the root of both these misdirected tendencies.

V.3. The Successes of the Thought of the *UC*

However, although the thought of the *UC* does harbor this life-denying tendency at its core, it would be a mistake to dismiss these four essays as complete failures that have little bearing on Nietzsche's mature philosophy. It should not be overlooked that these early works already contain statements of various ideas of Nietzsche's in what is basically their mature form, and

---

31. On this subject cf. the excellent discussion in Meier, 2019, pp. 73–74.

32. Given this *fundamental* difference between the conception of the philosopher in the *UC* and that of the mature Nietzsche, I must disagree with Brooks's (2018, pp. 130–131) claims that "the older Nietzsche [. . .] understood himself to be the redeeming philosopher-artist depicted in the combined teaching of *SE* and *WB*" and that "Nietzsche is both the herald for the redeeming philosopher and a kind of redeeming philosopher, just as Zarathustra was both a herald for the overman and a kind of overman." The similarities in the cultural role of the young and mature Nietzsche's conception of the philosopher do not warrant such a strong blanket statement, especially regarding the *redeeming* role of the philosopher. This is not to say that the *UC*, and especially *SE*, had no positive influence on Nietzsche's further development—a subject I treat below.

The Failures—and the Successes—of the *Untimely Considerations* | 191

by paying attention to them we will come to see also the continuity of the *UC* with Nietzsche's later works, at least in these partial aspects.

While the death of God is not announced as such in the *UC*—Nietzsche's first pronouncement of the famous words "God is dead" takes place in *GS* 108—the core of this dictum, which he sums up in *GS* 343 as the awareness "that the belief in the Christian God has become unbelievable," is present already in the *UC*. This is evident in the subject matter of *DS*, which is a critique of D. F. Strauss's attempt to establish a post-Christian morality and religion. The main thrust of the critique of *DS* is not that Strauss has abandoned Christianity prematurely or without good reasons, but rather that he failed to develop a genuinely post-Christian way of thinking. In particular, Strauss lacked the courage to actually face the consequences of a godless cosmos that does not care about humans at all and dealt with this simply by smuggling a baseless notion of cosmic providence into his "new faith" (cf. 1.197/41). The most direct statement in the *UC* of the end of Christianity as a cultural force, as a force that guides the thoughts and lives of humans in the West, is at 1.446–447/273, where Christianity is treated as "a bit of Oriental antiquity" that has been "thought through and pursued [. . .] to its logical conclusion." The possibilities of Christianity (and hence of the "Oriental," at least for the time being) having been exhausted, it is now time for the other major European cultural force, the Hellenic, to assert itself: "the Earth, which up to this point was sufficiently Orientalized, now yearns once more for Hellenization" (1.447/274).[33] The only other alternative that the *UC* recognize is barbarism, that is, life devoid of culture in any strong sense of the term: the life of the philistines.

The philistines of the *UC* (who make significant appearances in all four essays: cf. 1.164–173, 1.323, 1.389–390, 1.459–464/10–19, 157, 220–221, 285–289) prefigure quite faithfully the complacent and self-satisfied "last men," one of the key corollaries of the death of God. The philistines' key characteristic is their belief that *they* know what the truly important things in life are, and hence what the good life is—their "seriousness of life" comprises "profession and business, together with wife and child" (1.170/16), or providing a comfortable existence for themselves and their immediate family. All other concerns, in particular anything related to art, philosophy, or any other form of self-cultivation, is relegated to the

---

33. We can see traces of this approach already in *BT*, in what Nietzsche calls the "consistently cautious and hostile silence about Christianity" of this book (*BT* Attempt 5).

192 | The Young Nietzsche's Education

status of entertainment or *divertissement*. They certainly do not allow these concerns to put their own way of life into question: "the watchword of the philistine is: 'We should seek no further'" (1.168/14). These philistines are as much incapable of and/or unwilling to strive beyond what they already are, beyond their comfortable existence, as the last men who believe to have "invented happiness" (*Za* I Prologue 5). And, as the enthusiastic reaction of the crowd at the marketplace to Zarathustra's description of the last man shows, the last man is an object not so much of a prophecy as an already existing phenomenon. This comes up time and again in Nietzsche's critiques and diagnoses of modernity in his post-*Zarathustra* writings: He describes *BGE* as "in all essentials a *critique of modernity*" (*EH* BGE 2), and his genealogical analyses occasionally show a polemical edge against the present age in passages such as *GM* I.12 or *AC* 38.

This polemical tendency, as well as Nietzsche's general position of "untimeliness" (cf. Large, 1994), are connected in a ministerial way to another important facet of his thought that appears for the first time in the *UC* and remains central ever after: namely his concern with educating his readers, in the best case helping them become philosophers in their own right.[34] Although already *BT* addresses the German youth with the hope that they will come to "live resolutely" and create a new culture based on Wagner's tragic art (1.119/*BT* 88), it doesn't have any kind of educational strategy: It simply points the ambitious readers to Wagner and his cause. In contrast, the *UC* do have a specific audience they strive to address: the young souls, who are understood as having a particular psychological profile with particular needs and desires. The rhetoric of the *UC*, as well as the plan it has for the young souls, are derived from this understanding of their specific nature. The *UC* offer the young souls a teaching designed to address their spiritual problems, to help them orient themselves in a world they find themselves alienated from, and to employ their productive forces in the project Nietzsche envisions himself and Wagner to spearhead. Moreover, he presents this teaching with a rhetoric designed to appeal to their passions: On the one hand, Nietzsche appeals to their contempt for D. F. Strauss and their anger that his worthless book is celebrated as a "catechism for strong spirits" (1.201/45); he's explicitly siding with the disaffected young souls in their opposition to the established cultural forces and authorities.

---

34. As Lampert (2017, p. 85) notes, "that Platonic goal [i.e., "to produce new Platos" at 1.413/242] can be said to be Nietzsche's most basic political motive from the beginning to the end of his career."

The Failures—and the Successes—of the *Untimely Considerations* | 193

On the other hand, he appeals to their pride and to their desire to make their limited lifespan worth the while by telling them of the uniqueness of their existence and by promising them a happy and meaningful life if they develop it in the right way, if they follow the imperative *be yourself*. The basic idea of rhetorically seducing ambitious youths for a course of philosophic education is important to all of Nietzsche's subsequent works, although the profile of the intended audience changes in significant ways, and the rhetorical means get much more refined.[35] From the *UC* onward, Nietzsche's philosophical style constantly develops and changes, guided by the question of how best to reach the various kinds of readers he wants to reach, challenge them to examine their not-yet-reflected beliefs, and induce them to actively *lead* their lives.[36]

In the *UC* we find for the first time also the counterpart to the attitude of the last man incapable of making any distinctions. It is the attitude of the "Nietzschean humanism" of *HL* 2: the idea that human greatness consists in the constant striving for "extending the concept of 'the human being' and giving it a more beautiful substance" (1.259/97). While the quoted passage presents this idea as the "commandment" [*Gebot*] of the monumental individual, it finds a wider field of applicability in the thought of the *UC* in that it supports the activity of making distinctions—not just between oneself and others, but also and more importantly between oneself as one currently is and the ideal one holds up for oneself. It is because of its direct opposition of the monumental commandment to the philistine principle "we should seek no further" (1.168/14) that Nietzsche presents this commandment as exemplary to his readers and uses it as an important tool in the service of his educative effort in the *UC*. And for the same reason, this attitude of what Nietzsche will later call "self-overcoming"—most generally of what one currently is, and in the best case of the human as it was hitherto understood—will remain a central part of Nietzsche's pedagogy vis-à-vis his readers, even though the goals to which it should aim

---

35. Heinrich Meier describes how this stratification of intended audience is dramatized in *Zarathustra*. First, Zarathustra decides to speak to "companions" rather than to the people in general (*Za* I Preface 9; Meier, 2017, pp. 26–27). Second, he divides his disciples into the (merely) noble natures and the potential philosophers, with each of these groups being addressed in a different way (*Za* I On the Tree on the Mountainside; Meier, 2017, pp. 33–35). Finally, he decides to abandon his disciples when he realizes that none of them, not even his favorite disciple, have managed to lift themselves beyond the stage of the obedient believer, the "camel" (*Za* II The Soothsayer; Meier, 2017, p. 92).

36. On this cf. the valuable discussions in Conant (2001, pp. 216–226 and p. 240n7).

194 | The Young Nietzsche's Education

will be different from those of the self-sacrificing Schopenhauerian human being. The characters held up by the later Nietzsche as the goals for one's self-overcoming include the "philosophers of the future" from *BGE*, the "sovereign individual" from *GM* II.2, or the "Hyperboreans" from *AC*. They also include, with a crucial caveat, the slogan *Übermensch*. The *Übermensch* namely appears in Nietzsche's works in two very different senses. The first of these is the *Übermensch* as "the meaning of the Earth" from *Za* I Preface 3, as the goal of the futuristic teaching, as the being whose coming about is supposed to redeem all existence that is meaningless and would forever remain meaningless without it. This usage of the *Übermensch* is a reflection of the young Nietzsche's belief in a similar redeeming event, which we saw play itself out in the course of the *UC*. But Zarathustra never uses the phrase "the meaning of the Earth" in *Za* II–IV; its thematic replacement is the statement *"the heart of the Earth is of gold"* (*Za* II On Great Events), which implies that the Earth and life have worth on their own and do not need the *Übermensch* (or anyone else) to give meaning and value to them. The *Übermensch* thus becomes a much more limited concept, an image of the perpetual self-overcoming of the human, in line with Nietzsche's usage of this word in his other writings. Already in *D* 27 Nietzsche describes a passion that has been given an illusion of permanence as "a new suprahuman [*übermenschlichen*] concept which elevates humanity." In *AC* 4, Nietzsche describes the higher human type whose side he takes in similarly relational terms, as a type "which is, in relation to humanity as a whole, a kind of *Übermensch*." In *EH* Books 1, Nietzsche explicitly says he uses the word *Übermensch* "as the designation of a type of supreme achievement, in contrast to "modern" humans, to "good" humans, to Christians and other nihilists." In *EH* Destiny 5 Nietzsche first continues with the same point, saying that Zarathustra's type of the human being is "a relatively superhuman type, is superhuman precisely in its relation to the *good* [human being]"; a couple of lines earlier he determines that this relative *Übermensch* is "the really truthful individual," that is, the knower whose life is oriented on the truth and nothing besides the truth. He then flips the perspective of this opposition and points out that " 'the good and the just' would call [Zarathustra's] *Übermensch* the *devil.*" In sum, the *Übermensch* is for the mature Nietzsche a symbol of the ceaseless striving to push human limits—in particular the limits of human *knowledge*—ever further and higher, a striving he first articulated in *HL* 2 and that he worked to promote in his readers ever since.

Another matter that deserves to be highlighted is the seriousness with which the *UC* deal with the problem of suffering. Of course, the sufferings

The Failures—and the Successes—of the *Untimely Considerations* | 195

inherent in the very effort to simply keep on living have been highlighted already in *BT* in the form of the "wisdom of Silenus" (1.35/*BT* 23).[37] But while *BT* frames these sufferings simply as the undifferentiated "terrors and horrors of existence" (1.35/*BT* 23), the *UC* explore in much greater detail the manifold forms in which humans suffer from life. It is no exaggeration to say that in the *UC*, every kind of human existence is examined with an eye to the peculiar sorts of suffering it entails. Here belongs "the suffering under *convention*" (1.455/281), the suffering resulting from our incapacity to express our needs because of the alienated character of modern language. The philistines suffer from the bad conscience that results from their avoidance of their particular genius (1.338, 1.463/172, 288), as well as from the sense of the meaninglessness of their existence, from the creeping sense that their ordinary existence is a pointless bad infinity (1.378/210), which they cover up with *divertissements*. On the other hand, the young souls who heed the command of their conscience to *be yourself* face their own sufferings that are even greater than those of the philistines. There are the manifold sufferings inherent in the striving for truthfulness, which they are voluntarily to take upon themselves in the process of their becoming a redeeming genius (1.371–372/203–204).[38] Furthermore, this process is risky and dependent on forces beyond oneself—and this results in the "sufferings of someone who is developing" that arise from the uncertainty of attaining the completion of one's project (1.439–441/267–269). And, at the highest level of insight that the *UC* recognize, "the greatest sufferings that exist for the individual" (1.451–452/278) await: namely the suffering caused by the unbearable tension between one's philanthropy and one's knowledge of the nature of human life, the suffering of knowing that however much one may strive, the redeeming insight of the genius will remain a preserve of a small group, and the vast majority of human beings will continue to lead lives that amount to senseless suffering.

---

37. This passage obliquely shows the ubiquity and longevity of the recognition of the sufferings of human existence. Nietzsche's immediate source for this story is Plutarch (*Moralia, Consolation to Apollonius* 27); Plutarch is quoting a now-lost work of Aristotle; and Aristotle says in the quoted passage that "this is such an old and ancient belief with us that no one knows at all either the beginning of the time or the name of the person who first promulgated it." More generally, recognition and attempted justification of the miseries inherent in human existence are already a staple of pre-philosophic reflection on human existence across time and space, as universal as the miseries themselves.

38. Nietzsche will always speak clearly about the dangers and difficulties of knowing, and of the—at least up to a certain point—unbearable character of the truth; *BGE* 39 is a characteristic late discussion of this issue.

196 | The Young Nietzsche's Education

As discussed above, the mature Nietzsche no longer thinks that the life of knowledge is suffering, let alone the greatest suffering of all—quite the opposite. Already in his next book, in *HA* 235, he addresses again the tension between one's philanthropy and one's knowledge of human affairs, but no longer as an insoluble and unbearable tension. Here, the tension between "the warmest heart" and "the highest intelligence" is resolved unambiguously in favor of knowledge. In its desire to institute a perfect state in which humans would no longer suffer—a state akin to that which the redemptive event should bring about—"the warmest heart" wants not only something that may well be impossible, but also something that goes against the conditions of its own existence. For "the warmest heart" is a *passionate* heart, and the only way to establish a perfect state without suffering is to populate it solely with "enfeebled individuals," with last-man–like people no longer capable of such a passion as "the warmest heart" itself exhibits. Thus, Nietzsche concludes, "the warmest heart desires the abolition of its own foundation, the destruction of itself, which is to say it desires something illogical, it lacks intelligence." And therefore, "the sage has to resist these extravagant desires of unintelligent goodness, because [their] concern is the continuance of [their] type and the eventual creation of the highest intelligence." The status of philanthropy that wants to remove suffering from human affairs is reduced because, on examination, this philanthropy has shown itself to be a self-defeating enterprise. Knowledge, as the love of necessity (cf. Meier, 2019, p. 74), now determines the limits on the love of humanity—limits that are necessary if both these passions are to coexist and if they are not to engage in self-contradictory projects. The solution of *HA* 235 remained decisive for Nietzsche ever since, as evident, for example, from *BGE* 87.

However, the suffering inherent in human existence, suffering that the vast majority of humans have to find a way of dealing with, remains a major concern of Nietzsche's thinking throughout his career. One example of central importance to Nietzsche's mature thought is the famous sentence "the human being would much rather will *nothingness* than *not* will" that appears in *GM* III.1 and III.28, thus framing the body of *GM* III. What emerges from the overall argument of *GM* III is that a crucial reason behind the world-historical success of Christianity is precisely that it was able to provide the vast numbers of subjected and miserable human beings with a reason for their suffering, namely that it is the punishment for their sins (*GM* III.15); with ways to redirect and discharge their vengeful affects that they cannot turn against their masters, even if this means turning these

The Failures—and the Successes—of the *Untimely Considerations* | 197

affects against oneself (*GM* III.16–20); and with a goal—a goal in the illusory Beyond, but a goal nevertheless—at which they could aim their willing, and for the sake of which the ascetic practices should be performed. The function of the life-denying ascetic ideals is precisely to give meaning to the sufferings of human existence by presenting them as a path to an alleged better existence after death. The ascetic ideals gave meaning to human suffering, and "thus far it has been the only meaning" (*GM* III.28), at least for the vast majority of humanity. Their enormous historical success is the result of them fulfilling the essential function of making suffering meaningful and giving it a place in the overall psychic economy of their followers, while having no competition in the form of a life-affirming ideal that could fulfill the same function.

What brings all these insights of the *UC* together is their close relation to the human soul, of which they all speak in one way or another. Be it the death of the Christian God who served as the capstone of a moral structure (cf. *TI* Skirmishes 5) that effectively knew no rival in Europe for almost two millennia, or the rise of the last man who, without such a God, fails to cultivate his desiring in any direction whatsoever and instead sinks into a self-satisfied comfortable life; be it Nietzsche's wish to promote the striving beyond what one currently is, his account of how one may get to know oneself and one's genuine needs (i.e., knowledge of what striving beyond oneself means in one's particular case), and his efforts to educate his readers and to induce them to such a striving on their own part; or be it the manifold ways in which we experience life as suffering and even as unbearable—all these insights of the *UC* speak of psychic phenomena and can be explicated in the terms of the erotic-historic soul.

I would moreover like to contend that the psychological theory of the *UC*, the theory of the erotic-historic soul whose cornerstones can be found in *HL* 1 and *SE* 1, is in its core the same as that of the mature Nietzsche, which is discussed in most detail in *BGE*. This soul is composed of desires as mutually conflicting driving forces of our action, and of memory-based higher structures such as conscience through which the desires express themselves and from which the human soul receives its complexity. In *BGE* 12 we find the soul characterized as a "social structure of the drives and affects": in terms of a multitude of "wills," or desires, that exist alongside each other and vie with each other for domination, that is, for the capacity to direct the entire human being toward their own satisfaction at the expense of the competing wills or desires. *BGE* 19 expands on this by constructing willing itself in terms of this manifold structure: In each act

198 | The Young Nietzsche's Education

of what is commonly called "willing" we actually deal with "commanding and obeying, on the basis, as already said, of a social structure composed of many 'souls,'" and we identify our "self" with that will or desire that prevailed over the others. The conflicting nature of our desires furthermore necessitates that the chaos that is their natural state be ordered in some way, as otherwise we would not be capable of any higher psychic functions than satisfaction of our immediate physiological needs. In other words, human beings necessarily need *a* morality: "morality being understood as the doctrine of the relations of supremacy under which the phenomenon of 'life' comes to be" (*BGE* 19).[39] He expands on this understanding of morality as a tool of psychic organization in *BGE* 188: Each morality is, he says, "a piece of tyranny against 'nature'; also against 'reason.'"[40] *BGE* 188 continues by explaining that any morality is above all a compelling force that strives to keep the activities of the soul within boundaries determined by the ruling desire of the soul in question, and as such it not only limits the expression of other desires within that soul, but it also sets the terms in which the other drives may express themselves: A morality of any sort entails "the need for limited horizons"—a phrase that originates in *HL* 1 (1.251/90)—for horizons of significance formed by the ruling desire itself. It is thanks to these manifold forms of compulsion that humans have set upon themselves and each other that manifold human capacities were able to develop into the immense height and breadth in which we can observe them throughout human history, into the astonishing diversity of human ways of life, acting, and thinking: Out of such a "single-minded" compulsion "something always develops, and has developed, for whose sake it is worth while to live on Earth; for example, virtue, art, music, dance, reason, spirituality—something transfiguring, subtle, mad, and divine."

As always, it is thinking in particular that draws Nietzsche's attention when he goes on to say that it was precisely the compulsion of morality through which "the European spirit has been trained to strength, ruthless curiosity, and subtle mobility." Needless to say, Nietzsche himself, and we ourselves, are the heirs and beneficiaries of this long compulsion. And

---

39. That Nietzsche speaks here of "life" rather than of "the human being" implies that a similar, albeit simpler structure exists also in other living beings—an idea that harks back to Aristotle's conception of the soul as the specific form of a given kind of living being (cf. *De anima* II.1).

40. For a similar and more thorough account of Nietzsche's understanding of morality, cf. van Tongeren 1989.

The Failures—and the Successes—of the *Untimely Considerations* | 199

just as in *SE* 1 conscience was understood a memory-based structure that compares our current existence with the kind of existence that our ruling desire prescribes to us, so it is in *BGE* 158: "to our strongest drive, the tyrant in us, not only our reason bows but also our conscience." "Reason" is understood here instrumentally, as a tool that calculates the best course of action on behalf of a desire that sets the goal for it. In terms of the erotic-historic soul, this makes it yet another memory-based structure, "historical" in the sense of *HL* 1.

The opposite case—the lack of a ruling desire and of a stable structure of command within a soul, the lack of a morality that compels the other desires to obedience and servitude to the ruling desire's goal—is what the mature Nietzsche calls *decadence*. Decadence understood as "anarchy of the atoms, disintegration of the will" (*CW* 7; cf. *TI* Skirmishes 35) can be used as a description of the condition that Nietzsche diagnosed in *HL* as the "historical sickness"; but decadence is a much wider term that encompasses many more problems than just the oversaturation with historical learning that was the core problem in *HL*.[41] A telling example is the fact that Wagner, who in the *UC* was hailed as the exemplary artist and one who has managed to learn a lot without succumbing to the historical sickness (1.442/269), is in *CW* (esp. Epilogue) precisely the exemplary decadent, the "*most instructive case*" of the modern soul divided against itself. Here it is important to note that this revaluation of Wagner's spiritual health does not imply a denial of the capacity for learning ascribed to him in *WB*.

BGE 230 expands this account of the soul by describing knowledge and experience as something to be digested and incorporated [*einverleibt*] by the soul—again a notion that appears already in *HL* 1 (1.251/89). Our soul tends to approach the things it encounters in the world with "a strong inclination to assimilate the new to the old, to simplify the manifold, and to overlook or repulse whatever is totally contradictory." This process of assimilating the new into the preexisting structure is, like the useful kinds of history in *HL* 2–3, also a process of falsification: The new things and experiences are not examined for what they are by themselves but are taken in terms of their utility for our goals and forced into the roles we prescribe to them. This process of "filing new things in old files" leads to "growth," or the feeling thereof: It is the feeling of being ever more in control of our world, of making our world conform to an ever-greater degree to our

---

41. Cf. Conway (1999, pp. 60–67) for a more detailed account of decadence in the late Nietzsche.

200 | The Young Nietzsche's Education

structures of meaningfulness. A part of this basic way of relating to our world is also the "apparently opposite drive" toward ignorance and "the limiting horizon" that is regulated by the strength of our nature—just as in *HL* 1, there are limits to how much we can process and incorporate, and matters whose relevance to our goals we fail to see remain outside of our mental horizon. These two drives, toward incorporation and exclusion, are two sides of the same coin: Their combined effect is the limiting of our world to matters we find meaningful and the ever-greater integration of such matters into our structures of meaningfulness. In this way, our world becomes ever more "our," and we come to see ourselves as ever more "at home" in it.

At this point in *BGE* 230 Nietzsche introduces an innovation that has no thematic parallel in *HL*: namely "the sublime inclination of the knower, who treats and *wants* to treat things in a profound, multiple, and thorough manner," which is as such opposed to our natural way of approaching the world, dubbed "the fundamental will of the spirit" by Nietzsche.[42] Knowledge as the desire to understand things as what they are by themselves stands in a peculiar opposition to our basic tendency to incorporate them in terms or horizons of the ruling passion.[43] This opposition carries several important implications for Nietzsche's cognitive psychology. First of all, it means that if we are at all to know things as they are, we first need to get to know ourselves and our soul and become aware of the distorting tendencies that our particular needs and desires implant into the way we look

---

42. As Meier (2019, pp. 270) points out, the description of "this fundamental will of the spirit" makes clear that it is the same thing as what Nietzsche elsewhere calls "the will to power" (cf. *BGE* 9 in particular). My discussion of *BGE* 230 here is indebted to Meier's reading thereof (2019, pp. 269–273) also more generally.

43. From this we can also see why truth—in the sense of seeing things as they are in themselves rather than in terms of their utility for our goals—is "deadly" for Nietzsche. Things often—in the case of a regular person, much more often than not—are not what we would like or need them to be, and becoming aware of this gap between what a thing is and what we have so far taken it to be, becoming aware of our hitherto-deluded way of seeing and acting, can deal a painful blow to our confidence that we know how to satisfy our ruling passion, how to get what we want. It leads to a state of *aporia* in which the previous way of acting or thinking is no longer feasible (and may have even come to light as violent, shameful, disgusting, or otherwise unacceptable in the light of our current self-understanding), and no new and better way is immediately in sight. Moreover, this is the case not just for the regular person, but (up to a certain point) also for the knower who, after all, willingly seeks out such truths about themselves: "anyone who ever built a 'new heaven' first found the power to do so in their *own hell*" (*GM* III.10).

The Failures—and the Successes—of the *Untimely Considerations* | 201

at the world. Knowledge requires *self-knowledge*: Only by carrying out this reflexive turn can the being for whom its own being is at stake find out how its existential investments distort its way of seeing, and subsequently take distance from its own biases and correct them. Second, this clearly is no easy task: It requires that one consciously and deliberately oppose one's most natural tendency, and this over a long period of time. It requires a "moral" training in the sense of *BGE* 188, an *askesis* of wisdom, a long and arduous training in searching for one's biases and correcting them.[44] Third, this process of coming to see, oppose, and correct the distorting tendencies of the fundamental will of the spirit is a difficult and painful undertaking, a process of strict self-discipline, a kind of cutting oneself open and severing the ligaments of one's cognitive apparatus in order to replace them with new and more adequate connections—which explains why Nietzsche calls it "a kind of cruelty of the intellectual conscience and taste."[45] Fourth and finally, an endeavor like this requires a powerful driving force that would provide us with the strength to oppose our natural tendency to distort the world according to our wishes, a power that would outweigh the power of this natural tendency. The passion for knowledge, whose goal is precisely to know things as they are by themselves, can fulfill this crucial function, at least for those in whom it had become the ruling passion.[46]

In *BGE* 23, Nietzsche characterizes his psychology as "morphology and *the doctrine of the development of the will to power*." How does this psychology of the will to power relate to the erotic-historic soul? Well, just like *eros*, the will is constituted by a lack: We will what we do not yet have. Normal

---

44. The word *askesis* originally denoted athletic training, and the ancient philosophic tradition came to use it as a name for various kinds of practices and spiritual exercises whose purpose was to improve the order of one's soul and thus to orient one's life on the activity of philosophizing. For examples of such usage, see *Gorgias* 527e; *Cleitophon* 407b; Xenophon's Socrates (*Memorabilia* I.2.23); or Diogenes Laertius VI.48, 71 (in reference to Diogenes the Cynic). Nietzsche speaks of this kind of *askesis*, e.g., in *D* 195, where he mentions "the practical asceticism of all Greek philosophers." The current meaning of "asceticism" that implies self-denial or mortification of the flesh—the sense in which also Nietzsche speaks of "ascetic ideals" in *GM* III—is the result of the later Christian appropriation of the philosophic usage (Hadot, 1995, p. 128). Cf. van Tongeren, Schank, & Siemens (2004, pp. 155–173) for an exhaustive account of Nietzsche's usage of the word.

45. However, unlike the pain caused by scientific history, these are genuine growing pains (cf. Chapter II.3).

46. This has important implications for the thinker's striving to become what they are—see the next section.

202 | The Young Nietzsche's Education

willing or desiring has a particular object or goal; the "power" in the will to power is not such a goal. It is rather a general characteristic of the goals we tend to seek. If we hear in the word "power" the Greek *dynamis* or the Latin *potentia*, the will to power shows itself to us as the will to increase our capacities for thinking and action, or to extend our current possibilities.[47] The will to power is thus continuous with the core of what I called "Nietzschean humanism" in my discussion of monumental history. It is also a polemical counterpoint to the doctrines of Spinoza and Schopenhauer, according to which life strives *merely* to preserve itself (*BGE* 13).

In short, the mature Nietzsche's psychology in principle follows the erotic-historic model of the soul from the *UC*. His main focus is on the "erotic" part of the soul: on the desires, on their internal conflicts, and on ways of ordering them into a single structure not torn by mutual strife; in a word, on the "politics of the soul," as Thiele (1990) puts it. The Platonic tripartite model of the soul, in which each of the three "parts" (and, at least in the case of the appetitive "part," their sub-parts) has its own desire to satisfy, and caring for the soul means harmonizing these "parts" under the rule of the rational "part," is clearly an inspiration for Nietzsche.[48] Both Plato and Nietzsche examine the reality of psychic conflict among the various desires that constitute the soul: They examine both *what* rules the soul and *how* it rules, what kind of *regime* the ruling passion establishes within the soul (cf. Acampora, 2013, pp. 195–196). Both also examine the various possible ways of resolving our psychic conflict, that is, ways of ordering the soul into a single, ordered, and non-self-contradictory whole (inasmuch as this is in human capacities). Of course, Nietzsche doesn't think "reason" should rule the entire human being, or that it even *could* do so (cf. *BGE* 191); but Plato too discusses the three parts of the soul as each having desires and pleasures of their own (*Republic* 580d–3a), and such a desiring reason is surprisingly close to Nietzsche's "passion for knowledge." I believe it could be shown that many features of Nietzsche's mature writings, such as decadence (see above) or his typological enterprise in *AC*, can and should be understood in terms of this conception of the soul as a plurality of contesting parts. That, however, is beyond the scope of this study.[49]

---

47. So Heidegger (1991, vol. I, p. 64), who also defines power as "will as willing out beyond itself" [*Über-sich-hinaus-wollen*].

48. On this subject cf. the excellent discussion in Parkes (1994, pp. 305–334, and Chapter IX in general).

49. Fink (2003, p. 118) has a particular blind spot here, claiming—in a discussion of the late Nietzsche!—that "Nietzsche clarifies his psychological preconceptions and the structure of the psyche itself nowhere clearly."

The Failures—and the Successes—of the *Untimely Considerations* | 203

Of course, the psychological understanding is much more refined in the later works, not least through the historicization of origin of the structures of the soul (e.g., *GM* passim); Parkes (1994, p. 331) calls this "the increasing realization of how much more of the 'foreign' past comes to us through 'the blood.' " The result of this procedure is historicization and immanentization of many features of the human soul that would otherwise seem to be "natural" or "transcendental," such as the distinction between *good* and *evil*, or the existence of *bad* conscience (as opposed to a conscience working in the service of our ruling passion). It also led him to the recognition that philosophy is nothing self-evidently good and valuable, but rather that for the greatest part of human history, philosophy and independent thinking in general has been considered criminal to the highest degree (*GM* III.9; *TI* Skirmishes 45; *AC* 13). But since it is in *HL* where Nietzsche first tells us that he considers the doctrine "of the lack of any cardinal difference between human and animal" true (1.319/153), this historicization does not constitute a substantially different model of the soul. Thus, the late Nietzsche's framework for thinking about the soul is in its central features the same as the one he first developed in the *UC*.

V.4. The Thought of the *UC* as a Means to Overcome Itself

Nietzsche's thinking in the *UC* contains also two moments that, although by themselves they fall short of the perspective of Nietzsche's later philosophy, were nevertheless instrumental in helping him attain that perspective. Although the thinking of the *UC* led Nietzsche into the crisis triggered by the Bayreuth festival, these two moments moved him not to remain stuck in it and to emerge from it with the recognition of his earlier errors.

The first of these is the voluntary acceptance of the suffering of truthfulness (1.371/203). This is admittedly a moral attitude: The suffering of truthfulness is accepted not for one's own sake, but rather in order to bring about the redemptive event and thus to justify the world that would otherwise remain meaningless. We could describe it as a kind of "piety of knowledge" in the language of *GS* 344, although a different kind than the one discussed in that aphorism. Whereas the scientist described in *GS* 344 is unconditionally opposed to lies and untruths of any kind, their attitude being "I do not want to deceive," Nietzsche's attitude is far removed from this, as is evident already from the very first page of *DS*, where he tells us that "delusions can be of the most salutary and blessed nature" (1.159/6). In *HL* Nietzsche agrees with Goethe's idea that scientific knowledge should be kept away from the general public and contribute to life "only by means

204 | The Young Nietzsche's Education

of an *enhanced praxis*" (1.301/137), and he explicitly warns against the spread of "doctrines I hold to be true, but also deadly" precisely because of their corrosive effects on the solidarity of a people, which would then dissolve into "systems of individual egoisms" (1.319/153). We saw that the image of Wagner in *WB* is a monumental fiction that has little to do with Nietzsche's private understanding of Wagner at that point, and this essay ends with the hope that Wagner's fictions will become myths that will give meaning to the lives of the free human beings of the future (*WB* 11). In the thinking of the *UC*, truth is to be the preserve of an elite group, a group among whose members Nietzsche counts himself. Because the *UC* understand truth as essentially hostile to life, this "privilege" is actually an act of self-sacrifice on their part for the benefit of lesser humans.

But it was precisely this attitude of desiring the truth at any cost, regardless of how painful or difficult to bear it may be, that allowed—or rather *forced*—Nietzsche not to close his eyes in the face of the fiasco of Bayreuth. He had to face the facts that the project he had just presented in the *UC* was never going to happen and that he was tricked by Wagner's big words into publicly supporting a man who was much more of an actor than Nietzsche had supposed. Nietzsche could have followed Wagner's example, thrown out whatever of his own ideas was no longer applicable, and pretended that everything was going swimmingly. Had he done this, he could have enjoyed a comfortable existence as one of the Maestro's foremost disciples at a time after "the greatest victory an artist has ever achieved" (*HA* II Preface 1), as Nietzsche described the first Bayreuth festival in retrospect. But this was never a real option. For Nietzsche, the attitude of accepting the suffering of truthfulness was not a pose, but a genuine commitment. To abandon it for the sake of living comfortably alongside Wagner would be completely unheroic and unphilosophic; it would mean giving up everything that had defined him until then. And so he had to suffer from truthfulness once more and examine where his thinking had gone wrong. Nietzsche's pessimistic attitude of wanting the truth at any cost led him also to examine the truth behind the presuppositions of this attitude itself. As he tells us in *EH* HA 1, in the period of *HA* he formulated critiques of concepts like "the genius," "the saint," "the hero," "faith," "conviction," "pity," and "the thing in itself"—almost all of which play a prominent role in the *UC*. And, as we saw, in *D* 550 at the latest he achieves the rejection of the idea of the insoluble conflict between truth and life that was the main premise of his early pessimism. The practical attitude issuing from his pessimism came to overcome the

The Failures—and the Successes—of the *Untimely Considerations* | 205

thinking behind it—just as Nietzsche will later say that it was in fact the Christian morality of unconditional honesty that made the Christian faith unbelievable, that in this way the Christian God abolished himself. As he says in *GS* 357 and repeats in *GM* III.27, "We see *what* it was that really triumphed over the Christian God: Christian morality itself, the concept of truthfulness that was understood ever more rigorously, the father confessor's refinement of the Christian conscience, translated and sublimated into the scientific conscience, into intellectual cleanliness at any price." Just as the practice of Christian faith abolished its theoretical basis and thus itself, so did the practice of Schopenhauerian pessimism abolish its theoretical basis in Nietzsche's case. In the note 27 [80] (8.500) from 1878, Nietzsche indeed interprets the attitude of the Schopenhauerian human being as what drove him to "skepticism against everything revered and held up high, everything I have defended until then (also against the Greeks, Schopenhauer, and Wagner)," and says that this "*detour*" was how he came to his "*height*." This "height," although in 1878 it can't yet be Nietzsche's mature philosophical outlook, is a height in relation to the earlier Schopenhauerian-pessimistic position. His mature outlook, even though Nietzsche is fond of calling it a kind of pessimism as well ("pessimism of *strength*" in *BT* Attempt 1, or "*Dionysian* pessimism" in *GS* 370), is rather an overcoming of pessimism. As it is described in *BGE* 56, Nietzsche came to it by thinking pessimism "through to its depths"—that is, by uncovering and examining its premises by the practice of unconditional truthfulness—and by consequently opening his eyes "to the opposite ideal." This ideal entails the affirmation of everything there was and is, and even the affirmation of the eternal return of everything there was and is—the eternal return being the "highest formula of affirmation that is at all attainable" (*EH* Za 1). We can thus sketch a path from the denial of the livability of the truthful life in the *UC* to a full affirmation of the whole—a path on which the pessimistic ideal of unconditional truthfulness was, at least initially, an indispensable guideline.

The second matter of particular importance in this respect is the doctrine of *be yourself*. Here we must distinguish between its function as a universal ideal for the project of the *UC* and its personal-individual dimension, in which it is an exhortation to specific self-chosen individuals—the young souls in *UC*—as well as to Nietzsche himself. Both these senses are clearly present in *SE* 1: Nietzsche first laments the present rule of "publicly opining pseudo-human beings" and speculates that because of it, the present age may be the "least human chapter of history" (1.338–339/172). But he opens the next paragraph by emphasizing that the effort to *be yourself*

206 | The Young Nietzsche's Education

is of supreme importance to our lives "even if the future were to give us no cause for hope" (1.339/173). In this personal-individual dimension it was to remain one of Nietzsche's central positive doctrines. He changed the wording of this doctrine from *be yourself* to *become who you are*, but this doesn't substantially change its content: It rather serves to emphasize the paradox of exhorting us to become what we think we already are. The doctrine appears in this new wording in *GS* 270 as the voice of Nietzsche's own conscience (and in *GS* 255 it describes his ambition as a teacher), and he chose it—in a significantly modified form[50]—as the subtitle for *EH*, his intellectual autobiography.

However, this is not to say that the doctrine as it is presented in the *UC* is the same as in the mature Nietzsche and that it hasn't undergone important developments after the *UC*. Acampora (2013, ch. 5), who contrasts the account of Wagner's becoming-himself in *WB* (which is the principal example of this process in the *UC*) with Nietzsche's account of his own becoming-himself in *EH*, points out several important differences between these two accounts. First, the Wagner of *WB* becomes himself by undergoing heroic struggles with himself as well as with the world, whereas the Nietzsche of *EH* claims that "no trace of *struggle* can be demonstrated in my life; I am the opposite of a heroic nature" (*EH* Clever 9). Second, while Wagner became himself by pursing his artistic ideals and realizing them with ever-greater fidelity, in *EH* Clever 9 Nietzsche asserts that "to become what one is, one must not have the faintest notion *what* one is," that the process of becoming-oneself is not under our conscious control and direction; and even that in cases such as Nietzsche's, when one's task is as enormous as the revaluation of all values, "*nosce te ipsum* would be the recipe for ruin." These two points of direct contrast (Acampora, 2013, p. 154) lead us to consider further divergences between these two accounts.

Third of these is that while the Wagner of *WB* is devoted to his ideals, the Nietzsche of *EH* emphasizes the importance of selfishness in the sense of self-love and self-care (indicated by words such as "self-love" [*Selbstsucht*] or "self-preservation" [*Selbsterhaltung*]). This selfishness means putting oneself

---

50. The subtitle of *EH* is "How One Becomes What One Is." First, this is no longer an imperative, but an answer to a question. Second, the question is not how to become who we are, but how to become *what* we are. Taken together, these changes imply that Nietzsche has fulfilled what was earlier the imperative of his conscience, that he is now in position to explain the inner workings of this process to us, and that he now understands it as closely related to one's psycho-physiological type, to the "what" of one's nature.

The Failures—and the Successes—of the *Untimely Considerations* | 207

and one's own bodily well-being in the first place, paying the greatest attention to seemingly small things such as "the choice of nutrition, of place and climate, of recreation" (*EH* Clever 8), which Nietzsche discusses in detail on his own example in *EH* Clever 1–8. This search for the optimal conditions of one's day-to-day existence is guided by the question "How do *you*, among all people, have to nourish yourself to attain your maximum of strength, of *virtù* in the Renaissance style, of moraline-free virtue?" (*EH* Clever 1), that is, by the effort to gather and increase one's powers without wasting them in struggling with unimportant but annoying everyday problems: "our *great* expenses are composed of the most frequent small ones" (*EH* Clever 8). Here I would add that this emphasis on the body[51] does not have a precedent in the *UC*; it was thematically introduced in *WS* 5 as the turning from the "first and last things" to the "*nearest things*" that encompass precisely the small, everyday conditions of our embodied existence. It receives its most forceful expression in *EH* Clever 10, where Nietzsche declares that

> These small things—nutrition, place, climate, recreation, the whole casuistry of selfishness—are inconceivably more important than everything one has taken to be important so far. Precisely here one must begin to *relearn*. [. . .] All the problems of politics, of social organization, and of education have been falsified through and through because one mistook the most harmful individuals for great individuals—because one learned to despise "little" things, which means the basic concerns of life itself.

The goal of this Nietzschean selfishness isn't merely that we feel good about ourselves and our lives (though that certainly is *a* goal of it too): It is rather the accumulation of our productive forces. As Acampora (2013, p. 184) describes it, it aims "not at preserving mere existence or sheer survival [. . .] but rather at achieving a certain 'self-sufficiency that overflows and gives to men and things' (*GS* 55)."

Another way of describing this kind of selfishness is the metaphor of pregnancy, which Nietzsche uses in *D* 552. In a state such as pregnancy, says Nietzsche, we do everything "in the unspoken belief that it has somehow to benefit that which is coming to be within us." At the same time,

---

51. Understood as *Leib* rather than *Körper*, as the living, ensouled body, as the interrelated unity of our psychic and physical powers that forms a single mortal whole. Cf. Hutter (2006, pp. 26–31).

208 | The Young Nietzsche's Education

we do not know or care what is it that grows in us or what will become of it, what kinds of effects will it have: It is "a pure and purifying feeling of profound irresponsibility," in which our only care is for ourselves and for the conditions in which *we* live, so that our "offspring" may turn out as well as possible. Nietzsche is quite emphatic on the benefits of living in such a "pregnancy":

> It is *in this state of consecration* that one should live! It is a state one can live in! And if what is expected is an idea, a deed—towards every bringing forth we have essentially no other relationship than that of pregnancy and ought to blow to the winds all presumptuous talk of "willing" and "creating"! This is *ideal selfishness*: continually to watch over and care for and to keep our soul still, so that our fruitfulness shall *come to a happy fulfilment!*

And by living in such a way—not caring for what we "want" to do or achieve, but rather keeping ourselves healthy and prepared for whatever thoughts or deeds may come to us when their time arrives—"we watch over and care for to the *benefit of all*." This is the best way of using our powers on an everyday basis.

What are these thoughts or deeds that should come out of our selfishness or self-care? They are the particular works or tasks that come to our sight in the course of our life and that we take upon ourselves. To be sure, the tasks *we* in particular choose for ourselves are to a large degree dependent on the kind of person we already are, but this doesn't mean they are a matter of simple self-expression. They rather contribute significantly to our further growth and becoming, to the process of ordering our soul in new and more complex ways. As Acampora (2013, p. 186) puts it, in accomplishing one's tasks "One does not simply realize some potency already there, fully formed, from the start; nor does one make oneself into something other than what one already is. Rather, *becoming what one is* is realized through an interactive process in which the constitutive rank ordering of drives is achieved by virtue of a form of ruling expressed in engaging others." In Nietzsche's case, these tasks were his engagements with philosophical problems and spiritual opponents. He tells us that he sought out to engage with such problems and enemies that "require us to stake all our strength, suppleness, and fighting skill—opponents that are our equals" (*EH* Wise 7). There is thus a transformative dimension to Nietzsche's "practice of war" (*EH* Wise 7): "his

The Failures—and the Successes—of the *Untimely Considerations* | 209

agones represent his efforts to engineer, harness, and direct in the future the efficient force that is the will to power that he *is*" (Acampora, 2013, p. 191). At the same time, Nietzsche's choice of worthy and victorious opponents to fight seeks to challenge their strengths rather than their weaknesses, and thereby formulate alternatives that can overcome the hitherto victorious causes he attacks. Another consequence of this approach is the polemical bent it gives to his arguments: Acampora (2013, p. 188) says that "virtually all his positive views are inseparable from the positions he battles such that his 'practice of war' plays a significant role in shaping both *what* ideas he expresses and *how* he does so." Nietzsche's practice of war thus transforms him by giving him occasions for a full exercise of his powers and thereby for psychic growth and integration; it challenges his opposition in its strong points, precisely where it hitherto was able to prevail over enemies, that is, at the core of its appeal; and it shapes the expression of his ideas in writing. Nietzsche's philosophic works are the results of this practice of war, artifacts of his spiritual becoming. This assessment can be applied already to the *UC*, which Nietzsche retrospectively characterized as "thoroughly warlike" (*EH* UC 1) and as "attempts at assassination" (*EH* UC 2).

What all these differences amount to is a significant change of orientation between the early doctrine of *be yourself* and the mature account of "becoming what one is" in *EH*. The thematic effort to *be yourself* is no longer to be the chief object of one's desire. One's immediate task is rather to develop a "casuistry of selfishness" (*EH* Clever 10) that seeks out the optimal conditions for one's body, learning to live according to the needs of one's psychophysiological (or *leiblich*) nature, an effort to live well in an everyday sense so as to achieve the optimum of strength. This strength is then to be utilized, expressed, and increased by carrying out particular tasks that come to one's sight. These tasks or *agones* are "both *expressive* of the order of rank that [one] is and *effective* in rendering that ordering" (Acampora, 2013, p. 193). These tasks or *agones* are not to be taken as of absolute importance, but rather as partial expressions of whatever we are, or of whatever we are pregnant with—which will show itself in due time. "Becoming what one is" is not itself a task, as it was the case in *SE* (cf. the end of Chapter III above); it is rather by taking up and completing various tasks that one becomes what one is; tasks are ultimately ministerial. Meier (2019, p. 102) describes the central integrative role of the task (meaning his overarching task of revaluation of all values) in Nietzsche's becoming-himself as follows: "It is the task through which Nietzsche gets to know himself; through which he determines his nature, the order of rank of his capacities,

210 | The Young Nietzsche's Education

his passions, his virtues, and his skills; the task puts him into position to become *one* and allows him to integrate his personal history and to see it as meaningful." Finally, both Acampora (2013, p. 196) and Meier (2019, p. 67) point out that "becoming what one is" is not a process of realizing a pre-given end state to which we would proceed teleologically: Failure is a genuine possibility, and self-knowledge is essential for avoiding wrong turns.[52] We saw above that Nietzsche dealt with his crisis—which he perceived as a serious danger of losing himself—by a thorough self-examination, by a reflection on who he was, how he lived, and how he acted.

To summarize, "becoming what one is" is for the mature Nietzsche not something that we can willfully and deliberately accomplish, nor is it a matter of fulfilling some entelechic destiny that would await us. It is rather a process of ordering and maximizing the drives and capacities of our nature, of the type of human being that we are; it is making it possible for a "destiny" that is appropriate to our nature to come to our sight and being able to seize it. The crucial difference between *be yourself* of *SE* and *becoming what one is* of *EH* is not so much in what is done, but in the *how*, in the attitude that underlies these two strivings. Whereas in *SE* it is a heroic struggle that gets all-too-easily subsumed under that other heroic struggle to redeem the world, regardless of personal consequences, what we find in *EH* is, above all else, the concern with one's genuine good and with knowledge thereof. *Becoming what one is* means freedom as opposed to servitude to a (*any*) morality; it means the focus on *Leib* and the "nearest things" that constitute its material good, as opposed to the overly "spiritual" conception of the human in *SE*; and it means the orientation on the *agathon*, as opposed to the *kalon*.[53]

---

52. Meier (2019, p. 122) emphasizes that just as there isn't any personal providence for the mature Nietzsche (cf. *GS* 277), there also isn't any kind providential world-order with regard to our projects; we only get what we manage to make ourselves.

53. Another major difference between the account of *SE* and of *EH* is that the later Nietzsche employs only a *retrospective* teleology, which can be seen only once the process of becoming-oneself has been completed (cf. Meier, 2019, p. 102). This differs from the *prospective* teleology of *SE* (1.340/174), which wants to extrapolate the retrospective teleological account of how we have become what we are (at this point) to our future becoming as well. The later Nietzsche's critique of the early Nietzsche in this regard would be that *prospectively* we can only focus on particular tasks to guide us in our growth and to serve as means of our growth; the teleological perspective is valid only in the retrospect. As Meier (2019, p. 102) describes it, "before [Nietzsche] gets to see his task and himself, he of necessity sees a different picture."

The Failures—and the Successes—of the *Untimely Considerations* | 211

But despite the significant differences of the articulation of "becoming what one is" that we find in *EH*, the doctrine of *be yourself* from the *UC* was still beneficial to Nietzsche on his path to becoming himself. It cannot be overlooked that its presentation in *SE* and its exemplification in *WB* form the first articulation of one of the major concerns of Nietzsche's thought. The basic point that education is fundamentally self-education is affirmed in *WS* 267 and later. As mentioned above, "become what you are" is a dictate of Nietzsche's conscience in *GS* 270, and thus obtains its power from his awareness of his mortality and ephemerality. Given that the later Nietzsche still holds (in broad terms) an "erotic-historic" conception of the soul, his method of self-knowledge, of getting to know such a soul, is also "erotic-historic" (in the sense of taking into account both the ordering of our desires and our personal history), just as the method outlined in *SE* 1 is. Self-knowledge is not simply a matter of knowing how our desires are organized, but also of how they have developed, waxed and waned, conflicted and integrated with each other, until our soul has assumed the shape it has at the point where we come to be able to articulate this self-knowledge, this account of who or what we are and how we have become this. Both the "erotic" and the "historic" dimensions remain present here, and they are as intertwined as in *SE* 1, if not more so. Finally, it would be a mistake to think, despite Nietzsche's optimistic language, that even in *SE* he thinks that we can *fully* understand what we are ahead of the fact. He tells us explicitly there that our true self is *"immeasurably* high above you, or at least above what you commonly take to be your self" (1.340–341/174; emphasis added), and he is aware of the uncertainty inherent in the process of becoming-oneself (cf. 1.449/267)—although these aspects are much more marginal than in *EH*, and are treated more as problems to be dealt with than as elements constitutive of this process.

I would like to suggest that despite the somewhat inadequate formulation of the doctrine *be yourself* in the *UC*, already this formulation had proved sufficient in guiding Nietzsche toward his "destiny," that is, toward becoming a philosopher. He tells us that in this doctrine, as presented in *SE* and *WB,* "an unequaled problem of education, a new concept of self-discipline, self-defense to the point of hardness, a way to greatness and world-historical tasks was seeking its first expression" (*EH* UC 3). The expression of, and the solution to, this problem is not yet adequate, but the problem itself is already present. And this problem understood *as a problem* led Nietzsche to diagnose the crisis that followed the *UC* and the fiasco of Bayreuth in terms of losing his task (as can be seen from the discussion in

212 | The Young Nietzsche's Education

EH HA 3–4), that is, of him running away from his true self. He understands his crisis through the logic of becoming what one is, and therefore this logic, as formulated already in the *UC*, provides the grounds for the eventual overcoming of the crisis. If his (spiritual) sickness was his fear or refusal to become what he is, overcoming this sickness meant following his own prescription and returning to himself.

We have copious evidence for this understanding of the *UC*—especially of *SE*—on Nietzsche's part from his correspondence across the years between their publication and the writing of *EH*. In a draft intended for Lou von Salomé from December 1882 (KGB III.1, p. 299), he writes that "in Lucerne I gave you my work about Schopenhauer—I told you that my deepest and most fundamental sensibilities lie therein." He writes in the same vein to Georg Brandes six years later (letter from 19 Feb. 1888; KGB III.5, p. 260) that "the two works about Schopenhauer and Richard Wagner represent, as it seems to me today, more of a self-knowledge, and above all *vows to myself*, than an actual psychology of that maestro who is as deeply related as he is antagonistic to me." After Brandes reports having enjoyed *SE*, Nietzsche expands in response (letter from 10 Apr. 1888; KGB III.5, p. 287): "this short work [*SE*] serves as my sign of recognition: the person who does not find himself addressed *personally* by this work will probably have nothing more to do with me." A letter to Karl Knortz from 21 June 1888 (KGB III.5, p. 340) likewise highlights the importance of the *UC* for his intellectual development: "The *Untimely Considerations*, in a certain sense juvenilia, deserve the highest attention regarding my development. [. . .] the work about Schopenhauer, which I especially recommend you read, shows how an energetic and instinctively yes-saying spirit knows how to take the most beneficial impulses even from a pessimist." And in the note 41 [2] (11.670), Nietzsche likewise judges that "without even knowing it, I spoke [in *SE* and *WB*] only for myself, and in principle only about myself."

The second major judgment of the later Nietzsche is that the *UC*, and especially *SE*, are a *promise* or *vow* for the things to come, for his mature thought and body of work. Already in 1883, Nietzsche wrote to Peter Gast the following regarding *SE* and *Zarathustra* (letter from 21 Apr. 1883; KGB III.1, p. 364): "it is a curiosity: I wrote the *commentary* before the *text*. Everything is *promised* already in *Schopenhauer as Educator*, but there was still a long way to traverse from *Human, All Too Human* to the *Übermensch*." In August 1884 he wrote to Franz Overbeck (KGB III.1, p. 518): "I have *lived* just as I have prescribed it to myself (namely in *Schopenhauer as Educator*). [. . .] (its *error* is that it actually *doesn't* speak about Schopenhauer, but almost exclusively about me—but I didn't know that myself when I was writing it.).￼" A year later, in August 1885, we read in a draft to an unknown addressee (KGB III.3, p. 75): "my *Untimelies* mean *promises* for me: I do not know what they are for others. Believe me that I would not be alive anymore for a long time if I had evaded these promises even by a single step!" And finally, in the letter to Georg Brandes from 10 April 1888 (KGB III.5, p. 287), Nietzsche comments about *SE*: "in principle it contains the plan according to which I have lived until now: it is a strict *promise*." A promise to live truthfully and according to his ownmost nature, without any compromise in these two fundamental regards: Despite his incomplete youthful understanding of these two principles, Nietzsche always remained oriented on them, and this orientation was essential to his becoming what he is.

V.5. Conclusion

The examination of the *UC* from the perspective of the mature Nietzsche has shown us three central points. The first of these is that the thought of the *UC* is deeply marked by the idea of the fundamental and insoluble conflict between truth and life, the ultimate consequence of which is its life-denying character. Such thought cannot be considered philosophic in the sense in which the mature Nietzsche understands philosophy; it is rather just an expression of one's suffering from life. This issue, together with the central problem of the project of the *UC*—its connection to Wagner, who turned out to be nothing like Nietzsche had hoped—led to the fiasco of Bayreuth and to the crisis that Bayreuth triggered. In this crisis, Nietzsche had to reexamine and rethink all his views and beliefs, and especially give up the reliance on instinct that had shown itself to be untrustworthy (after all, it was the instinct that led him to Bayreuth).[54] The first fruit of the crisis was *HA*, a book that explicitly repudiates many of Nietzsche's earlier positions and is very different from Nietzsche's previous writings also in stylistic terms. The ultimate result of this process of rethinking was the abandonment of the thesis of the fundamental conflict between truth and life, and an affirmation of philosophy, of the life devoted to the truth, of the life for which truth is no longer an enemy but rather a *friend*, as the best possible way of life.

---

54. Cf. Meier (2019, p. 113) on the connection between the need to examine one's instincts and the figure of Socrates.

214 | The Young Nietzsche's Education

The second point is that the *UC* contain a surprisingly sophisticated psychological thinking, whose fundamental principles are the same as those of the psychology of *BGE*. Besides that, these four essays present virtually all the major concerns of Nietzsche's mature thought—concerns such as the death of God, the problem of suffering and life-affirmation, the structure of the human soul and the ways of unifying it, the critique of morality, education of his readers, or effecting a change on human life at large.[55] In (almost) all cases, his formulations of these concerns, and especially his proposed solutions to them, leave a lot to be desired. However, the *concerns* themselves never ceased to be concerns for Nietzsche, and in this sense the *UC* are the first full exploration of the intellectual space in which his thinking would continue to move throughout his career. As he says, already in the *UC* he "*beheld* the land" that he sought, and they are his "*vow*" (*EH* UC 3), his promise to himself to fully attain what he strives for already here, albeit not yet with full success.

The word *vow* [*Gelöbniss*] brings us to the third and final point. On a personal level—regarding Nietzsche's intellectual development after the *UC*—we cannot overlook the importance of Nietzsche's commitments to intellectual honesty and to becoming who he is. Although, again, his commitment to truth at any cost is in the *UC* a moralistic attitude (cf. Chapter V.2 above), and the doctrine *be yourself* would later undergo significant changes, they nevertheless proved to be crucial motive forces that helped Nietzsche overcome their own inadequacy. The commitment to truthfulness for its own sake pushed him away from the errors of the *UC*, and his wish to become what he is pulled him toward his mature self. When Nietzsche says that "in all psychologically decisive places I alone am discussed" in *WB* (*EH* BT 4), he is talking above all about the early model of "becoming

---

55. The late Nietzsche sees even the fanciful project of Bayreuth as a prefiguration of his actual world-historical task, of his spiritual founding of the "new party of life which would tackle the greatest of all tasks, raising humanity to higher levels" (*EH* BT 4). We cannot take seriously Nietzsche's claim that he "breaks the history of humanity in two" (*EH* Destiny 8) without considering *why* he believes he will have such an immense historical impact; and for this we need to understand what the failure of this first project was and what lessons he took from it. We thus cannot simply project *WB* onto the late Nietzsche, as Brooks (2018, p. 211) does; nor does it seem accurate to claim that the late Nietzsche opposed "the entire social and political framework of the modern West" (ibid.). To be sure, there are interesting parallels between the patterns first articulated in *SE* and *WB* and the task the late Nietzsche takes upon himself. But we would first have to understand the latter task to competently discuss these parallels.

what you are" that he showcases on Wagner, and on which he understood his own becoming as well at this point. When he claims the *UC* speak of "Schopenhauer and Wagner *or*, in one word, Nietzsche" (*EH* UC 1), and that he used these two men just as Plato used Socrates, namely "as a semiotic for Plato" (*EH* UC 3)—as semiotics for Nietzsche himself—the content of these "semiotics" are the commitments to unconditional truthfulness and to *be yourself* which were central to his self-understanding. These two commitments are integral parts of Nietzsche's becoming what he is, a stage of his development without which the mature Nietzsche cannot be imagined.

~

My final assessment of the *UC* is as follows. These essays are a beautiful document of Nietzsche's path to philosophy—but the goal, the perspective of the philosopher in the full sense of the word, the perspective that encompasses and affirms the whole of being, is not yet present in them. As such, they deserve particular attention of those who are on the path to philosophy themselves, who wish genuinely to philosophize. We can find much to learn in them, from the achievements of these early works (which I see in their understanding of the human soul and of the problem of modern culture), from their failures (especially their ultimately life-denying position and their excessive hopes for changing or even redeeming the world), and from how Nietzsche dealt with them. For Nietzsche himself the *UC* served as a ladder on which he climbed up to the height of his mature thought, and which he then discarded or greatly modified. And for us, here and now, they remain a testimony to the thinker's seriousness in grappling with the problematic nature of human existence, of the existence of the entity for whom alone its own being is at stake; and they are an inspiration for—as well as a challenge to—our own striving to understand ourselves and the world.

Bibliography

Acampora, C. D. (2013). *Contesting Nietzsche*. University of Chicago Press.

Ansell-Pearson, K. (2013). Holding on to the sublime: On Nietzsche's early "unfashionable" project. In J. Richardson & K. Gemes (Eds.), *The Oxford handbook of Nietzsche* (pp. 226–251). Oxford University Press.

Aristotle (1936). *De Anima*. In Aristotle, *On the soul, Parva Naturalia, On breath* (W. S. Hett, Trans.). Loeb Classical Library.

Aristotle (1998). *Politics* (C. D. C. Reeve, Trans.). Hackett.

Aristotle (2002). *On poetics* (S. Benardete & M. Davis, Trans.). St. Augustine's Press.

Banham, G., Schulting, D., & Hems, N. (Eds.) (2012). *The Continuum companion to Kant*. Continuum.

Berger, K. (2017). *Beyond reason: Wagner contra Nietzsche*. University of California Press.

Borchmeyer, D., & Salaquarda, J. (Eds.) (1994). *Nietzsche und Wagner. Stationen einer epochalen Begegnung* (Vols. 1–2). Insel Verlag.

Braatz, K. (1988). *Friedrich Nietzsche—Eine Studie zur Theorie der Öffentlichen Meinung* (Monographien und Texte zur Nietzsche-Forschung 18). De Gruyter.

Breazeale, D. (1997). Introduction. In *Nietzsche 1997* (pp. vii–xxxiii).

Breazeale, D. (1998). Becoming who one is: Notes on *Schopenhauer as Educator*. *New Nietzsche Studies, 2*(3–4), 1–25.

Brobjer, T. H. (2008). *Nietzsche's philosophical context: An intellectual biography*. University of Illinois Press.

Brooks, S. (2018). *Nietzsche's culture war: The unity of the Untimely Meditations*. Palgrave Macmillan.

Cavell, S. (1990). *Conditions handsome and unhandsome: The constitution of Emersonian perfectionism*. University of Chicago Press.

Church, J. (2015). *Nietzsche's culture of humanity: Beyond aristocracy and democracy in the early period*. Cambridge University Press.

Church, J. (2019). *Nietzsche's unfashionable observations: A critical introduction and guide*. Edinburgh University Press.

218 | Bibliography

Cicero, M. T. (1942). *De Oratore, Books I & II* (E. W. Sutton, Trans.). Loeb Classical Library.

Cicero, M. T. (1998). *Gespräche in Tusculum/Tusculanae Disputationes* (O. Gigon, Ed.). Artemis & Winkler.

Colli, G. (1999). Nachwort. In *Kritische Studienausgabe Bd. 1* (pp. 901–919). De Gruyter.

Conant, J. (2001). Nietzsche's perfectionism: A reading of *Schopenhauer as Educator*. In R. Schacht (Ed.), *Nietzsche's postmoralism* (pp. 181–257). Cambridge University Press.

Conant, J. (2014). *Friedrich Nietzsche: Perfektionismus & Perspektivismus* (J. Schulte, Trans.). Konstanz University Press.

Conway, D. W. (1999). The birth of the soul: Toward a psychology of decadence. In J. Golomb, W. Santaniello, & R. Lehre (Eds.), *Nietzsche and depth psychology* (pp. 51–71). State University of New York Press.

Dannhauser, W. (1990). Introduction to *HL*. In *Nietzsche 1990* (pp. 75–86).

Diels, H., & Kranz, W. (Eds.) (1960). *Die Fragmente der Vorsokratiker* (9th ed., Vols. 1–3). Weidmannsche Verlagsbuchhandlung.

Diogenes Laertius (1925). *Lives of eminent philosophers* (R. D. Hicks, Trans., Vols. 1–2). Loeb Classical Library.

Drochon, H. (2016). *Nietzsche's great politics*. Princeton University Press.

Eckermann, J. P. (2011). *Gespräche mit Goethe in den letzten Jahren seines Lebens*. Deutscher Klassiker Verlag.

Emden, Ch. (2006). Toward a critical historicism: History and politics in Nietzsche's second *Untimely Meditation*. *Modern Intellectual History, 3*(1), 1–31.

Fink, E. (1970). *Metaphysik der Erziehung im Weltverständnis von Plato und Aristoteles*. Vittorio Klostermann.

Fink, E. (1992). *Nietzsches Philosophie* (6th ed.). Kohlhammer Verlag.

Fink, E. (2003). *Nietzsche's philosophy* (G. Richter, Trans.). Continuum.

Franco, P. (2018). Becoming who you are: Nietzsche on self-creation. *Journal of Nietzsche Studies, 49*(1), 52–77.

Freud, S. (2016). *Das Unbehagen in der Kultur* (L. Bayer & K. Krone-Bayer, Eds.). Reclam.

Fustel de Coulanges, N. D. (1980). *The ancient city: A study on the religion, laws, and institutions of Greece and Rome* (W. Small, Trans.). Johns Hopkins University Press.

Gadamer, H.-G. (1990). *Wahrheit und Methode: Grundzüge einer philosophischen Hermeneutik (Gesammelte Werke 1)*. Mohr Siebeck.

Gadamer, H.-G. (2004). *Truth and method* (J. Weinsheimer & D. G. Marshall, Trans.). Continuum.

Geisenhanslüke, A. (1999). Der Mensch als Eintagswesen. Nietzsches kritische Anthropologie in der Zweiten Unzeitgemässen Betrachtung. *Nietzsche-Studien, 28*, pp. 125–140. De Gruyter.

Bibliography | 219

Gmirkin, R. E. (2016). *Plato and the creation of the Hebrew Bible*. Routledge.

Goethe, J. W. von (1982). *Italian journey* (W. H. Auden & E. Mayer, Trans.). North Point Press.

Goethe, J. W. von (2000). *Goethes Werke, Hamburger Ausgabe in 14 Bänden* (E. Trunz, Ed.). DTV/C. H. Beck.

Golder, H. (1990). Introduction to DS. In *Nietzsche 1990* (pp. 3–14).

Golomb, J. (1999). Nietzsche's "new psychology." In J. Golomb, W. Santaniello, & R. Lehre (Eds.), *Nietzsche and depth psychology* (pp. 1–19). State University of New York Press.

Gray, R. T. (1995). Translator's afterword. In *Nietzsche 1995* (pp. 395–413).

Gutman, R. W. (1968). *Richard Wagner: The man, his mind, and his music*. Harcourt, Brace, & World.

Haar, M. (1996). *Nietzsche and metaphysics* (M. Gendre, Trans.). State University of New York Press.

Hadot, P. (1995). *Philosophy as a way of life: Spiritual exercises from Socrates to Foucault* (M. Chase, Trans.). Blackwell.

Hadot, P. (2002). *What is ancient philosophy?* (M. Chase, Trans.). Belknap Press of Harvard University Press.

Hegel, G. W. F. (1970). *Werke Bd. 12: Vorlesungen über die Philosophie der Geschichte*. Suhrkamp.

Hegel, G. W. F. (1988). *Introduction to the philosophy of history* (L. Rauch, Trans.). Hackett.

Herodotus (1975). *The Histories, Books I and II* (A. D. Godley, Trans.). Loeb Classical Library.

Heidegger, M. (1962). *Being and time* (J. Macquarrie & E. Robinson, Trans.). Blackwell.

Heidegger, M. (1976). Vom Wesen der Wahrheit. In *Wegmarken* (*Gesamtausgabe Bd. 9*) (pp. 177–202). Vittorio Klostermann.

Heidegger, M. (1991). *Nietzsche, Volumes One and Two* (D. F. Krell, Trans.). Harper Collins.

Heidegger, M. (1996). *Nietzsche, Erster Band* (*Gesamtausgabe Bd. 6.1*). Vittorio Klostermann.

Heidegger, M. (2000). Wer ist Nietzsches Zarathustra? In *Vorträge und Aufsätze* (*Gesamtausgabe Bd. 7*) (pp. 99–124). Vittorio Klostermann.

Heidegger, M. (2003). *Zur Auslegung von Nietzsches II. Unzeitgemässer Betrachtung* (*Gesamtausgabe Bd. 46*). Vittorio Klostermann.

Heidegger, M. (2006). *Sein und Zeit (19. Auflage)*. Max Niemeyer Verlag.

Heidegger, M. (2008). *The basic writings* (D. F. Krell, Trans.). Harper Perennial Modern Thought.

Heidegger, M. (2016). *Interpretation of Nietzsche's second untimely meditation* (U. Haase & M. Sinclair, Trans.). Indiana University Press.

Huang, J. (2017). "Nachweis aus Aristoteles' *Politik*, übertragen von Jacob Bernays." *Nietzsche-Studien, 46*, 242. De Gruyter.

220 | Bibliography

Huenemann, Ch. (2013). Nietzsche's illness. In J. Richardson & K. Gemes (Eds.), *The Oxford handbook of Nietzsche* (pp. 63–81). Oxford University Press.

Hume, D. (2007). *A treatise of human nature* (D. F. Norton & M. J. Norton, Eds.). Clarendon Press.

Hutter, H. (2006). *Shaping the future: Nietzsche's new regime of the soul and its ascetic practices.* Lexington Books.

Hutter, H. (2009). Nietzsche's thumotic politics: A programmatic statement with an eye on Agnes Heller. In K. Terezakis (Ed.), *Engaging Agnes Heller: A critical companion* (pp. 193–221). Lexington Books.

Hutter, H. (2013). The Nietzsche cure: New kinds of "gymnastics of willing." In H. Hutter & E. Friedland (Eds.), *Nietzsche's therapeutic teaching: For individuals and culture* (pp. 3–12). Bloomsbury.

Janaway, C. (2003). Schopenhauer as Nietzsche's educator. In N. Martin (Ed.), *Nietzsche and the German tradition* (pp. 155–185). Peter Lang.

Janz, C. P. (1978). *Friedrich Nietzsche Biografie* (Vols. 1–3). Carl Hanser Verlag.

Jenkins, S. (2014). Nietzsche's use of monumental history. *Journal of Nietzsche Studies, 45*(2), 169–81.

Jensen, A. K. (2016). *An interpretation of Nietzsche's* On the uses and disadvantage of history for life. Routledge.

Johnson, D. R. (2001). Nietzsche's early Darwinism: The "David Strauss" essay of 1873. *Nietzsche-Studien, 30*, 62–79. De Gruyter.

Kant, I. (1980). *Vorlesungen über die philosophische Enzyklopädie.* In *Kant's gesammelte Schriften* (Vol. XXIX.1,1). De Gruyter.

Kant, I. (2006). *Toward perpetual peace and other writings on politics, peace, and history* (D. L. Colclasure, Trans.). Yale University Press.

Kant, I. (2016a). *Kritik der reinen Vernunft.* In W. Weischedel (Ed.), *Werke in sechs Bänden* (Vol. 2). WBG.

Kant, I. (2016b). Beantwortung der Frage: Was ist Aufklärung? In W. Weischedel (Ed.), *Werke in sechs Bänden* (Vol. 6, pp. 51–61). WBG.

Kaufmann, W. (1978). *Nietzsche: Philosopher, psychologist, antichrist.* Princeton University Press.

Kaufmann, W. (1982). Nietzsches Philosophie der Masken. *Nietzsche-Studien, 10*, 111–131. De Gruyter.

Kierkegaard, S. (1983). *Fear and trembling, Repetition* (H. V. Hong & E. H. Hong, Trans.). Princeton University Press.

Kuchtová, A. (2024). *The ungraspable as a philosophical problem: The stubborn persistence of humanism in contemporary phenomenology.* Brill.

Lampert, L. (1993). *Nietzsche and modern times: A study of Bacon, Descartes, and Nietzsche.* Yale University Press.

Lampert, L. (2001). *Nietzsche's task: An interpretation of* Beyond good and evil. Yale University Press.

Bibliography | 221

Lampert, L. (2017). *What a philosopher is: Becoming Nietzsche*. University of Chicago Press.

Large, David (1978). The political background of the foundation of the Bayreuth Festival, 1876. *Central European History, 11*(2), 162–172.

Large, Duncan (1994). On "untimeliness": temporal structures in Nietzsche or: "The day after tomorrow belongs to me." *Journal of Nietzsche Studies, 8*, 33–53.

Large, Duncan (2012). Untimely Meditations. In P. Bishop (Ed.), *A companion to Friedrich Nietzsche: Life and works* (pp. 86–107). Camden House.

Lear, G. R. (2011). Mimesis and psychological change in *Republic* III. In P. Destrée & F.-G. Herrmann (Eds.), *Plato and the poets, Mnemosyne supp. vol.* 328, pp. 195–216. Brill.

Lemm, V. (2007a). Animality, creativity and historicity: A reading of Friedrich Nietzsche's *Vom Nutzen und Nachtheil der Historie für das Leben*. *Nietzsche-Studien, 36*, 169–200. De Gruyter.

Lemm, V. (2007b). Is Nietzsche a perfectionist? Rawls, Cavell, and the politics of culture in Nietzsche's "Schopenhauer as Educator." *Journal of Nietzsche Studies, 34*, 5–27. Pennsylvania State University Press.

Lemm, V. (2011). History, life, and justice in Friedrich Nietzsche's *Vom Nutzen und Nachtheil der Historie für das Leben*. *CR: The New Centennial Review, 10*(3), 167–188. Michigan State University Press.

Lipták, M. (2023). Alienated citizens: Hegel and Marx on civil society. *Filozofia, 78*(9), 760–776.

Machiavelli, N. (1998). *The Prince* (2nd ed., H. C. Mansfield, Trans.). University of Chicago Press.

Meier, H. (2017). *Was ist Nietzsches Zarathustra? Eine philosophische Auseinandersetzung*. C. H. Beck.

Meier, H. (2019). *Nietzsches Vermächtnis. Ecce Homo und Der Antichrist. Zwei Bücher über Natur und Politik*. C. H. Beck.

Montinari, M. (1982). *Nietzsche lesen*. De Gruyter.

Most, G. W. (2002). On the use and abuse of Ancient Greece for life. *Cultura Tedesca, 20*, 31–53.

Most, G. W. & Fries, T. (1994). ‹(«)›: Die Quellen von Nietzsches Rhetorik-Vorlesung. In T. Borsche, F. Gerratana, & A. Venturelli (Eds.), *Centauren-Geburten. Wissenschaft, Kunst und Philosophie beim jungen Nietzsche* (pp. 17–46). De Gruyter.

Neymeyr, B. (2020). *Kommentar zu Nietzsches "Unzeitgemäßen Betrachtungen" (Nietzsche-Kommentar Bd. 1/2)* (Vols. 1–2). De Gruyter.

Nietzsche, F. W. (1967 ff.). *Nietzsche Werke. Kritische Gesamtausgabe* (G. Colli & M. Montinari, Eds.). De Gruyter.

Nietzsche, F. W. (1974). *The gay science* (W. Kaufmann, Trans.). Vintage Books.

Nietzsche, F. W. (1975 ff.). *Nietzsche Briefwechsel. Kritische Gesamtausgabe* (G. Colli & M. Montinari, Eds.) De Gruyter.

222 | Bibliography

Nietzsche, F. W. (1982). *The portable Nietzsche* (W. Kaufmann, Ed. & Trans.). Penguin Books.

Nietzsche, F. W. (1989a). *Beyond good and evil* (W. Kaufmann, Trans.). Vintage Books.

Nietzsche, F. W. (1989b). *On the genealogy of morals and Ecce Homo* (W. Kaufmann & R. J. Hollingdale, Trans.). Vintage Books.

Nietzsche, F. W. (1990). *Unmodern Observations* (W. Arrowsmith, Ed.). Yale University Press.

Nietzsche, F. W. (1995). *Unfashionable Observations* (R. T. Gray, Trans.). Stanford University Press.

Nietzsche, F. W. (1997). *Untimely Meditations* (R. J. Hollingdale, Trans.). Cambridge University Press.

Nietzsche, F. W. (1998). *On the Genealogy of Morality* (M. Clark & A. J. Swensen, Trans.). Hackett.

Nietzsche, F. W. (1999). *Friedrich Nietzsche, Sämtliche Werke. Kritische Studienausgabe in 15 Bänden* (G. Colli & M. Montinari, Eds.). DTV/de Gruyter.

Nietzsche, F. W. (2005a). *The Anti-christ, Ecce Homo, Twilight of the idols, and other writings* (J. Norman, Trans.). Cambridge University Press.

Nietzsche, F. W. (2005b). *Human, all too human* (R. J. Hollingdale, Trans.). Cambridge University Press.

Nietzsche, F. W. (2006). *Daybreak* (R. J. Hollingdale, Trans.). Cambridge University Press.

Nietzsche, F. W. (2007). *The birth of tragedy and other writings* (R. Speirs, Trans.). Cambridge University Press.

Nietzsche, F. W. (2016). *Anti-education: On the future of our educational institutions* (D. Searls, Trans.). New York Review of Books.

Parkes, G. (1994). *Composing the soul: Reaches of Nietzsche's psychology*. University of Chicago Press.

Pascal, B. (1995). *Pensées and other writings* (H. Levi, Trans.). Oxford University Press.

Patočka, J. (1989). *The natural world and phenomenology*. In E. Kohák (Ed. & Trans.), *Jan Patočka: Philosophy and selected writings* (pp. 239–273). University of Chicago Press.

Patočka, J. (1996). *Heretical essays in the philosophy of history* (E. Kohák, Trans.). Open Court.

Patočka, J. (2002). *Plato and Europe*. (P. Lom, Trans.). Stanford University Press.

Patočka, J. (2006). *Co jsou Češi?* [*What are the Czechs?*] In K. Palek & I. Chvatík (Eds.), *Jan Patočka: Sebrané spisy* [*Collected Works*] (Vol. 13, pp. 253–324). Oikoymenh.

Patočka, J. (2022). *The selected writings of Jan Patočka: Care for the soul* (I. Chvatík & E. Plunkett, Eds.). Bloomsbury Academic.

Pearson, J. S. (2018). United we stand, divided we fall: the early Nietzsche on the struggle for organization. *Canadian Journal of Philosophy*. https://doi.org/10.1080/00455091.2018.1475183.

Bibliography | 223

Picht, G. (1988). *Vorlesungen und Schriften: Nietzsche.* Klett-Cotta.

Pinker, S. (2019). *Enlightenment now: The case for reason, science, humanism, and progress.* Penguin Books.

Pippin, R. B. (2010). *Nietzsche, psychology, and first philosophy.* University of Chicago Press.

Plato (1900 ff.). *Platonis Opera* (Vols. 1–5, J. Burnet, Ed.). Clarendon Press.

Plato (1988). *The Laws* (T. L. Pangle, Trans.). University of Chicago Press.

Plato (1991). *The Republic* (A. Bloom, Trans.). Basic Books.

Plato (1997). *Complete works* (J. M. Cooper, Ed.). Hackett.

Plutarch (1928). *Consolation to Apollonius.* In *Plutarch's Moralia in fifteen volumes* (Vol. II, F. C. Babbitt, Trans.). Loeb Classical Library.

Polybius (1922). *The Histories.* (W. R. Paton, Trans.). Loeb Classical Library.

Prange, M. (2013). *Nietzsche, Wagner, Europe* (Monographien und Texte zur Nietzsche-Forschung 61). De Gruyter.

Richardson, J. (2015). Nietzsche vs. Heidegger on the self: Which I am I? In J. Constancio, M. J. Mayer Branco, & B. Ryan (Eds.), *Nietzsche and the problem of subjectivity* (pp. 343–366). De Gruyter.

Rose, P. L. (1992). *Wagner: Race and revolution.* Yale University Press.

Salaquarda, J. (1984). Studien zur Zweiten Unzeitgemässen Betrachtung. *Nietzsche-Studien, 13,* 1–45. De Gruyter.

Schaberg, W. H. (1995). *The Nietzsche canon: A publication history and bibliography.* University of Chicago Press.

Schacht, R. (1990). Introduction to *SE.* In Nietzsche (1990), pp. 149–161.

Schacht, R. (1995). *Making sense of Nietzsche: Reflections timely and untimely.* University of Illinois Press.

Schmitt, C. (1996). *Roman Catholicism and political form* (G. L. Ulmen, Trans.). Greenwood Press.

Schmitt, C. (2008). *Römischer Katholizismus und politische Form.* Klett-Cotta.

Schopenhauer, A. (1966). *The world as will and representation* (Vols. 1–2, E. F. J. Payne, Trans.). Dover Publications.

Schopenhauer, A. (1986). *Sämtliche Werke* (Vols. 1–5, W. Frhr. von Löhneysen, Ed.). Suhrkamp.

Schopenhauer, A. (2000). *Parerga and Paralipomena* (Vols. 1–2, E. F. J. Payne, Trans.). Clarendon Press.

Siemens, H. (2001). Agonal configurations in the *Unzeitgemäße Betrachtungen. Nietzsche-Studien, 30,* 80–106. De Gruyter.

Silk, M. S., & Stern, J. P. (1981). *Nietzsche on tragedy.* Cambridge University Press.

Stewart, J. (2021). *Hegel's century: Alienation and recognition in a time of revolution.* Cambridge University Press.

Strauss, D. F. (1872). *Der alte und der neue Glaube: ein Bekenntniß.* Verlag von S. Hirzel.

Strauss, D. F. (1874). *The old faith and the new: A confession* (M. Blind, Trans.). Asher and Co.

224 | Bibliography

Strauss, D. F. (1997). *The old faith and the new: A confession* (M. Blind, Trans.). Prometheus Books.

Strauss, L. (1963). *The political philosophy of Hobbes: Its basis and its genesis*. Phoenix Books.

Strauss, L. (1988). *What is political philosophy? And other studies*. University of Chicago Press.

Strauss, L. (1995). What is liberal education? In *Liberalism ancient and modern* (pp. 3–8). University of Chicago Press.

Strong, T. B. (2000). Learning to love: Nietzsche on love, education and morality. In B. N. Ray (Ed.), *Contemporary political thinking* (pp. 71–101). Kanishka Publishers.

Šajda, P. (2011). The choice of oneself: Revisiting Guardini's critique of Kierkegaard's concept of selfhood. *Filozofia, 66*(9), 868–878.

Taylor, Q. P. (1997). *Republic of genius: A reconstruction of Nietzsche's early thought*. University of Rochester Press.

Thiele, L. P. (1990). *Friedrich Nietzsche and the politics of the soul: A study of heroic individualism*. Princeton University Press.

Tongeren, P. J. M. van (1989). *Die Moral von Nietzsches Moralkritik. Studie zu "Jenseits von Gut und Böse."* Bouvier Verlag.

Tongeren, P. J. M. van (2000). *Reinterpreting modern culture: An introduction to Friedrich Nietzsche's philosophy*. Purdue University Press.

Tongeren, P. J. M. van, Schank, G., & Siemens, H. (eds.) (2004). *Nietzsche-Wörterbuch, Band 1: Abbreviatur—einfach*. De Gruyter.

Tucker, R. C. (ed.) (1978). *The Marx-Engels reader (2nd ed.)*. W. W. Norton & Company.

Valiquette Moreau, N. (2017). Musical mimesis and political ethos in Plato's *Republic*. *Political Theory, 45*(2), 192–215.

Wagner, R. (1966). *Richard Wagner's prose works* (Vols. 1–8, W. A. Ellis, Trans.). Broude Brothers.

Wagner, R. (1983). *Dichtungen und Schriften. Jubiläumsausgabe in zehn Bänden* (D. Borchmeyer, Ed.). Insel Verlag.

Wagner, R. (2014). *Beethoven* (R. Allen, Trans.). The Boydel Press.

Xenophon (1923). *Memorabilia, Oeconomicus, Symposium, Apology* (E. C. Marchant & O. J. Todd, Trans.). Loeb Classical Library.

Zinn, H. (2015). *A people's history of the United States*. Harper Perennial Modern Classics.

Zuckert, C. H. (1970). *The morality of history: A Study of Friedrich Nietzsche's Untimely Meditations* (Doctoral dissertation). University of Chicago.

Zuckert, C. H. (1976). Nature, history and the self: Friedrich Nietzsche's Untimely Considerations. *Nietzsche-Studien, 5*, 55–82. De Gruyter.

Index

AC. See *The Antichrist*
Acampora, C. D., 62n39, 206–210
Achilles, 58, 97n20
active forgetting, 46, 47, 51
Adeimantus, 94
Aeneid, 172
Aeschylus, 152n31
affirmative history, 54n23
Afterphilologie (Rohde), 16, 16n5
agonism, 2n1
  in *betrachten*, 11n9
Alexander the Great, 58, 97n20, 141n23
Allen, Garrett, 94
Anaxagoras, 121
Ansell-Pearson, K., 2n1, 64n42
The Antichrist (*AC*), 5, 176, 177, 190,
  194, 203
  life-affirmation in, 185–186
  redemption in, 182n18
antiquarian history
  of Goethe, 105n35
  in *HL*, 54n22, 55–56, 59–60, 64n42
anti-Semitism, of Wagner, R., 131,
  131n4, 145n27
AOM. See *Assorted Opinions and
  Maxims*
Aristotle, 59n32, 71, 138n18, 173,
  195n37, 198n39
Arrowsmith, William, 92n12
askesis, 201, 201n44

Assorted Opinions and Maxims (*AOM*),
  55, 176n11, 177n12, 183, 183n19
Audience and Popularity (Wagner, R.),
  168n3
Augenblick (Wagner, R.), 134, 134n10
authenticity, 4, 88n6

barbarism
  in *DS*, 20, 21n11, 22–23, 22n17,
    23n23, 35–36, 65, 85
  Goethe on, 22n17
  of philistines, 20, 21n11, 22–23,
    22n17, 23n23, 35–36, 191
Bayreuth. See also *Richard Wagner in
  Bayreuth*
  founding of, 133–134
  philosophical monasticism and, 164,
    164n46
  Wagner, R., and, 5, 8, 14, 126,
    167–175, 171nn7–8, 211–213
  as Wagner's permanent home, 134
Beethoven (Wagner, R.), 13, 21n12
Beethoven, Ludwig van
  Strauss, D., and, 27, 30–31,
    30nn34–35
  Wagner, R., and, 147
Being and Time (Heidegger), 56n27,
  88n6, 134n10
belief/faith, 187n25
  in Christianity, 205

226 | Index

belief/faith *(continued)*
in *HL*, 203–204
suffering and, 32
truth and, 186–188
of Wagner, R., 136, 136n15
best way of life *(pos bioteon)*, 10, 23
betrachten, 11n9
Beyond Good and Evil (BGE), 5, 7, 49,
50, 55, 78n59, 119n57, 120n59,
145n27, 165, 173, 176, 184–90,
195n38, 196, 205, 214
Christianity in, 179
conscience in, 89n7
erotic-historic soul in, 197–202
HL and, 199–200
Meier on, 200n42
morality in, 198
self-knowledge in, 201
self-overcoming in, 194
WB and, 179
will to power in, 201–202
Bias, 153n32
Bildung, 20, 21n13
Bildungsphilister (cultivated philistines),
21–22, 22n15
*The Birth of Tragedy Out of the Spirit of
Music (BT)*, 3, 122n62, 180n14
Christianity in, 191n33
pessimism in, 205
suffering in, 195
untimeliness in, 192
Wagner, R., and, 13, 16–17
WB and, 151
Bismarck, Otto von, 39n46, 122
Braatz, K., 23n23, 24n25
Brandes, Georg, 9, 77n56
on *SE*, 212–213
Brezeale, D., 2, 113n46, 119n56, 125n65
Brobjer, T. H., 2, 58n31
Brooks, S., 5–6, 8n6, 39n46
on barbarism, 21n11
on *Bildung*, 21n13

on *DS*, 28n30
on *HL*, 50n13, 54, 64n42
Nietzsche's Culture War by, 5
on *SE*, 99n23, 104n32, 122,
181n16, 190n32
on *WB*, 133n6, 143n25, 148, 150,
181n16, 190n32
BT. See *The Birth of Tragedy Out of the
Spirit of Music*
Buddhism, 52n16

The Case of Wagner (CW), 107n37,
132, 163n45, 168n2, 174, 176
decadence in, 199
Cavell, S., 94
Christianity. See also *The Old Faith
and the New*
in *BGE*, 179
in *BT*, 191n33
conscience in, 205
faith in, 205
"God is dead" and, 27, 191, 197
life-denial in, 70, 70n47
monasticism in, 67
morality of, 33, 176–177, 205
Nietzsche's break from, 1, 26–27
pity in, 176
scientific history and, 69–72
in *SE*, 70n47, 103–104, 103n30, 117
unity of style in, 70n47
Wagner and, 132
Chronicle of Kosmas, 172
Church, J., 3, 3n4, 5–6, 8n6
on *DS*, 28n30
on *HL*, 40, 52nn17–18, 55n24,
57n29, 63n41, 82n63
on memory, 48
on nihilism, 180n14
on *SE*, 90n8, 91n10, 92n11,
93n13, 104n31, 106n36, 110n40,
118n55
on *UC*, 178n13, 188n29

on *WB*, 136n13, 152n31
on *Za*, 181n16
Cicero, 5, 54n21
Colli, G., 2, 13
comparing, in *HL*, 48, 48n9
Conant, James, 49n10, 193n36
  on *SE*, 92n11, 94n16, 97n19,
    98n22, 119n56
conscience, 15n4, 49, 126, 197, 203,
  206
  in *BGE*, 89n7, 199, 201
  in Christianity, 205
  in *GS*, 211
  of philistines, 155, 195
  in *SE*, 88–90, 88n6, 89n7, 94–95,
    115n50, 199
Cosmos, in *DS*, 31–32, 37n41
courage, 76
  in *DS*, 28
  of Kant, 68n45
  of philistines, 26, 31–34, 38
  in *SE*, 100n26
  in *WB*, 152
critical history
  in *HL*, 54nn22–23, 56, 61–63
  Rousseau and, 105n35
cultivated philistines (*Bildungsphilister*),
  21–22, 22n15
CW. See *The Case of Wagner*
cynicism, in *HL*, 71–72, 93

D. See *Daybreak*
Dannhauser, W., 47n7
Darwin, Charles, 32–34, 36
*David Strauss the Confessor and the
  Writer* (*DS*), 2, 3, 5, 7, 66, 95
  barbarism in, 20, 21n11, 22–23,
    22n17, 23n23, 35–36, 65, 85
  Brooks on, 28n30
  Church on, 28n30
  Cosmos in, 31–32, 37n41
  courage in, 28

critique of German culture in, 19–26
divertissement in, 107
genius in, 16, 19, 34, 36–37, 41
"God is dead" and, 27, 191
Goethe in, 22n17, 24n23, 27,
  29–30, 40
good life in, 24, 28, 34, 36–37,
  37n41
happiness in, 27
HL and, 96
main subject of, 35n40
philistines in, 13, 21–42, 22nn14–
  15, 35n40, 72, 81, 120
Schopenhauer in, 14, 15, 22n14,
  31, 40
SE and, 118
self-cultivation in, 13, 29, 35, 38,
  39–40
truth in, 178
unity of style in, 28, 35, 65, 85
Wagner, R., and, 13, 18–19
WB and, 127, 154, 165
Daybreak (*D*), 1, 187n28, 189–190,
  194, 204
  desiderata in, 189
  pregnancy in, 207–208
De Oratore (Cicero), 54n21
decadence, 199
degeneration, 56
desiderata
  in *Daybreak*, 189
  in *HL*, 50, 69, 73–74
  in *SE*, 91, 126
  in *WB*, 137, 142, 143n25
Diogenes Laertius, 201n44
Dionysia
  Wagner, R., and, 171
  in *WB*, 151
divertissement (entertainment)
  in *DS*, 107
  of philistines, 23, 23n24, 28n33,
    29, 35, 38, 120, 192, 195

228 | Index

divertissement (entertainment)
(*continued*)
in *SE*, 94, 108, 109, 117
Wagner, R., and, 171, 188
in *WB*, 135, 151, 155, 163
Drochon, H., 77n55, 118n54,
122n62, 127n66, 133n7
DS. See *David Strauss the Confessor and
the Writer*

Ecce Homo (*EH*), 5, 10, 14, 167–69,
175, 179, 182n18, 187n25, 188,
192, 194, 204, 214–15
life-affirmation in, 185–186
SE and, 126, 210, 210n53
self-overcoming in, 206–207,
206n50, 209–211
Übermensch in, 194
Wagner, R., and, 14–15, 168n3,
169, 174
Eckermann, J. P., 20n8, 22n17,
24n23, 27, 30, 38, 69, 105n34
educator, in *SE*, 96–105, 98n22,
125n65
EH. See *Ecce Homo*
Eleusis, 148–149
Emden, Ch., 54, 54n22, 60n34
Emerson, Ralph Waldo, 94, 94n16
Empedocles, 79, 106, 106n36, 112,
177
WB and, 148
entertainment. See *divertissement*
Enthusiasmus, 67n44
Epictetus, 98n22
erotic-historic soul
in *BGE*, 197–198
in *HL*, 7, 44–52, 197
in *SE*, 87–96, 197, 211
eternal glory among the mortals (*kleos
aenaon thneton*), 57
existentialism, 4

Fachidiotismus, 20
faith. *See* belief
Faust (Goethe), 29
Faust II (Goethe), 27, 104n32
FEI. See *On the Future of Our
Educational Institutions*
Fincke, Elise, 3
Findende (finders), 24
Fink, E., 3, 6, 85, 148, 185n23,
202n49
Five Prefaces to Five Unwritten Books,
18
"For the Introduction of the Complete
Edition of 'Untimely Ones,'" 18
forgetting. *See also* active forgetting
Darwin and, 33
in *HL*, 46–47, 46nn4–5
Four Noble Truths, of Buddhism,
52n16
Franco, P., 92n11
Franco-Prussian War, 19
Freud, Sigmund, 59n32

Gadamer, H.-G., 21n13
Gast, Peter, 132, 164n46, 212
The Gay Science (*GS*), 164n46, 173,
175, 176n11, 179, 203, 210n52
conscience in, 211
"God is dead" in, 191
pessimism in, 205
self-overcoming in, 206
Gebildetheit, 20
Geisenhanslüke, A., 56n27
genius
in *DS*, 16, 19, 34, 36–37, 41
in *HA*, 204
in *HL*, 55, 79
morality of, 186
philanthropy and, 102, 144, 178,
186
Plato and, 77n55, 122n62

Index | 229

redemption by, 180, 183, 183n20, 184, 195
in *SE*, 7, 92–93, 111–118, 113n46, 113n48, 119n56, 121, 173
self-knowledge and, 92–93
suffering of, 180
truth of, 180
Gersdorff, Carl von, 15, 40, 83n64, 143n26
Gervinus, G., 29
Gesamtkunstwerk (Wagner, R.), 130, 171n8
Glaucon, 94, 157n35
GM. See On the Genealogy of Morality
"God is dead," 27, 191, 197
Goethe, J. W. von, 20
antiquarian history of, 105n35
on barbarism, 22n17
in *DS*, 22n17, 24n23, 27, 29–30, 40
Faust by, 29
Faust II by, 27, 104n32
HL and, 43, 49n11, 63n41, 82, 203–204
Iphigenia in Tauris by, 105n34
Maxims and Reflections by, 49n11
Observations in the Sense of the Wanderers by, 49n11, 92n12
on perspectivism, 49n10
Schopenhauer and, 100n25, 104–105, 104n31, 105n35
on scientific history, 82
Torquato Tasso by, 105n34
Wilhelm Meister's Journeyman Years by, 29n32, 49n11
Golomb, J., 182n18
good life
in *DS*, 24, 28, 34, 36–37, 37n41
in *HL*, 43–44
in *UC*, 106n36
Gray, R. T., 14n2, 99n24
on *WB*, 133n6

great enlightenment, in *SE*, 111, 114
The Greek State, 122n62, 173
GS. See The Gay Science
gymnastics, in *WB*, 157, 158–159, 158n38, 159n39, 164n47

HA. See Human, All Too Human
Hadot, Pierre, 1, 66, 67, 118, 149, 164n47, 201n44
happiness, 1, 104n33, 178, 189–190
in *DS*, 27
in *HL*, 46n5, 52, 57, 69
redemption and, 187
in *SE*, 89, 109–111
in *WB*, 162
Hartmann, Eduard von, 31, 72–73, 72n48
heaven, of philistines, 28–31
Hegel, G. W. F., 33, 71–72, 103, 107, 148n28
cynicism and, 71–72
Heidegger, M., 6, 114
Being and Time by, 56n27, 88n6, 134n10
on critical history, 61n36
on *HL*, 56, 56n27, 61n36, 77, 77n54, 85, 86
Wagner, R., and, 134n10
on willpower, 202n47
Heraclitus, 57, 57n29, 147
Herodotus, 148n28
Hesiod, 148n28
historia magistra vitae, in *HL*, 52–62
HL. See On the Utility and Liability of History for Life
Hölderlin, F., 25, 38
Socrates and Alcibiades by, 102
Homer, 16, 62n39, 148n28, 166, 172
Homer's Contest, 153n32
horizons of significance, in *HL*, 47, 47n7, 86, 198

230 | Index

Human, All Too Human (HA), 3, 10, 55, 167, 176n11, 183n19, 185, 212
  genius in, 204
  philanthropy in, 196
  SE and, 100n26
  truth in, 213
  Wagner, R., and, 168n3, 169
Hume, David, 126
Hutter, H., 1, 21n10, 75n52, 155, 159, 162, 182, 185, 207n51
  on *WB*, 164n47

Iphigenia in Tauris (Goethe), 105n34
ironic existences, in *HL*, 70, 93

Janz, C. P., 14, 129, 133n8, 140n21, 143n26, 168, 171n7
Jenkins, 55n24
Jensen, A. K., on *HL*, 46n4, 53n19, 54, 54n23, 55n24, 76n53, 83n64
Jesuitism, 188
Judaism in Music, 131
justice
  in *HL*, 75–80, 117n52
  life-denial and, 75, 76
  in *SE*, 114
  suffering and, 76
  in *WB*, 76, 161

Kant, I., 1, 5, 33, 67n44
  courage of, 68n45
  nihilism and, 180n14
  Schopenhauer and, 67–68, 100–101
  in *SE*, 67
  What Is Enlightenment? by, 87n3
kleos aenaon thneton (eternal glory among the mortals), 57
Knortz, Karl, 10, 212
Kukučín, Martin, 60
Kulturkampf (Bismarck), 39n46
Kulturkritik, 7
Kulturstaat (Bismarck), 122

Lampert, L., 3–5, 10, 77n54, 88n4, 94n16, 106n36, 122n61, 132, 152, 163
  on Plato, 192n34
  on *WB*, 143–144
Large, David, 131n3, 140n21
Large, Duncan, 2, 11, 54, 88n4, 94n17, 192
  on *WB*, 133n6
Laws (Plato), 156–158
laziness, in *SE*, 87–89, 87n3, 95n18
Lear, Gabriel Richardson, 158n36
Lemm, Vanessa
  on *HL*, 46n4, 53, 62n38, 76
  on *SE*, 118n54
Lenin, V., 34n39
Lessing, G., 23n21, 36, 38, 40
The Life of Jesus (Strauss, D.), 26, 37
life-affirmation, 185–186
  Emerson and, 94n16
  in *SE*, 105–115, 177–178, 184n21
  suffering and, 197
  Wagner, R., and, 169
life-denial, 177–178, 184, 188
  in Christianity, 70, 70n47
  in *HL*, 52, 62, 75, 76
  justice and, 75, 76
  in *SE*, 125
  truth and, 213
  in *UC*, 8
  in *WB*, 163
Livy, 58n31
Ludwig II, 130–131, 131n2

Machiavelli, N., 58, 58n31
Maier, Mathilde, 187n26
Marx, K., 34, 103n29
master morality, 176–177
Materials for a Treatise About the Terrible Mischief Done Nowadays to the German Language (Schopenhauer), 37n42
Maxims and Reflections (Goethe), 49n11

Index | 231

Meier, H., 5, 88n4, 126, 169n5, 177, 187n27, 196, 209, 210, 210n52, 210n53, 213n54
  on *BGE*, 200n42
  on *Za*, 181–182, 193n35
memory
  in *HL*, 44–49, 45n3, 46nn4–5, 49n10
  in *SE*, 89, 199
Meysenbug, Malwida von, 18, 40
monasticism
  in Christianity, 67
  philosophic, 164, 164n46
Montinari, M., 133, 158n38
monumental history
  in *HL*, 48n9, 54nn21–22, 56, 56n25, 57–59
  Nietzschean humanism and, 57, 202
morality
  in *BGE*, 198
  of Christianity, 33, 176–177, 205
  of genius, 186
  in *HL*, 198
  life-affirmation and, 184–187
Most, G. W., 54, 84n66

Nachlass, 2
Neymeyr, B., 11n8, 20n9, 23n21
  on *HL*, 54n21, 61n37, 69n46, 73n49
  Nietzsche-Kommentar by, 3
  on Schiller, 57n30
  on *SE*, 87n3, 99n24, 100n27, 120n60, 123n63
Nietzsche, Elisabeth, 168, 168n3
Nietzsche, Friedrich Wilhelm. *See specific topics*
Nietzschean humanism, 57, 193, 202
Nietzsche-Kommentar (Neymeyr), 3
Nietzsche's Culture War (Church), 5
nihilism, 1, 74, 176, 188, 194
  Church on, 180n14
  redemption and, 179–180

objectivity, in *HL*, 68, 76, 76n53
Observations in the Sense of the Wanderers (Goethe), 49n11, 92n12
The *Old Faith and the New* (Strauss, D.), 5, 13–41
  German and English editions of, 27n28
On Authorship and Style (Schopenhauer), 37n42
On Conducting (Wagner, R.), 20n9
On Musical Criticism (Wagner, R.), 158n38
On Philosophy at the Universities (Schopenhauer), 123n63
On the Basis of Morality (Schopenhauer), 32n37
On the Future of Our Educational Institutions (*FEI*), 18, 19, 38n44, 119n57
On the Genealogy of Morality (*GM*), 162n42, 174–77, 184n22, 186n24, 192, 194, 200n43, 201n44, 203, 205
  active forgetting in, 46, 47, 51
  Schopenhauer in, 100n26
  suffering in, 196–197
On the Pathos of Truth, 79, 114n49
On the Utility and Liability of History for Life (*HL*), 2, 5, 6, 193, 203
  antiquarian history in, 54n22, 55–56, 59–60, 64n42
  BGE and, 199–200
  Brooks on, 50n13, 54, 64n42
  Christianity and, 27
  Church on, 52nn17–18, 55n24, 57n29, 63n41, 82n63
  comparing in, 48, 48n9
  critical history in, 54nn22–23, 56, 61–63
  curing historical sickness in, 75–85
  cynicism in, 71–72, 93
  desiderata in, 50, 69, 73–74

232 | Index

On the Utility and Liability of History for Life (*HL*) (continued)
DS and, 96
erotic-historic soul in, 7, 44–52, 197
excess of history in, 64–68
faith in, 186–187
forgetting in, 46–47, 46nn4–5
genius in, 55, 79
Goethe and, 43, 49n11, 63n41, 82, 203–204
good life in, 43–44
happiness in, 46n5, 52, 57, 69
Heidegger and, 56, 56n27, 61n36, 77, 77n54, 85, 86
historia magistra vitae, 52–62
horizons of significance in, 47, 47n7, 86, 198
ironic existences in, 70, 93
Jensen on, 46n4, 53n19, 54, 54n23, 55n24, 76n53, 83n64
justice in, 75–80, 117n52
life-denial in, 52, 62, 75, 76
memory in, 44–49, 45n3, 46nn4–5, 49n10
monumental history in, 48n9, 54nn21–22, 56, 56n25, 57–59
negative countermeasures in, 80–82
Neymeyr on, 54n21, 61n37, 69n46, 73n49
objectivity in, 68, 76, 76n53
philanthropy in, 79
plastic force in, 51, 53, 64–65, 136n13, 138
positive countermeasures in, 83–85
Renaissance and, 54n22, 55, 60, 63n41
sapping of will to growth in, 68–73
Schopenhauer in, 61n37
scientific history in, 63–64, 63n41, 64n42, 68–75, 81–83, 82n62
SE and, 105–106, 113n47, 117, 118, 121, 127

self-cultivation in, 86
self-overcoming in, 52
Strauss, L., and, 53n20
suffering in, 46n4, 63, 64, 76, 83
suprahistorical humans of, 51, 51n15, 52n17, 75, 83n64
truth in, 75–80
WB and, 134n10, 165
Zuckert on, 56, 74–75, 76n53, 83n64
On the Will in Nature (Schopenhauer), 32n37
Opera and Drama (Wagner, R.), 154
Overbeck, Franz, 9, 184n21, 212

Parkes, G., 6, 49n11, 94n16, 116, 132, 136n14, 142, 151, 202n48, 203
Pascal, B., 23n24
Patočka, Jan, 59n32, 63n41, 74, 90n9, 148n28, 158, 172
Pearson, J. S., 73n49, 119n56
Pedro II, 167–168
perspectivism, 49, 49n10
pessimism, 31–32, 174–175, 204–205
in *BT*, 205
in *GS*, 205
Phaedrus (Plato), 97n19, 189
philanthropy
genius and, 102, 144, 178, 186, 195
in *HA*, 196
in *HL*, 79
in *SE*, *102*
suffering and, 196
Wagner, R., and, 136n15, 138, 150
philistines
barbarism of, 20, 21n11, 22–23, 22n17, 23n23, 35–36, 191
conscience of, 195
courage of, 26, 31–34, 38
divertissements of, 23, 23n24, 28n33, 29, 35, 38, 120, 192, 195

Index | 233

in *DS*, 13, 21–42, 22nn14–15,
  35n40, 72, 81
heaven of, 28–31
Romanticism and, 24
self-cultivation of, 191–192
self-knowledge of, 22, 23
style of, 34–39
supremacy of, 25
philology, 17, 24–25, 35, 54n22
Philology of the Future! (Wilamowitz-
  Möllendorff), 16–17
*Philosophy in the Tragic Age of the
  Greeks*, 18
Picht, G., 3
Pippin, R. B., 91n10
Pittacus, 153n32
pity, 79, 176, 176n11, 204
plastic force, in *HL*, 51, 53, 64–65,
  136n13, 138
Plato, 48, 57n29, 62n39, 67, 71, 77,
  79, 97, 121–122, 202, 215
genius and, 77n55, 122n62
Homer and, 16, 166
Lampert on, 122n61, 192n34
Laws by, 156–158
Phaedrus by, 97n19, 189
Protagoras by, 98n22
Republic by, 62, 94–95, 108,
  110n38, 150, 150n30, 156–160,
  157nn34–35, 173
WB and, 148–151, 150n30,
  156–160, 157nn34–35, 158n36,
  159n40, 166
Plotinus, 98n22
Plutarch, 68, 195n37
Politics (Aristotle), 59n32, 173
Polybius, 54n21, 142–143
pos bioteon (best way of life), 10, 23
practice of war, 40n49, 208–209
Prange, M., 14, 16n5, 129, 145n27
pregnancy, 207–208
Prince (Machiavelli), 58n31

Protagoras (Plato), 98n22
pudenda origo (shameful origin), 1
Pythagoras, 79

Quellenforschung, 30

Ranke, Leopold von, 63
redemption
  in *AC*, 182n18
  by genius, 180, 183, 183n20, 184,
    195
  happiness and, 187
  nihilism and, 180n14
  in *SE*, 119
  truth and, 182–183
  in *Za*, 120n58, 181, 181n16, 182,
    190n32
Renaissance, *HL* and, 54n22, 55, 60,
  63n41
Republic (Plato), 62, 94–95, 108,
  110n38, 150, 150n30, 156–160,
  157nn34–35, 173
Richard Wagner in Bayreuth (*WB*), 2,
  3, 5, 8, 10, 129–166, 172
  becoming Richard Wagner in,
    135–140
  BGE and, 179
  Brooks on, 133n6, 143n25, 148,
    150, 181n16, 190n32
  BT and, 151
  Christianity in, 132
  Church on, 136n13, 152n31
  courage in, 152
  desiderata in, 137, 142, 143n25
  the Dionysian in, 151
  divertissement in, 135, 151, 155, 163
  DS and, 127, 154, 165
  experience of Wagner's art in,
    146–151
  free human beings of future in,
    161–166
  Gray on, 133n6

234 | Index

Richard Wagner in Bayreuth (*WB*)
(continued)
gymnastics in, 157, 158–159,
158n38, 159n39, 164n47
happiness in, 162
HL and, 134n10, 165
Hutter on, 164n47
justice in, 76, 161
Large on, 133n6
life-affirmation in, 163
as monumental fiction, 204
Plato and, 148–151, 150n30,
156–160, 157nn34–35, 158n36,
159n40, 166
SE and, 127, 214n55
self-overcoming in, 206–207
Socrates and, 151
suffering in, 137, 143n26, 154, 178
Taylor on, 145n27
tyrannical will in, 136, 136n13, 137
Wagnerian musical education in,
153–161
Zuckert on, 143n25
Richardson, J., 93n14
Rohde, Erwin, 14, 14n2, 15, 15n4,
85, 86n67
Afterphilologie by, 16, 16n5
SE and, 164n46
WB and, 129–130
Romanticism
pessimism in, 175
philistines and, 24
Rousseau, J.-J., 104, 105, 106n36
critical history of, 105n35

Salaquarda, J., 48n9, 72n48, 73n49
Salomé, Lou von, 9, 212
Schiller, F., 30, 38n44, 51n14, 98n22
Neymeyr on, 57n30, 98n21, 117n53
Universal History lecture by, 117n53
Wallenstein by, 29
Schmitt, Carl, 34n39
Schopenhauer, A., 3, 3n3, 7

in *DS*, 14, 15, 22n14, 31, 40
in *GM*, 100n26
Goethe and, 100n25, 104–105,
104n31, 105n35
in *HL*, 61n37
Kant and, 67–68, 100–101
*Materials for a Treatise About the
Terrible Mischief Done Nowadays to
the German Language* by, 37n42
Nietzschean humanism and, 202
nihilism and, 180n14
On Philosophy at the Universities by,
123n63
On the Will in Nature by, 32n37
On Authorship and Style by, 37n42
On the Basis of Morality by, 32n37
pessimism of, 31, 174–175, 205
on philistines, 22n14
pity and, 176, 176n11
redemption and, 180, 180n14
suffering and, 31
UC and, 185n23
vegetarianism and, 15
virtues of, 101–102
Wagner, R., and, 113n45, 155–156,
169, 169n6, 174–175, 212, 215
The *World as Will and Representation*
by, 101, 102n28, 108, 112n43,
118n55, 155–156
Schopenhauer as Educator (*SE*), 2, 4,
5, 6, 9
Brandes on, 212–213
Brooks on, 99n23, 104n32, 122,
181n16, 190n32
Christianity in, 70n47, 103–104,
103n30, 117
Church on, 90n8, 91n10, 92n11,
93n13, 104n31, 106n36, 110n40,
118n55
Conant on, 119n56
conscience in, 88n6, 89–90, 89n7,
199
courage in, 100n25

desiderata in, 91, 126
divertissement in, 108, 109, 117
DS and, 118
educator in, 96–105, 98n22
EH and, 126, 210, 210n53
erotic-historic soul in, 87–96, 197, 211
genius in, 7, 92–93, 111–112,
113n46, 113n48, 114–118,
119n56, 121, 173
great enlightenment in, 111, 114
HA and, 100n26
happiness in, 89, 109–111
HL and, 105–106, 113n47, 117,
118, 121, 127
justice in, 114
Kant in, 67
laziness in, 87–89, 87n3, 95n18
Lemm on, 118n54
life of culture in, 115–125
life-affirmation in, 105–115, 177–
178, 184n21
life-denial in, 125
memory in, 89, 199
Neymeyr on, 87n3, 99n24, 100n27,
120n60, 123n63
philanthropy in, 102
redemption in, 119
Rohde and, 164n46
self-cultivation in, 93, 93n13, 99,
107, 114, 117
self-knowledge in, 89–93, 111n42
self-overcoming in, 205, 210
Strong on, 112n44
suffering in, 109, 110, 112, 178
Taylor on, 118n55
truth in, 101, 105n35, 106–109,
178
untimeliness, 107
WB and, 127, 214n55
Zuckert on, 104nn31–32, 113n45,
120n58, 121
Schwärmerei, 67, 67n44
scientific history

in *HL*, 63–64, 63n41, 64n42, 68–
75, 81–83, 82n62
suffering from, 64
SE. See *Schopenhauer as Educator*
Second Alcibiades (Plato), 93
self-cultivation
in *DS*, 13, 29, 35, 38, 39–40
in *HL*, 86
of philistines, 191–192
in *SE*, 93, 93n13, 99, 107, 114, 117
in *UC*, 95, 126–127
Zuckert on, 41n50
self-knowledge, 210
in *BGE*, 201
genius and, 92–93
of philistines, 22, 23
in *SE*, 89–93, 111n42
in *UC*, 4
self-overcoming
in *BGE*, 194
in *EH*, 206–207, 206n50, 209–211
in *GS*, 206
in *HL*, 52
in *SE*, 205, 210
in *UC*, 203–213
in *UH*, 66
in *WB*, 206–207
Seven Sages, 153n32
shameful origin (*pudenda origo*), 1
Siemens, H., 2n1, 84n66
on *betrachten*, 11n9
"Skirmishes of an Untimely One"
(*Streifzüge eines Unzeitgemässen*),
11
slave morality, 176–177
socialism
Strauss, D., and, 33–34
vegetarianism and, 15
Socrates, 23, 93, 94–95, 110n38,
157nn34–35, 159–160, 213n54,
215
persecution of, 121–122
tragedy and, 151

236 | Index

Socrates and Alcibiades (Hölderlin), 102
Socrates and Greek Tragedy (Nietzsche), 16
Solon, 153n32
Spinoza, B., 202
Strauss, David Friedrich, 2, 5, 7. See
   also *David Strauss the Confessor
   and the Writer*
   Beethoven and, 27, 30–31, 30nn34–
      35
   Goethe and, 27, 29–30
   socialism and, 33–34
Strauss, Leo, 5, 21, 39
   HL and, 53n20
Streifzüge eines Unzeitgemässen
   ("Skirmishes of an Untimely
   One"), 11
Strong, Tracy, 90n8, 98n22
   on *SE*, 112n44
Suchende (seekers), 24
suffering
   in *BT*, 195
   in Buddhism, 52n16
   faith and, 32
   of genius, 180
   in *GM*, 196–197
   in *HL*, 45, 46n4, 63, 64, 76, 83
   justice and, 76
   philanthropy and, 196
   Schopenhauer and, 31
   from scientific history, 64
   in *SE*, 109, 110, 112, 178
   in truth, 9, 178, 203–204
   in *UC*, 194–197
   Wagner, R., and, 15
   in *WB*, 137, 143n26, 154, 178
suprahistorical humans, of *HL*, 51,
   51n15, 52n17, 75, 83n64

Tacitus, 58n31
Taylor, Q. P., 3
   on *HL*, 53n19
   on horizons of significance, 47n7

on *SE*, 118n55
on *WB*, 145n27
Thales, 153n32
Thus Spoke Zarathustra (*Za*), 3, 5, 10,
   133, 172, 185, 194
   Church on, 181n16
   futuristic teaching in, 181–182
   Meier on, 193n35
   philistines and, 192
   pity in, 176n11
   redemption in, 120n58, 181,
      181n16, 182, 190n32
Torquato Tasso (Goethe), 105n34
Treaty of Trianon, 60n35
Tristan and Isolde (Wagner, R.), 130
truth, 188–190, 200n43
   belief and, 186–187
   in *DS*, 178
   of genius, 180
   in *HA*, 213
   in *HL*, 75–80
   life-denial and, 213
   nihilism and, 179
   pessimism toward, 204–205
   redemption and, 182–183
   in *SE*, 101, 105n35, 106–109,
      178
   suffering in, 9, 178, 203–204
   in *UC*, 204, 214–215
Tusculan Disputations (Cicero), 5
Twilight of the Idols, 197, 199, 203
tyrannical will, in *WB*, 136, 136n13,
   137

Übermensch, 179, 181, 194, 212
UC. See *Untimely Considerations*
unity of style
   in Christianity, 70n47
   in *DS*, 28, 35, 65, 85
untimely (*unzeitgemäss*), 11, 11n8, 40,
   101, 107, 192–193
   Wagner, R., and, 14n2

Index | 237

Untimely Considerations (UC), 1–6,
2nn1–2, 3n3, 8n6. *See also specific
essays*
Church on, 178n13, 188n29
failure of project of, 170–176
life-denial in, 8, 177–184
Schopenhauer and, 185n23
self-cultivation in, 95, 126–127
self-knowledge in, 4
self-overcoming in, 203–213
sickness of thought in, 176–188
successes of thought of, 190–203
suffering in, 194–197
truth in, 204, 214–215
value of existence in, 106n36
Wagner, R., and, 14–19, 15n4
unzeitgemäss. See untimely

Valiquette Moreau, N., 157n34
vegetarianism, 67n43
Wagner, R., and, 15, 15n3
Voltaire, 36, 40

Wagner, Cosima, 14, 18–19, 131n3,
169n6
Wagner, Richard, 2, 3, 3n3, 7, 69,
94, 179–180. *See also The Case
of Wagner; Richard Wagner in
Bayreuth*
Aeschylus and, 152n31
anti-Semitism of, 131, 131n4,
145n27
Audience and Popularity by, 168n3
Augenblick of, 134, 134n10
Bayreuth and, 5, 8, 14, 126, 167–
175, 171nn7–8, 211–213
Beethoven and, 147
Beethoven by, 13, 21n12
BT and, 13, 16–17
CW and, 174
Dionysia and, 171
divertissement and, 171, 188

DS and, 13, 18–19
EH and, 168n3, 169, 174
faith of, 136, 136n15
Gesamtkunstwerk by, 130, 171n8
HA and, 168n3, 169
life-affirmation and, 169
On Conducting by, 20n9
On Musical Criticism by, 158n38
Opera and Drama by, 154
philanthropy and, 136n15, 150
on philology, 17
popular success of, 168, 168n2
redemption of, 180
Romantic pessimism of, 175
Schopenhauer and, 113n45, 155–
156, 169, 169n6, 174–175, 212,
215
suffering and, 15
Tristan and Isolde by, 130
UC and, 14–19, 15n4
untimeliness and, 14n2, 192
vegetarianism and, 15, 15n3
Wallenstein (Schiller), 29
The Wanderer and His Shadow (WS),
173, 207, 211
WB. See Richard Wagner in Bayreuth
We Philologists, 129
Weltgericht, 77, 77n56
What Is Enlightenment? (Kant), 87n3
Wilamowitz-Möllendorff, Ulrich von,
16–17
Wilhelm I, 167–168
Wilhelm Meister's Journeyman Years
(Goethe), 29n32, 49n11
will, 25, 68–73
will to power
in *BGE*, 201–202
Heidegger on, 202n47
The World as Will and Representation
(Schopenhauer), 101, 102n28,
108, 112n43, 118n55, 155–156
WS. See The Wanderer and His Shadow

238 | Index

Xenophon, 159, 201n44

Za. See *Thus Spoke Zarathustra*
Zinn, H., 62n39
Zuckert, Catherine, 2, 5, 33–34
  on the erotic-historic soul, 44–45

on *HL,* 56, 74–75, 76n53, 83n64
on *SE,* 104nn31–32, 113n45,
  120n58, 121
on self-cultivation, 41n50
on suprahistorical humans, 51, 51n15
on *WB,* 143n25